THE
CASSELL

Atlas of the

ANCIENT
WORLD

4,000,000 – 500 BC

John Haywood

with

Charles Freeman • Paul Garwood
Judith Toms

CASSELL

Project director	Peter Furtado
Cartographic manager	Richard Watts
Advisory editors	Jeremy Black *Professor of History, University of Exeter, UK*
	K.M. Chaudhuri *Vasco da Gama Professor of European Exploration, European University Institute, Florence, Italy*
	Barry Cunliffe *Professor of European Archaeology, University of Oxford, UK*
	Brian M. Fagan *Professor of Anthropology, University of California, Santa Barbara, USA*
	J.E. Spence *Associate Fellow, Royal Institute of International Affairs, UK*
Academic advisors	J.I. Catto *Oriel College, University of Oxford, UK*
	Professor Robin Cohen *University of Warwick, UK*
	Professor J.H. Elliott *Regius Professor of Modern History, University of Oxford, UK*
	Professor Harold James *Princeton University, New Jersey, USA*
	Professor Maldwyn A. Jones *University of London, UK*
	Dr Stuart Kewley *University of Cambridge, UK*
	Dr Stewart Lone *Australian Defence Force Academy*
	Dr Oswyn Murray *Balliol College, University of Oxford, UK*
	Professor A.J.S. Reid *The Australian National University*
	Professor Francis Robinson *Royal Holloway, University of London, UK*
	Professor John K. Thornton *Millersville University, Pennsylvania, USA*

This page:
Gold mask from Mycenae, c.1500 BC

Opposite above left:
Saharan rock paintings, c.3500 BC

Opposite centre left:
Bell-Beaker drinking cups, c.2000 BC

Opposite centre right:
Assyrian bas-relief of lion hunt, c.650 BC

Opposite below right:
Chavín textile of fanged god, c.400 BC

Following page:
Decorated skull from Jericho, c.8000 BC

Art director	Ayala Kingsley
Art editor	Martin Anderson
Cartographic editor	Tim Williams
Editors	Susan Kennedy
	Peter Lewis
(Encyclopedic dictionary)	BCS Publishing
Cartographer	Nathalie Johns
Picture research	Claire Turner
Production	Clive Sparling
Editorial assistance	Marian Dreier
Typesetter	Brian Blackmore
Illustrations	Charles Raymond
Proof reader	Lynne Elson
Index	Ann Barrett

AN ANDROMEDA BOOK

Produced and prepared by
Andromeda Oxford Ltd
11–15 The Vineyard
Abingdon
Oxfordshire OX14 3PX

© Andromeda Oxford Ltd 1998

First published in the UK
by Cassell plc
Wellington House
125 Strand
London WC2R 0BB

ISBN 0-304–35040–0

10 9 8 7 6 5 4 3 2 1

Printed in Italy Petruzzi Città di Castello - PG

Contents

INTRODUCTION

Four million years of biological and cultural evolution are covered in this story of the development of humankind from its origins on the African savanna to the appearance of the literate civilizations and classical empires. The story is the product of research in many disciplines, but the central thread comes from thousands of archeological excavations, of inconspicuous scatters of stone tools and animal bones, hunting camps and farming villages as well as towns and spectacular cities.

Archeologists study and explain changes in societies, indeed in humanity itself, over immensely long periods of time. Why, for example, did some societies acquire farming skills? And how and why did humans cross from Siberia into Alaska and colonize the Americas? The archeologist tries to account for such developments in terms of social organization as well as technology and environmental change.

The key intellectual framework for our most distant past derives from the evolutionary theories of Charles Darwin, formulated in 1859. The theory of evolution by natural selection made it possible to imagine a vast antiquity, a blank timescape for human evolution to unfold over hundreds of thousands, if not millions, of years. Darwin and his contemporaries could only guess at the timescales involved. Today, study of the DNA in our body cells tells us that the hominid line – of which *Homo sapiens sapiens* is the culmination – separated from the other apes between four and five million years ago. Today, archeology tells us that human ancestors appeared in Africa and moved out to populate the rest of the world almost two million years ago, and that modern humanity may also have originated there. With its help, we can not only wonder at the art of 30,000 years ago, but also build up chronologies based on scientific analysis as well as on techniques of stylistic comparison. Archeology reveals that literate civilizations developed independently in many places around the world. Historians using written sources, and archeologists using material remains, can then collaborate in piecing together a narrative of these civilizations.

Modern scholars think of evolution like the branches of a tree, with new species emerging as the endlessly proliferating limbs and twigs, which derive from a trunk of remote common ancestors. Human societies have evolved in many ways; but there are similarities, especially in social and political organization and in the ways in which people make their livings. A flexible classification of human societies into "prestate societies" and "state-organized societies" was made by the American anthropologist Elman Service.

The simplest prestate societies were small family bands, egalitarian groups with communal leadership based on experience. Usually hunters and gatherers of plant foods, band societies prevailed for an immensely long time, until the beginnings of farming. Some survived to modern times.

Early farmers lived in permanent villages, and needed new social institutions to settle quarrels and establish land ownership. Many village societies were "tribes", egalitarian groups with kin-based organization to regulate land ownership and undertake communal tasks. "Chiefdoms" were a development of tribes; power lay in the hands of a few people who controlled trade and accumulated wealth. "State-organized societies" or civilizations operated on a larger scale than chiefdoms. They involved cities and saw the development of a writing system. Early civilizations were centralized, with power concentrated in the hands of a supreme ruler at the pinnacle of a socially stratified society.

Four major themes dominate the long early chapter of our history: the origins of humanity, the evolution and spread of humans, the beginnings of agriculture, and the emergence of civilizations. All of these are bound up with the ways in which food has been secured. For 99 percent of all human history, people lived by hunting and gathering. Our earliest ancestors probably used fleetness of foot and opportunism to scavenge their meat from lion and leopard kills. Hunting may have begun at the same time as modern humans appeared. Stone-tipped spears, then barbed antler projectiles and spearthrowers allowed hunters to shoot game from a safe distance. When the bow-and-arrow came into use some 10,000 years ago, humans could hunt animals of every size and birds on the wing. And as the ice sheets retreated, people intensified the quest for food and permanent settlements began to emerge at some favored sites.

Hunting is often seen as the glamorous part of foraging, but edible plant foods formed the essential diet of humanity for four million years. Our ancestors knew which plants to eat as staples, and which to fall back on in lean times. It was only when populations rose at the end of the Ice Age that people began to plant wild grasses and tubers deliberately to extend the range of wild forms that had been gathered for millennia. And, in a remarkably short time – perhaps three thousand years – the growing of crops and the domestication of animals spread very widely.

Farming accelerated the pace of cultural change. At first, civilizations like those of the Egyptians, the Shang and the Sumerians were independent entities. Gradually, though, states became reliant on each other. By 500 BC, empires, much larger entities, played a leading role. But the first four million years had created human biological and cultural diversity and laid the foundations of our own world ■

USING THIS ATLAS

This atlas is part of a six-volume chronological set covering the Ancient (1), Classical (2), Medieval (3), Early Modern (4), 19th Century (5), and Modern (6) worlds. To help the user pinpoint straight away which era any particular map relates to, pages are numbered first by volume, and then by 2-page spread within that volume. Thus, map spread 14 in volume 1 is identified by the page number 1.14.

World map spreads outline global history on the date shown. Different typographical categories (see table opposite) denote different kinds of political or social entity. The text on these spreads includes many cross-references to other relevant spreads. The timelines here are organized by region.

Regional map spreads cover a part of the world over a specific period. Maps for a continent or major region are grouped in a section, named in the heading on the right-hand side of the spread. These sections also appear in the Contents page.

Maps are shown in true cartographic projections. North is generally at the top of the page. Some distortion is evident in those maps that cover huge areas of the world (e.g. Asia). Where necessary location maps have been included.

Each regional map has certain standard features: thick grey lines denote major borders, thin grey lines internal borders. Campaigns or journeys are shown by lines with arrowheads; thicker grey arrows are used for mass movements of people. Trade routes are thinner lines, with arrowheads when the trade is one-way. All map-key items are referred to in text. The main text explains and amplifies the information on the map.

The timelines on regional maps are arranged in geographical or thematic sections. Civilizations, cultures, and dynasties are shown with colored bands; broad historical phases (such as "Bronze Age") are indicated with grey bands. Every regional map also has several numbered "pointers", whose captions offer further historical detail on the places marked. Finally, the panel bottom right cross-refers to other spreads with related information, listing their numbers and themes.

A substantial encyclopedic section at the end of the book contains an A–Z guide to the people, places, and events of the period. It is cross-referenced both within the section and to the information that appears on the map spreads.

The index provides detailed references to the text, timelines, pointer captions and map keys. Space constraints have precluded indexing every location on the maps themselves.

TYPOGRAPHICAL CONVENTIONS	
World maps	
FRANCE	state or empire
Belgian Congo	dependency or territory
Mongols	tribe, chiefdom or people
Anasazi culture	cultural group
Regional maps	
HUNGARY	state or empire
Bohemia	dependency or territory
Slavs	tribe, chiefdom or people
ANATOLIA	geographical region
⚔	battle
•	site or town

Human evolution began as the Earth's climate started to cool during the Miocene epoch (25–5 million years ago), and culminated about one million years ago in the Pleistocene Ice Age. During the early Miocene the global climate was warmer than today. Widespread tropical forests in Africa and Eurasia supported diverse populations of early hominoid apes, including a common ancestor of gorillas, chimpanzees and humans.

By the end of the Miocene ice caps had formed at the Poles, and drier conditions in Africa caused tropical forests to shrink. In east Africa, probably the birthplace of the hominids, this was exacerbated by geological movements that led to the uplift of the East African plateau and the formation of the Rift Valley. The ancestral hominids were confined to shrinking "islands" of forest surrounded by open woodland and savanna. As a result they learned to walk on two legs, allowing them to cover long distances on the ground.

The oldest known hominid, 4.4-million-year-old *Ardipithecus ramidus*, was probably bipedal, and the slightly later species *Australopithecus afarensis* certainly was, although (like later australopithecines) it retained a good tree-climbing ability. By 3 million years ago the australopithecines had evolved into two types, known as robusts and graciles. The robusts (named for their massive jaws and teeth) were not human ancestors. The gracile *Australopithecus africanus* had smaller teeth and jaws, and lived on plant foods and meat scavenged from the carcasses of the savanna's herd animals. The first hominid to be considered human, *Homo habilis*, appeared about 2.4 million years ago. This lived in a similar way to the gracile australopithecines, but had a larger brain – almost half the size of a modern human's, compared with a third, for australopithecines and chimpanzees. Whereas the australopithecines used simple tools such as stones and sticks, *Homo habilis* made sharp flakes and chipped pebble tools for butchering large animals. This simple toolmaking culture is known as the Oldowan, for the early hominid fossil site of Olduvai Gorge in the Rift Valley.

About 1.9 million years ago *Homo habilis* was replaced by *Homo erectus*, with a brain size about two-thirds that of modern humans. Over the next million years this proportion grew to three-quarters, the brain evolving rapidly as the climate fluctuated from dry glacial periods to moister, warmer inter-glacial periods. There was little time to adapt physically to new conditions, and intelligent animals that could cope by modifying their

**Map labels:**
0 — 600 km
0 — 400 mi

Hadar — Aa
Bodo — He
Middle Awash — Ar
Melka Kunture
Gadeb
Omo — Ra, other — Ra
West Turkana — He
Ileret — Ra, Hh, He
Koobi Fora — Ra, Hh, He
Chesowanja — Ra
Olorgasailie
Peninj — Ra
Olduvai Gorge — Ra, Hh, He.
Ndutu — other
Laetoli — Aa, other
Kalambo Falls
Kabwe — other

Timeline entries:

1,600,000 Earliest evidence of the use of fire, at Chesowanja, Kenya and Swartkrans (South Africa)

1,800,000 Populations of *Homo erectus* reach south and southeast Asia

c.2,000,000 Stone choppers, from Olduvai Gorge, Tanzania, initiate the Oldowan culture

c.3,500,000 "Lucy", the most complete *Australopithecus afarensis* found, lives at Hadar, Ethiopia

c.3,600,000 Hominid bipedal footsteps from this date have been found at Laetoli, Tanzania

c.2,400,000 Date of the oldest known stone tools, from Hadar, Ethiopia and the start of the African Lower Paleolithic

1,000,000 Beginning of the modern (Pleistocene) Ice Age

1,000,000 *Homo erectus* reaches Europe and Asia

TIMELINE

| 4,000,000 years ago (ya) | 3,000,000 ya | 2,000,000 ya | 1,500,000 ya | 1,000,0 |

Homo habilis
Homo erectus
Australopithecus africanus
Ardipithecus ramidus
Australopithecus afarensis
Robust Australopithecines
Oldowan culture
LOWER PALEOLIT•

PLIOCENE EPOCH
TERTIARY PERIOD

probable range of early hominids

probable range of *Homo erectus*, c.500,000 years ago

range of Neanderthals, c.100,000 ya

Mousterian culture, c.100,000 ya

southeast Asian chopper-flake technology

fossil site

fossil site with finds of uncertain species

tool cultures

Oldowan, 2-1.2 million years ago (mya)

Acheulian, 1.5 mya-150,000 ya

major species found at fossil site

Ar   *Ardipithecus ramidus*

Aa   *Australopithecus afarensis*

Aaf *Australopithecus africanus*

Ra   *Australopithecus robustus*

Hh   *Homo habilis*

He   *Homo erectus*

Hsn *Homo sapiens neanderthalensis*

other other forms of archaic *Homo sapiens*

evidence of Neanderthal ritual burial

use of fire by *Homo erectus*

conjectural spread of *Homo erectus*

ancient coastline, in glacial periods

Pliocene rainforest in Africa

**Map labels:**

Greenland

Bury St Edmunds
La Chapelle-aux-Saints
Hsn
Neander Valley
Hsn
Steinheim
other
wanscombe
He
Pontnewydd
He
Boxgrove
He
Le Moustier
Hsn
Schöningen
Krapina
Hsn
Vértesszöllös
He
a Ferrassie
Hsn
Circeo
Hsn
Petralona
other
Tbilisi
Yerevan
He
atapuerca
He
Mt Carmel
Hsn
Teshik Tash
Hsn
Gibraltar
Hsn
Torralba-Ambrona
Dederiyeh
Hsn
Shanidar
Hsn
mas
ries
He
Ternifine
He
Hadar
Hh
Salé
He
Qafzeh
Hsn, other
Kebibat
other
Yayo
He

EAST AFRICAN RIFT VALLEY

see inset

Madagascar

Zhoukoudien
He
Lantian
He
Langtandong
He
Bailongdong
He
Yunxian
He
Yuanmou
He
Tham Khuyen
He
Narmada
He
Ban Mae
Tha
Trinil
He
Solo
He
Sangiran
He

Makapansgat
Aaf
Sterkfontein
Ra
Kromdraai
Ra
Taung
Aaf
Swartkrans
Ra, Hh
Elandsfontein
other

Timeline (left lower):

100,000 Modern humans begin their migration out of Africa

135,000 Date of the earliest anatomically modern human fossils, from Omo, Ethiopia

300,000 Possibly the oldest known human structure; a hut is found at Terra Amata, France

400,000 The earliest surviving wooden tool, a spear (found in Schöningen, Germany)

500,000 ya

250,000 ya

H. s. sapiens

Archaic *Homo sapiens*

H. s. neanderthalensis

Acheulian culture

Mousterian culture

MID PALEOLITHIC

PLEISTOCENE EPOCH

QUATERNARY PERIOD

behavior had evolutionary advantages. *Homo erectus* mastered the use of fire, and was a more able toolmaker than *Homo habilis*, using the symmetrical hand-ax (a butchery tool) of the Acheulian culture.

Homo erectus was the first hominid to live outside Africa. Perhaps as early as 1.8 million years ago it had spread through tropical south and southeast Asia and colonized temperate areas of Europe and northern China before one million years ago. *Homo erectus*, however, did not reach Australia or the Americas. It could survive in temperate climates but not in Arctic and sub-Arctic ones, usually prefering to live in savanna, steppe and open woodlands: the same hand-ax technology was widespread. However in southeast Asia it adapted to tropical forest life, using flake and chopper tools and bamboo. The isolated *Homo erectus* populations began to evolve in different ways after 500,000 years ago. In Africa and Europe a variety of large-brained forms showed a mixture of archaic and modern human characteristics. In Europe between 230,000 and 150,000 years ago, archaic *Homo sapiens* evolved into *Homo sapiens neanderthalensis*, its physique adapted to life on the cold steppes and tundras of Ice Age Eurasia. These Neanderthals developed the Mousterian toolmaking technique, which was also widely used by hunter–gatherer groups in North Africa and the Middle East (often called the Near East by archeologists). In Africa archaic humans evolved until anatomically modern humans, *Homo sapiens sapiens*, appeared by 135,000 years ago

The earliest known anatomically modern *Homo sapiens sapiens* had appeared in Africa by 135,000 years ago (ya). By 90,000 years ago anatomically modern humans existed in the Middle East; by 75,000 years ago they were in east Asia and by 40,000 in Europe and Australia. By the end of the Ice Age 10,000 years ago, only some oceanic islands, Antarctica and some parts of the high Arctic remained completely uninhabited.

Two rival explanations have been offered for these facts. One argues that the modern human races developed directly from the regional *Homo erectus* populations: modern Africans evolved from *Homo erectus* via African archaic *Homo sapiens*; modern Europeans from *Homo erectus* via European archaic *Homo sapiens* and Neanderthals and so on. Critics point out that parallel evolution of this sort over such a wide area is implausible and that there is no supporting fossil evidence. The second explanation, known as the single-origins or "out of Africa" model, is supported by genetic evidence suggesting that all modern humans derive from African ancestors who lived between about 285,000 and 150,000 years ago, and that all modern non-African humans are descendants of a single group of this ancestral population that migrated out of Africa around 100,000 years ago. According to this model, the descendants of this group spread across Eurasia. The anatomically modern humans had better developed speech abilities than the archaic natives, who could not compete with the newcomers and gradually became extinct.

This model is more compatible with the fossil and archeological evidence than the first. Between 120,000 and 90,000 years ago the African climate was more moist than it is today and bands of hunters and gatherers could have crossed the Sahara. The earliest known fossils of modern humans outside Africa date to about 90,000 years ago and were found in Israel – just the place and date predicted by the single-origins theory. Only in Africa have forms intermediate between archaic and modern humans been found. In Europe, the Neanderthals and early modern humans formed distinct populations that coexisted for over 10,000 years: the Neanderthals did not evolve into modern humans. In east and southeast Asia, the *Homo erectus* populations were replaced by modern humans with no trace of intermediate forms.

When the first modern humans reached the Middle East, the global climate was beginning to enter one of the most severe glacial periods of the Ice Age. Human technology was probably inadequate for survival in the arctic climates of Europe and central Asia, and these areas were left to the hardier Neanderthals. Instead the moderns moved east, reaching China and southeast Asia around 75,000 years ago. Here they developed boat- or raft-building skills and

115,000 Onset of the last glaciation of the (Pleistocene) Ice Age

90,000 Anatomically modern humans living at Qafzeh, Israel

40,000 Anatomically modern humans begin to colonize Europe: they live alongside the indigenous Neanderthals

32,000–14,000 Period of cave art traditions in Europe

The Americas
Europe
Middle East
Africa
East and South Asia

100,000 years ago
80,000 ya
60,000 ya
40,000 ya
30,000 ya

c.120,000 Middle Stone Age flake-tool technology is well established in tropical Africa

120,000–90,000 Periods of higher rainfall make the Sahara habitable by humans

c.75,000 Glaciation causes Africa to become arid: the Sahara becomes impassable by humans

75,000 Anatomically modern humans inhabit China and southeast Asia

45,000 Date of the oldest known musical instrument, a flute, found in north Africa

35,000 Anatomically modern humans hunt large game in Eurasia

35,000 Australian aboriginal hunter–gatherer traditions emerge

28,000 The Solomon Islands are settled

vegetation zones 18,000 ya

- tundra
- forest
- grassland
- semidesert
- desert
- ice cap 18,000 ya
- ice cap 12,000 ya
- ice cap 10,000 ya
- selected fossil sites of anatomically modern humans, with date
- other early modern human sites, with date
- Paleoindian fluted point tradition sites, 12,000–10,000 ya
- migration of anatomically modern humans, 100,000–11,000 ya
- possible marine migration route
- range of Neanderthals, c.100,000 ya
- limit of habitation, c.10,000 ya
- ancient coastline at peak of the last glaciation, 18,000 ya

SUNDA ancient land bridge

Greenland Ice Sheet

Taymyr Ice Sheet

BERINGIA

Berelekh 14,000

Scandinavian Ice Sheet

Bisovaya 14,000

Dyukhtai Cave 18,000

Malaya Siya 34,000

Mal'ta 21,000

Cresswell Crags 12,000

early modern humans in Europe 40,000

Mladec 33,000

Cro Magnon 25,000

early modern humans in Middle East 90,000

early modern humans in central Asia 35,000

Zhoukoudian 18,000

Zasaragi 50,000

Skhul 90,000

Dar es-Soltane 40–30,000

Haua Fteah 47,000

Qafzeh 90,000

Linjiang 67,000 ?

Okinawa 32,000

Omo 130,000

early modern humans in Southeast Asia 75,000

Tabon 24–22,000

Niah Cave 40,000

SUNDA

Madagascar

origin of ancestral modern humans 200,000–135,000

Wadjak 50–25,000

early modern humans reach Solomon Islands 28,000

Bobangara 38,000

SAHUL

early modern humans reach Australia and New Guinea 40,000

Border Cave 115,000

Klasies River Mouth 120,000

Devil's Lair 34,000

Lake Mungo 33,000

Bluff rockshelter 30,500

Kow Swamp 14,000

TASMANIA 31,000

11,000–9000 Folsom culture replaces Clovis culture among Paleoindians

11,500 Beginning of Clovis culture in North America

15,000 Possible date of the first settlement of North America, at Bluefish Cave (Alaska)

28,000 The last Neanderthals become extinct, in southern Spain

20,000 ya

10,000 ya (8000BC)

20,000–14,000 Dyukhtai tradition: earliest settlement of northeast Asia

18,000 Height of the last glaciation: sea levels are 100–130m lower than today

10,000 The beginnings of agriculture in the Middle East

10,000–3000 ya Higher rainfall makes the Sahara habitable again

by 40,000 years ago had reached New Guinea and Australia (then linked into one vast island continent), probably by a series of island-hopping voyages. Though the distances to be covered were relatively short as the sea levels were lower than today (a large amount of water was locked up in ice caps), these early sea voyages were a great achievement, even if possibly accidental:

About 40,000 years ago, modern humans moved into Europe. By this time they had evolved modern mental characteristics and sufficient technology to flourish on the frigid Eurasian steppes and tundras. Within 12,000 years the Neanderthals were extinct. The Eurasian steppes and tundras were favorable for late Ice Age hunters because of the herds of reindeer, horse, bison and mammoth that ranged across them. By 35,000 years ago hunting bands had reached deep into central Asia and by 20,000 years ago others, perhaps moving north from China, had entered northeastern Siberia. The area now covered by the Bering Straits was a cold plain which some bands crossed to reach the Americas by 15,000 years ago. Further progress into the Americas was blocked by massive ice sheets. Between 14,000 and 12,000 years ago these began a retreat and hunting–gathering bands – the Paleoindians – could reach the heart of North America. The earliest Paleoindian sites are characterized by beautifully worked fluted projectile points used for big-game hunting. The Paleoindians spread rapidly through the Americas and had reached Patagonia in South America by 11,000 years ago ∎

F arming communities arose independently in many parts of the world between 10,000 and 5000 BC as a response to the environmental changes that followed the end of the Ice Age. The warmer climate was a mixed blessing: sea levels rose as the ice sheets melted, flooding huge areas of lowland hunting grounds. The savannas, steppes and tundras, all abundant in big game, shrank as the forests advanced.

In many areas, hunter–gatherers began to exploit small game birds, fish and plants to a greater extent than before. It was among these communities that agriculture first arose. Probably the first stage was planting the seeds of favored wild plant foods to guarantee their continuing availability. Next was the domestication of food plants by breeding strains with desirable characteristics. Because their seeds had a high carbohydrate content and were easy to store, the most important domesticated plant foods were strains of the cereals – wheat, barley, oats, rice, millet and maize – that still form the staple food crops today. Relatively few animal species have been domesticated; most of those have been herd animals, whose tendency to "follow the leader" makes them easier to manage. Animal domestication began with the management and selective culling of wild herds. Penning the animals followed, then selective breeding for desirable qualities. Most early centers of agriculture were rich in wild plants and animals suitable for domestication. Elsewhere agriculture relied on the introduction of crops and livestock from established farming areas.

Some communities of hunter–gatherers moved from casual cultivation of wild plants (incipient agriculture) to a full farming economy far more quickly than others. Farmers have to work harder than hunter–gatherers, and few made the transition willingly. Rising populations probably forced many to adopt cultivation to supplement wild food supplies. In the Fertile Crescent of the Middle East, where farming first developed, (▷ 1.08) the transition from incipient agriculture to dependence on domesticated cereals took only three centuries, 8000–7700 BC, and domesticated animals replaced hunted wild animals a millennium later. In Mesoamerica a full farming way of life developed within a few centuries of the domestication of maize (▷ 1.28). In eastern North America hunting and gathering remained the main source of food for some three millennia after the first cultivation of domesticated food around 2500 BC. Even farmers who grew most of their food still exploited wild food sources.

Agriculture led to far-reaching technological developments. Most hunter–gatherers had to carry everything from camp to camp: farmers were sedentary, so weight became less critical. New tools, such as polished stone

Hawaiian Islands

EASTERN N AMERICA
goosefoot
gourds
marsh elder
sumpweed
sunflowers
c.1000

Bahamas

Cuba   Hispaniola
            Puerto Rico
Jamaica

c.2300

c.1000

MESOAMERICA
avocados
beans
cotton
gourds
maize
peppers
pumpkins
squashes
tomatoes
turkeys

c.3500

c.4000

LOWLAND S AMERICA
manioc
peanuts
pineapples

c.3000

c.2000

ANDES
alpacas
beans
chili peppers
gourds
guinea pigs
llamas
potatoes

c.1000

c.500

Timeline

The Americas

c.12,000 BC Jomon hunter–gatherers make the first pottery in Japan

Europe

5400–4500 Bandkeramik culture: first farmers of central Europe

6000 Farming spreads across southern Europe

Middle East

10,000 BC Natufian hunter–gatherers harvest wild cereals in Syria

9000 Wild sheep flocks are managed in the Zagros mountains, Iraq

9000–8000 Incipient agriculture (cultivation of wild cereals) in the Fertile Crescent

8000-7700 Wheat and barley are domesticated in the Fertile Crescent

6200 Copper smelting and textile manufacture in Chatal Huyuk (Turkey)

c.6000 The first cattle are domesticated in the Middle East

5000 Irrigation agriculture begins on the Mesopotamian plains

3800 The earliest bronze working is carried out in the Middle East

Africa

6000 Wheat, barley and sheep farming begins in Egypt

East and South Asia

8000 End of the last glaciation, worldwide

6500 Rice cultivation in the Yangtze valley

6000 Earliest evidence for farming in the Indian subcontinent

4500 Farming is adopted in the Ganges plain

10,000 BC   8000   6000   4000

transition to agriculture beginning,

before 8000 BC

before 6000 BC

before 3000 BC

before 500 BC

hunters and gatherers

uninhabited

textile find, with date

cotton

linen

silk

wool

earliest pottery, with date

earliest evidence for the
adoption of plow, with date

rice   early domestication of plant or animal

earliest use of the potter's
wheel, before 3000 BC

earliest centers of copper/
bronze metallurgy, 6000–2000 BC

early spread of wheeled vehicles,
4th millennium BC

Greenland

Iceland

3500

c.1200

3500

3500

SW STEPPES
horses

S EUROPE
cattle
geese
grapes
oats
olives
rye

3500

c.6000

6000

6000

4500

c.3000

c.6000

6000

6500

c.7000

CENTRAL ASIA
Bactrian camels
yaks

c.6000

11000

c.6000

2700

c.3000

c.1000

4000

c.7000

6000

5000

4500

c.5000

2600

CHINA
millet
rice
silk worms
soybeans

c.8000

c.2600

c.6000
3500

1400

SAHARA
bulrush millet
cattle

c.7000

W AFRICA
African rice
oil palms
water melons
yams

MIDDLE EAST
asses
barley
date palms
dogs
dromedary camels
flax
goats
lentils
onions
peas
pigs
sheep
wheat

INDIA
cotton
zebus

c.7000

300

1000

E AFRICA
sorghum

c.6000

Ceylon

SE ASIA
chickens
pigs
rice
taros
water buffalo
waterchestnuts

Philippine
Islands

SE ASIAN
ARCHIPELAGO
bananas
breadfruit
coconuts

Borneo   Celebes

c.2500

New Guinea   NEW GUINEA
sugar cane
sweet potatoes

Sumatra

c.2000

Java

Timor

Madagascar

750 Nomadism becomes
the dominant way of life
on the Eurasian steppes

1000–800 Maize is
introduced to South
America

1200 Maize is introduced
to southwest North
America

700 Maize is domesticated
in Mesoamerica

1500 Pastoral farmers
spread across the Eurasian
steppes

3650 Wheeled vehicles
in use on the Russian
steppes

2000 Farming becomes
the main source of food
in Peru

2000

3000 Copper and silk
manufacture are known
in China

2500 Desertification of
the Sahara drives nomadic
herding groups to the
edges of the desert

2000 Farming and
pastoralism begin in sub-
Saharan Africa

1500 Rice cultivation is
adopted in Korea

axes for clearing forest, hoes, sickles
and grindstones, appeared in early
farming cultures. Pottery became common
in early farming settlements where it was needed for
storage and cooking. Pottery led to other technological breakthroughs: the
kilns that were developed in some areas for baking pots also provided the
means for smelting and casting metals – copper and gold first, then bronze and
finally iron. The wheel too was first used as an aid to making pottery; only later
was it applied to transport. The spinning and weaving of plant and animal
fibers to make textiles also became important in early farming communities.

The social implications of the adoption of agriculture were just as far-
reaching. Farming peoples accumulated material possessions on a scale
far beyond anything possible among most hunter–gatherers. As a result,
differences in social status became more marked and the equality of hunter–
gatherer society gave way to complex and hierarchical social structures. Most
significantly, farming made possible an enormous increase in the human population. A single hunter–gatherer may need 25 square kilometers to make a
living even in favorable terrain. In contrast, even the most primitive forms of
agriculture can support up to 20 people on one square kilometer. Where food
production could be intensified by plowing or by irrigation, still greater populations were possible. If the typical unit of hunter–gatherer society was the
nomadic band of 30–50, simple farming methods, could support villages of
hundreds of people, and intensive methods, towns of thousands of people

By 2000 BC the revolutionary impact of agriculture had become clear. Farming was practiced on every continent and would overtake hunting and gathering as the way of life of most people well before the Christian era.

Not all early farming societies developed the same level of complexity. Poor soil, climate, endemic diseases of humans or livestock or a lack of suitable crops limited development in many areas. The greater the resources possessed by a society, the more complex it could become; in a few favorable environments (such as the northwest of North America), hunter-gatherer societies too achieved greater levels of social complexity.

Most early farming societies were kinship-based tribes of hundreds or a few thousand people living in villages or dispersed homesteads. Although they recognized ties of kinship, religion or language with others, each tribe was essentially independent. Differences of rank and status existed but leaders could rarely exercise coercive power over other tribes' people. Archeologically, such societies (known to anthropologists as "segmentary societies") can be recognized by communal burial practices, the remains of permanent homesteads and villages and communal works such as the megalithic tombs of prehistoric western Europe. In 2000 BC segmentary farming societies were dominant in south and southeast Asia, New Guinea, north Africa, northern Europe and parts of Mesoamerica and South America.

Where intensive agricultural techniques could be used, largescale hierarchical communities of up to 20,000 people, known as "chiefdoms", could develop. Rank and status were linked to lineage: the senior person of the senior lineage was the chief, who was thereby the ruler of the whole community. Chieftains could exercise coercive power, often through a warrior class, and support specialist craftsmen. Archeologically, chiefdoms show major construction projects requiring large resources of labor and wealth, such as Stonehenge in southern Britain (▷ 1.20). In chiefdoms the quantity and quality of grave goods placed with burials indicate the rank and status of the individual and a few burials are lavishly furnished. Chiefdoms commonly had a dominant central site such as a stronghold or ceremonial center, and smaller satellite settlements. In 2000 BC chiefdoms were established in the Middle East and southwest central Europe, in China and the Andes. In western Europe segmentary farming societies were giving way to chiefdoms at this time.

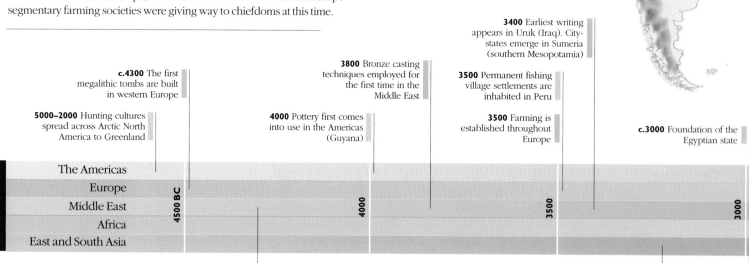

3400 Earliest writing appears in Uruk (Iraq). City-states emerge in Sumeria (southern Mesopotamia)

c.4300 The first megalithic tombs are built in western Europe

3800 Bronze casting techniques employed for the first time in the Middle East

3500 Permanent fishing village settlements are inhabited in Peru

5000–2000 Hunting cultures spread across Arctic North America to Greenland

4000 Pottery first comes into use in the Americas (Guyana)

3500 Farming is established throughout Europe

c.3000 Foundation of the Egyptian state

TIMELINE				
The Americas				
Europe	4500 BC			
Middle East		4000	3500	3000
Africa				
East and South Asia				

4300–3100 Uruk period in Mesopotamia. The first cities are built.

3200–1800 Chinese Longshan advanced farming cultures; first towns are built in China

3000 Ancestral Austronesians migrate from Taiwan to the Philippines

3000–1700 Pastoral farming is established on the central Asian steppes (Afanasevo culture)

hunter-gatherers
nomadic pastoralists
simple farming societies
complex farming societies/
chiefdoms
state societies
uninhabited
extent of bronze working,
c.2000 BC

2300 Beginning of the
Bronze Age in Europe

2334–2279 Sargon of
Akkad conquers
Mesopotamia, and sets up
the world's first empire

2000 Completion of the
main stage of Stonehenge
megalithic monument
(southern Britain)

2600 The earliest
monumental buildings are
built at Aspero, Peru

2000 Early Greeks settle
the Peloponnese

2500

2000

2630 The first pyramid is
built at Saqqara (Egypt)

2600–1800 The Indus
valley civilization
flourishes

2575–2134 The Old
Kingdom in Egypt

2040–1640 The Middle
Kingdom in Egypt

2500 The earliest bronze
tools are found in
southeast Asia

2000 Austronesians settle
in Melanesia

In river floodplains where agriculture could support communities of tens
of thousands, cities could develop. In these
large-scale societies the first states and civilizations
developed. Ties of kinship and lineage were insufficient to bind them, and
rulers devised ideologies to define the rights and obligations of their subjects.
Writing and mathematics were developed for administration. Although most
people still worked on the land, specialist occupations – craftsmen, shopkeep-
ers, merchants, soldiers, priests and bureaucrats – and social classes emerged.
Public building projects, such as city walls, roads, canals, temples and palaces,
could be undertaken for economic, defense, religious reasons, or for prestige.

In 2000 BC states existed in only a few areas. Independent city-states had
developed in Sumeria (southern Iraq) around 3400 and were widespread in
the Middle East by 2500, but declined in importance in Mesopotamia as militaristic rulers began to create territorial kingdoms and empires (▷ *1.10*). In
Egypt, the territorial kingdom formed the basis of the state from the start. A
centralized kingdom was created in about 3000, and by 2800 it held sway
throughout the Nile valley north of Nubia (▷ *1.17*). By 2300 a state civilization
had also developed in the Indus valley (▷ *1.26*).

Pastoral nomadism, an important form of intensive animal husbandry in
which farmers constantly move their herds from one poor pasture to another,
developed out of sedentary (single-center) pastoral farming, probably in the
Sahara where desertification spread after 3000 BC ∎

The fragility of the first civilizations was evident during the second millennium BC. Sumeria had vanished as a political entity shortly before 2000 BC, though its achievements were built upon by the Babylonian and Assyrian states which arose in the early second millennium (▷ 1.11). The rivalry between these two states was to endure until the middle of the first millennium. The other major power of the Middle East was the Hittite kingdom of Anatolia. One of the secrets of Hittite success is thought to have been their early mastery of iron working, in about 1500 BC. Meanwhile, Egypt expanded far south into Nubia and north into the Levant (▷ 1.18). In the eastern Mediterranean, the Minoans of Crete were replaced by the Mycenaean civilization that emerged on the Greek mainland around 1600. Around 1400 the Mycenaeans conquered Crete and introduced the Greek language; they also settled on Cyprus and in Anatolia (▷ 1.22).

This civilized world was thrown into chaos about 1200 by a wave of invasions. Mycenae was destroyed by invaders from the north, plunging Greece into a 400-year-long "dark age". Thracians, Phrygians and Anatolian Luvians overthrew the Hittite empire and nomadic Aramaeans occupied much of Mesopotamia. Egypt was invaded by mysterious Sea Peoples. Their fleets were driven from the Nile, but they settled in the Levant where they were known as the Philistines.

By 1000 stability was returning. The Hittites survived though as a shadow of their former selves. The Aramaeans had settled and were assimilating with the urbanized peoples of the conquered territories: their language became the common tongue of the Middle East for the next millennium. Assyria and Babylon were beginning to recover (▷ 1.12). The Levant was a mosaic of tiny states: of these, the Phoenician city-states and Israel acquired a historical importance out of all proportion to their size (▷ 1.14). Egyptian power was in decline and the Nubians, after a millennium of Egyptian domination, set up the kingdom of Kush. In sub-Saharan Africa, the transition to a farming way of life was beginning.

In Asia, the Indus valley civilization had collapsed around 1700; about 200 years later the Aryans, an Indo-European pastoralist people, migrated into India. In northern China the Neolithic Longshan cultures developed into the urbanized Shang state around 1766, marking the start of Chinese civilization. Around 1122 the Shang dynasty was ousted by the ruler of the Zhou sub-kingdom (▷ 1.27).

The Austronesian farming peoples continued to colonize the southeast Asian archipelagoes; by 2000 they had bypassed New Guinea and settled the western Pacific Bismarck archipelago around 1500 BC. The Lapita culture,

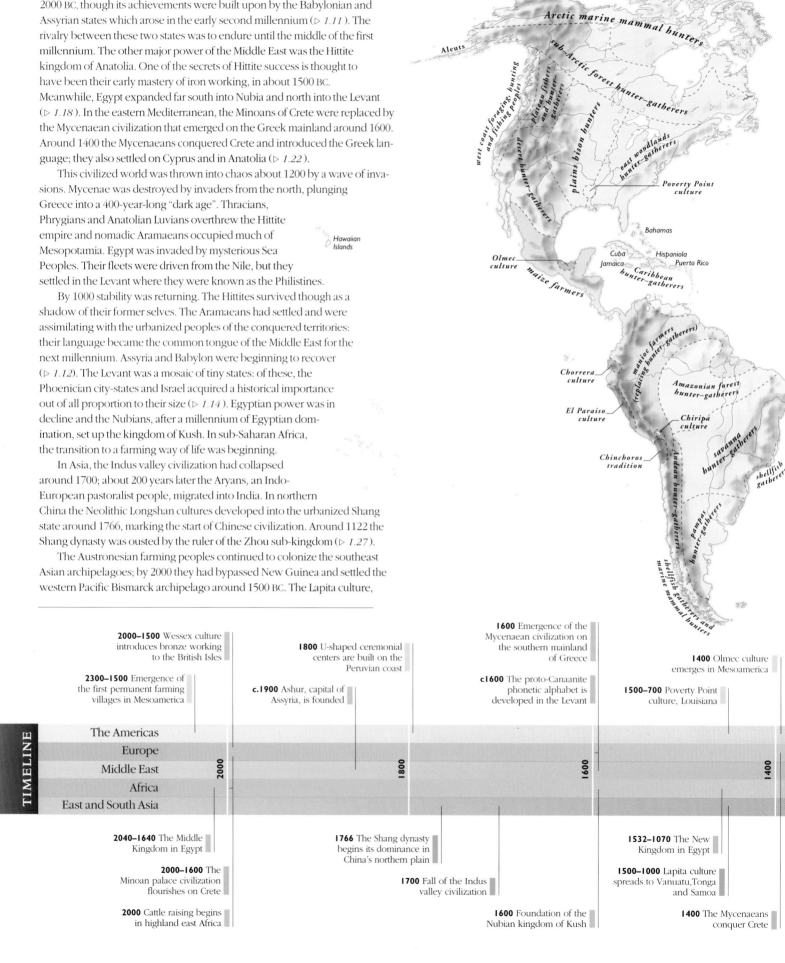

TIMELINE

	2000	1800	1600	1400
The Americas				
Europe				
Middle East				
Africa				
East and South Asia				

2000–1500 Wessex culture introduces bronze working to the British Isles

2300–1500 Emergence of the first permanent farming villages in Mesoamerica

1800 U-shaped ceremonial centers are built on the Peruvian coast

c.1900 Ashur, capital of Assyria, is founded

1600 Emergence of the Mycenaean civilization on the southern mainland of Greece

c1600 The proto-Canaanite phonetic alphabet is developed in the Levant

1400 Olmec culture emerges in Mesoamerica

1500–700 Poverty Point culture, Louisiana

2040–1640 The Middle Kingdom in Egypt

2000–1600 The Minoan palace civilization flourishes on Crete

2000 Cattle raising begins in highland east Africa

1766 The Shang dynasty begins its dominance in China's northern plain

1700 Fall of the Indus valley civilization

1600 Foundation of the Nubian kingdom of Kush

1532–1070 The New Kingdom in Egypt

1500–1000 Lapita culture spreads to Vanuatu, Tonga and Samoa

1400 The Mycenaeans conquer Crete

hunter-gatherers
nomadic pastoralists
simple farming societies
complex farming societies/
chiefdoms
state societies
uninhabited
extent of bronze working,
c.1000 BC
extent of iron working,
c.1000 BC

1200 Earliest Olmec
ceremonial centers in
Mesoamerica

1200 Collapse of Mycenae
and the beginnings of the
Greek "dark ages"

1200–1100 Hebrew tribes
settle west of the river
Jordan (Canaan)

1000 Spread of Phoenician
trading colonies in the
Mediterranean

c.1000 Iron working in
southern Europe

c.1100 Hillfort construction
begins in western Europe

1100 Development of the
influential Phoenician
alphabet

1350–1250 The Hittite
empire reaches its peak

1200–800 Karasuk culture
introduces advanced
bronze working to the
Asian steppes

1180 The Egyptians defeat
invasions of the Sea
Peoples

1122 Beginning of the
Zhou dynasty in China

1100 Iron working on the
Ganges plain

ancestral to the Polynesian culture,
developed here by 1500 and spread by
voyages of trade and exploration as far east
as Samoa and Tonga by 1000. This expansion was
made possible by the invention of the ocean-going outrigger canoe (▷ 2.26).

On the east Asian steppes the ancestors of the Turko-Mongol peoples took
up pastoral farming during the second millennium, under the influence of the
Iranian pastoralists of the western steppes. By 1000 far-reaching changes were
underway on the western steppes: the people of the Karasuk culture (probably Iranians) adopted transhumance, or seasonal migrations between summer
and winter pastures – only a step away from true pastoral nomadism.

In northern Europe the bronze-using Urnfield cultures (named for their
burial practices) spread across much of central, southern and western Europe.
By 1000 bronze working was almost universally practiced among European
farming cultures, most of which were now aristocratic chiefdoms (▷ 1.21).

In the Americas the Archaic period came to a close soon after 2000 BC,
with the emergence of fully developed regional hunter–gatherer cultures.
Some of these, such as the Poverty Point culture on the Mississippi, were
developing a degree of social complexity by 1000. In Mesoamerica, permanent farming villages appeared after 2000. By 1250 chiefdoms had emerged
among the Olmecs, farmers of the fertile floodplains by the Gulf of Mexico. In
South America complex societies continued to develop on the Pacific coast
and in the Andes, and farming spread into the Amazon basin (▷ 1.28) ■

The number and size of organized states in the Middle East, India and the Mediterranean rose sharply between 1000 and 500 BC. A succession of empires dominated the Middle East. The first was the Assyrian empire which stretched from the Zagros mountains to Egypt by the 7th century. Assyrian rule was harsh and in 625 the Babylonians rebelled and seized most of the empire for themselves (▷ 1.13). Then the Iranian Medes pushed west, conquering the Caucasus and eastern Anatolia. In 550 Cyrus II "the Great", an Iranian king, seized the Median kingdom and founded the Persian empire. He then took western Anatolia and the Babylonian empire. By 500 the Persian empire extended from Egypt to the Indus (▷ 1.15).

State-organized societies had also spread throughout the Mediterranean world. By 700 Greece was a patchwork of independent city-states: by 500 these cities, and Athens in particular, entered a period of intellectual creativity unparalleled in world history (▷ 1.24). The Greeks and Phoenicians also founded trading colonies throughout the Mediterranean. Although the Phoenicians lost their independence by 500, Carthage, their colony in north Africa, was the leading power of the western Mediterranean. The Greek cities of Sicily and southern Italy had a powerful influence, notably on the Etruscans who dominated northern Italy by 500. North of the Alps the Urnfield cultures of central Europe were replaced by the aristocratic iron-using Celtic Hallstatt culture c.600 (▷ 1.25).

States reappeared in the Indian subcontinent in the 9th century. The focus this time was the Ganges plain where Vedic Aryan chiefdoms began to coalesce into kingdoms and republics. By 500 the largest was the kingdom of Magadha. At the same time the Aryans extended southward, conquering the Dravidians and imposing Hindu religion on them (▷ 1.26). The Chinese Zhou kingdom expanded to the southeast after 1000, but what it gained in area it lost in internal cohesion. The Zhou kingdom was a decentralized feudal state and by the 8th century the powerful warlords had so undermined the power of the monarchy that it was power-less to prevent the kingdom from breaking up (▷ 1.27). Meanwhile the first chiefdoms emerged around 500 in Korea and in Van Lang in southeast Asia.

One far-reaching development of the early first millennium was the change in lifestyle of the Iranian peoples (Scythians, Sarmatians, Sakas and Yue Qi) of the Eurasian steppes from transhumant (seasonal) pastoralism to nomadic pastoralism. The steppe peoples had been pioneers in the use of horses: they had domesticated them for their meat around 4000 BC, they had harnessed them to wagons (4th millennium) and war chariots (2nd millennium) and by 1000 BC they had mastered

Arctic marine mammal hunters

Aleuts

sub-Arctic forest hunter-gatherers

west coast foraging, hunting and fishing peoples

plateau fishers and hunter gatherers

plains bison hunters

east woodlands hunter-gatherers

Adena complex

desert hunter-gatherers

maize farmers

Hawaiian Islands

Bahamas

Cuba *Hispaniola*
Jamaica *Puerto Rico*
Caribbean hunter-gatherers

Zapotec culture
Olmec culture
Maya

maize farmers

manioc farmers

Chorrera culture

Chavin culture

Yaya–Mama religious tradition

Paracas culture

savanna hunter-gatherers

Chinchoros tradition

shellfish gatherers

Andean hunter-gatherers

pampas hunter-gatherers

shellfish gatherers and marine mammal hunters

700–100 Adena culture burial mound builders in the eastern woodlands of North America

800 Zapotecs develop hieroglyphic script in Mesoamerica

700 City-states flourish in Greece and the Aegean

800–500 Greek colonization of the Mediterranean and Black Sea

c.750 Emergence of the Celtic Hallstatt Iron Age culture north of the Alps

900–700 Nomadism becomes the dominant way of life on the Eurasian steppes

800 Emergence of the Etruscan civilization in Italy

1000 Emergence of the kingdom of Israel

750–705 Assyrian power reaches its peak

612 The collapse of the Assyrian empire

TIMELINE					
The Americas					
Europe					
Middle East	1000	900	800	700	600
Africa					
East and South Asia					

1000–500 Formative period of Hinduism

900 The first states emerge on the Ganges plain

814 Foundation of the Phoenician colony of Carthage

712–671 Egypt is ruled by a Kushite dynasty from Nubia

600 Iron and bronze working develop in west Africa

800 The Aryans expand into southern India

600 Introduction of iron working into China

770–481 The "Springs and Autumns" period in China: the Zhou kingdom breaks up into minor states

c.590 The Nubian capital established at Meroë

Legend:
- hunter–gatherers
- nomadic pastoralists
- simple farming societies
- complex farming societies/chiefdoms
- state societies
- uninhabited
- empire
- extent of bronze working, c.500 BC
- extent of iron working, c.500 BC

507 A democratic system of government is established in Athens

509 Foundation of the Roman republic after the last king is expelled

525–404 Egypt is conquered by the Persians

539 Babylon is conquered by the Persians

550 Cyrus the Great founds the Achemenid Persian empire

550

500

c.563 Birth of Siddhartha Gautama, the Buddha, in northern India

500 The Bantu-speaking peoples begin to expand from their west African homeland

551 Birth of Confucius in China

c.540 Magadha becomes the dominant kingdom in the Indian subcontinent

riding on horseback. This development made the nomadic life possible by giving sufficient speed and mobility to manage large herds over vast ranges. By 500 BC the Iranian nomads had created a relatively homogeneous culture area from the Balkans almost to the borders of China. Nomadism had both beneficial and destructive consequences for the settled peoples of Eurasia. The nomads helped to forge trade links across Asia and by 500 BC Chinese silks found their way to the west along what would become known as the Silk Route. The mobility of the nomads also made them formidable raiders: Europe, the Middle East and China were troubled by their attacks for two thousand years.

Around 600 sub-Saharan Africa moved directly from the Stone Age to the Iron Age and the expansion of the Bantu-speaking peoples from their west African homeland continued. Over the next 1,500 years they became, through migration and cultural assimilation, the main linguistic group in Africa (▷ 1.16).

In Mesoamerica the Maya and Zapotec cultures emerged (▷ 1.28). Both Mesoamerican and Andean chiefdoms built impressive ceremonial centers. Farming was established in the Amazon basin by 500 BC and in several areas of North America cultivated plants were important supplements to wild foods. In the eastern woodlands hunters, gatherers and cultivators lived in semipermanent villages and developed complex cultures: the Adena people built communal burial mounds and ritual earthworks, made pottery and worked copper. Full farming economies, though, did not appear for many centuries ∎

Writing was invented as an aid to administration in communities that had grown so complex that human memory could no longer store all the information needed for efficient government. The earliest known writing has been found on clay tablets from the Sumerian city of Uruk (in modern Iraq), from about 3400 BC but, as this was already a complete system with over seven hundred signs, development must have begun much earlier.

The earliest Sumerian signs are pictographs – for example the sign for barley is a simplified picture of an ear of barley. More complex ideas were expressed by combining signs: thus a head and a bowl together meant "to eat". The signs were inscribed on wet clay tablets which were then dried. This proved to be a very durable medium and many thousands of clay tablets have survived (▷ 1.10). After about 2900 BC the signs were gradually simplified and inscribed with a rectangular-ended reed stylus. This left wedge-shaped strokes from which this script derives its name (cuneiform, from the Latin *cuneus*, "wedge").

Cuneiform was gradually refined so that a sign could also stand for the phonetic value of the word: if this system were used for modern English, the sign for "man" could also be used in combination with another sign, such as that for "age", to make another word, "manage". Syllable signs were also introduced, enabling cuneiform to record accurately all elements of human speech. Most early Sumerian documents were accounts and records of transactions. It was not until about 2400 that writing was used to record law codes, letters, chronicles, religious beliefs or for literature.

The Sumerian writing systems were widely adapted to other languages. Elamite and Indus valley pictographic derive from Sumerian pictographic (▷ 1.26) and although Egyptian hieroglyphic writing (a system that is almost as old as the Sumerian) was unique, the idea was probably based on Sumerian pictographs (▷ 1.17). Cuneiform was adapted successfully to the Akkadian, Assyrian, Babylonian, Elamite, Hittite, Hurrian and Urartian languages among others. Nevertheless, hundreds of different signs had to be learned, and scribes needed several years to master cuneiform and hieroglyphic scripts; as a result literacy remained the preserve of a tiny minority of specialists, and the cultural impact of its introduction was limited.

In the early 16th century BC the much simpler proto-Canaanite phonetic alphabet, with only 28 letters that stood for syllables which could be combined to spell out the sound of a word, was developed in the Levant or eastern Mediterranean coastal region (▷ 1.12). The letters were based on Egyptian hieroglyphs. By 1000 BC many variants of the proto-Canaanite script had developed, most important among them the Phoenician, Aramaic and the Arabian Sabean and Nabatean alphabets. The Aramaic alphabet was adopted by the Assyrians by the 8th century and replaced cuneiform as the main script of the Middle East. Adaptations of Aramaic were introduced into India in the 7th century and became the basis of modern Indian scripts and, ultimately, of the Indian-derived scripts of southeast and central Asia. Nabatean developed into the Arabic script in the 7th century AD while Sabean crossed the Red Sea to form the basis of Ethiopic, which was the only independent script to emerge in sub-Saharan Africa.

The Phoenician alphabet was the basis of the Old Hebrew and Greek alphabets. The Greeks adapted the Phoenician alphabet in the 8th century by introducing separate letters for consonant and vowel sounds (▷ 1.23). This was more precise than any syllabic alphabet. The Greek alphabet was in turn adapted to form new scripts by the peoples of Anatolia, the Balkans and Italy, including the Etruscans whose script was developed by the Romans into the Latin alphabet. Alphabetic scripts were easier to learn and use and they permitted literacy to become a widespread accomplishment, rather than just the preserve of professional scribes and administrators.

China, Mesoamerica and Polynesia each saw the independent development of writing. In Shang Dynasty China, a script with both pictographic and phonetic elements appeared around 1600 BC. Most early examples record the

results of divinations on animal bones, but the script was also used for record-keeping (▷ 1.27). This script was constantly refined and standardized over the centuries, and the modern Chinese writing system is still based on its principles. The Chinese script became the basis of Japanese and Korean scripts (though the Koreans later adopted an alphabetic script).

In Mesoamerica the Zapotecs began to develop a hieroglyphic script about 800 BC, from which the later Mesoamerican scripts derive (▷ 1.28). Of these, only the Mayan was a fully developed literary language capable of expressing all aspects of spoken language. Writing did not develop in the Andean civilizations although the Inca *quipu*, a mnemonic device made of knotted strings, fulfilled some of the functions of a simple script. Colored strings symbolized different commodities or services while the number of knots represented quantities held or required.

Another script to arise independently of any other was the hieroglyphic script developed in the Polynesian chiefdoms of Easter Island about AD 1500. Known as Rongorongo, it fell out of use before Europeans reached Easter Island and has not been deciphered ∎

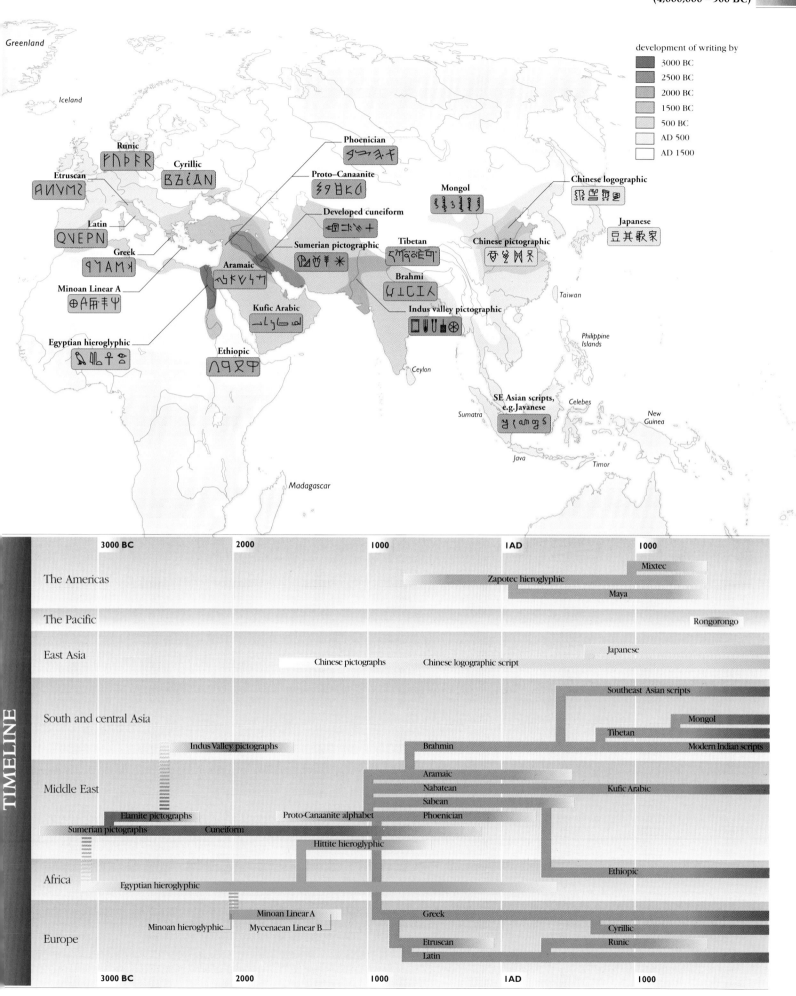

The earliest communities to rely on farming for most of their food grew up in the area known as the Fertile Crescent. This region of good soils and light but reliable rainfall extends in an arc from the foothills of Iraq's Zagros mountains, through south Turkey to western Syria, the Lebanon and Israel. Toward the end of the Ice Age it was colonized by plants such as wild emmer and einkorn wheat, wild barley, wild pulses, and almond, oak and pistachio trees. The supply of cereals and nuts was so rich that in some areas the hunter–gatherer population could settle in semi-permanent villages.

Among these sedentary hunter–gatherers were the Natufians of the Levant, whose way of life developed about 10,500 BC. Except for short stays at seasonal camps, the Natufians lived in villages of substantial wooden huts with stone foundations. They hunted gazelle intensively but their staple food was wild cereals, which they harvested with bone-handled reaping knives, stored in stone jars and processed with querns, grindstones, and mortars and pestles. Settled living and abundant food led them to abandon the egalitarianism of the nomadic hunter–gatherer band. A wide variation in the range and quality of goods found in individual burials points to the existence of social ranking.

During the 9th millennium they began to cultivate wild cereals close to their settlements. In some places, such as at Tell Mureybet in Syria, wild cereals may even have been introduced to areas where they did not naturally occur. The climate was changing and the natural range of wild cereals was shrinking, so these developments were probably an attempt to secure the food supply. Around 8000 BC these early farmers learned to breed wild cereals selectively for characteristics that increased the yield and made them easier to harvest. Within a few centuries domesticated strains of barley, emmer and einkorn wheat had appeared. Although cultivated plants were important to the economies of these transitional, or "proto-Neolithic", farmers, hunting and gathering continued to be crucial sources of food. As the population began to outstrip the environment's

capacity to support the old lifestyle, the dependence on farming increased. By about 7500 BC communities with a full farming economy had developed, marking the proper beginning of the Neolithic or "New Stone Age" (the period between the adoption of agriculture and that of metal working).

One of the most impressive proto-Neolithic sites is at Jericho, where a walled settlement of 1,500 people had grown up near a permanent spring by about 8000 BC. Domesticated barley and emmer wheat, pulses and figs were cultivated, but wild animals – gazelle and wild sheep and goats – were also important food sources. The people lived in huts built of sun-dried mud bricks, the earliest known use of what became the most important building material of the Middle East. Mud brick was easy to produce; when a house fell into disrepair it was simply knocked down and replaced by a new one. Over the centuries, successive rebuildings on the same site produced a high mound of debris,

**Map labels:**
spread of domesticated emmer wheat and barley to southeast Europe, 7th millennium
Aegean Sea
Ashikli Huyuk
Hacilar
Suberde
Can H
TAURU
Cyprus
Khirok
Mediterranea Sea

Legend:
- wild strains of einkorn wheat only
- wild strains of emmer and einkorn wheat, and barley
- distribution of wild sheep and goats
- southeastern limit of range of aurochs
- southern limit of dry farming
- area of Epipaleolithic Natufian sites, 10,500–8500
- △ proto-Neolithic settlement, 8500–7500
- aceramic Neolithic farming village, 7500–6500
- aceramic site with population of over 1000
- ◆ obsidian source
- distribution of Armenian obsidian
- distribution of Anatolian obsidian
- modern coastline and drainage where altered

0   300 km
0   200 mi

TIMELINE

	10000	9000	8000	7000	6000
Zagros/Taurus mts	11,000 Dogs are the first animals to be domesticated	9000 Management of wild sheep herds	8000–7700 Barley, emmer and einkorn wheat are domesticated	7000 Native copper is worked by cold hammering; 7000 Goats are domesticated.	6000 Cattle are domesticated; 6000 Development of irrigation in the Zagros foothills; 6700 Sheep are domesticated; 6500 Pigs are domesticated
Levant	Natufian hunter–gatherers; 10,500 Natufians harvest wild cereals, using stone sickles; 10,000 Buildings with stone foundations and semi-permanent settlements		8000 Mud brick is used for building; 8000 Emergence of the first farming communities; 7500 First use of flax for textiles		
General			7500 Long-distance trade in obsidian begins; 7000–6500 Permanent farming villages are widespread; lentils and peas are domesticated		6500 Pottery comes into general use

EPIPALEOLITHIC   PROTO-NEOLITHIC   ACERAMIC NEOLITHIC   NEOLITHIC

Black Sea

CAUCASUS MOUNTAINS

Kura

Caspian Sea

hunter–gatherers

Araks

ANATOLIA

Murat

Kizil Irmak

Acigol

Chiftlik

Bingol

⬛ 5

Chayonu

Cafer Huyuk

Nemrut Dag

Lake Van

Lake Urmia

2

Zawi Chemi Shanidar

ZAGROS MOUNTAINS

Gritille

Cyhan

Tigris

Great Zab

Tell Aswad

Qermez Dere

Karim Shahir

Jarmo

Tell Mureybet

MESOPOTAMIA

6

Abu Hureyra

1

Euphrates

Bouqras

Diyala

Ganj Dareh

Tepe Abdul Hosein

Ugarit

Orontes

Syrian Desert

Tepe Guran

Tamarkhan

Karkheh

LEVANT

Labwe

Ali Kosh

8

Choga Bonut

Tell Ramad

Beisamoun

Nahal Oren

Munhatta

Hatula

Ain Ghazal

Gosh

Jericho

I Khiam

3

Nahal Hemar

4

Beidha

Basta

Persian Gulf

HUMAN skulls, like this one found at Jericho, were often buried separately. Sometimes they were decorated with paint, shells and modeled clay features.

called a *tell* in Arabic, *huyuk* in Turkish and *tepe* in Persian. These settlement mounds are the most characteristic archeological sites of the region.

Farming also began to develop in southern Anatolia and the Zagros mountains. In the mountains hunter–gatherers intensified their management of flocks of wild sheep and goats. Animal bones from a settlement at Zawi Chemi Shanidar (9000 BC) show that the inhabitants killed mainly immature sheep. Since hunting would have resulted in a more random distribution of ages, the sheep had probably been penned and selectively culled. Pollen samples also suggest that wild cereals were cultivated at Zawi Chemi Shanidar. By the 7th millennium, domesticated sheep and goats were an important part of the economy of villages such as Chayonu (now in eastern Turkey).

Farming had not yet begun on the greater part of the fertile but almost rainless Mesopotamian plain. Only along the eastern edges, which caught some of the rainfall of the Zagros mountains, was farming possible before the development of irrigation and heat-resistant cereal strains in the 6th millennium.

The early farming communities had no pottery; this period of the Neolithic is known as the aceramic or prepottery Neolithic. The first pottery appeared by 7000 BC, but such was its usefulness for cooking and storage that its use had become widespread within five centuries. By this time bread wheat had also been developed, flax – the raw material of linen cloth – had been domesticated, as had the pig, and cattle were introduced from southeastern Europe where farming was just beginning.

The sedentary way of life meant that communities became less self-sufficient and long-distance trade, particularly in salt and toolmaking stone, became more important. The finest toolmaking stone, obsidian (volcanic glass), was traded over long distances. Obsidian from Anatolia has been found in early Neolithic sites almost as far south as the Red Sea, while obsidian from the region by Lake Van reached the Mediterranean and the Persian Gulf.

1 Abu Hureyra was a village of 300-400 people, living by hunting gazelles and harvesting wild cereals, c.9500.

2 Zawi Chemi Shanidar, a summer settlement c.9000, shows evidence for intensive management of wild sheep herds.

3 Jericho was a permanent settlement by 8500 BC, and was walled by 8000.

4 Nahal Hemar, an aceramic Neolithic site, has the earliest evidence for textile manufacture (flax).

5 At Chayonu, native copper was used 7300-6500 to make tools and ornaments.

6 Before 6000 BC Mesopotamia was only sparsely populated with hunter-gatherers.

7 Cultivation of emmer wheat and barley began in southeast Europe c.6000 BC, probably as a result of trade contacts with the Middle East.

8 Ali Kosh was one of the earliest farming communities on the Mesopotamian plain, founded 8000 BC.

See also 1.03 (rise of agriculture), 1.09 (MiddleEast), 1.16 (Africa)

By the time that pottery came into widespread use in the Fertile Crescent, around 6500 BC, the densest concentration of farming settlements was still to be found in the uplands of the Levant, southern Anatolia and the Zagros mountains, where there was reliable rainfall. Most villages had no more than a few hundred inhabitants and had social structures with relatively little distinction between rich and poor; the simple subsistence economies were based on cereals and herds of sheep, goats or cattle.

An important exception was the town-sized settlement which grew up around 6700 BC at Chatal Huyuk in Turkey. This settlement of densely packed mud-brick houses is the largest Neolithic settlement yet found. Long-distance trade in obsidian from nearby volcanoes, and improved agricultural yields resulting from the adoption of simple irrigation techniques, may have played a role in the town's growth. Chatal Huyuk had rich artistic traditions of wall-painting and sculpture, and a great many elaborately decorated shrines have been found. Many other crafts were practiced, including weaving, basketry, copper working (the earliest known evidence of copper smelting has been found here), fine stone toolmaking and pottery. Chatal Huyuk, however, was a precocious development. The local environment could not sustain longterm urban growth: the site was abandoned after about a thousand years and the pattern of dispersed settlements, typical of the rest of Neolithic Anatolia, was resumed.

The conditions for sustainable urban growth were first achieved in Mesopotamia. Farming was still confined to the fringes of the Mesopotamian plain in 6500 BC but it had spread throughout the region by 5500. The expansion of farming settlement across the plain is reflected by a series of cultures, each of which can be identified by a distinctive pottery style. The first of these was the Hassuna culture (6500–6000), centered on northern Mesopotamia and mostly within the dry farming zone. The Hassuna people grew emmer, einkorn and barley, bred sheep, goats, pigs and cattle and hunted a little. There is evidence for copper and lead

smelting and the Hassuna culture was the earliest to produce painted pottery and fire it in purpose-built kilns. Stamp seals, later used widely in Mesopotamia to indicate ownership, were also first used in the Hassuna culture.

The Hassuna culture was replaced around 6000 by the Halafian culture. A storehouse excavated at Arpachiyeh, containing a concentration of fine pottery, jewelry, sculpture and flint and obsidian tools, suggests that the Halafians were ruled by chiefs who amassed considerable personal wealth and controlled the community's trade contacts. The influence of the Halafian culture was confined almost entirely to the dry farming zone but the same was not true of the contemporary, and overlapping,

	earliest centers of copper working, 6000
	spread of copper working by 4500
	Hassuna culture, 6500–6000
	Samarran culture, 6000–5500
	Halafian culture, 6000–5400
	Ubaid culture, 5900–4300

settlement, though not necessarily occupied continuously throughout the period

	established before 6000
	established 6000–5400
	established 5400–4300
≈	evidence of irrigation, c.6000
Uruk	Ubaid period temple
	early pottery kilns
	find of Ubaid pottery outside main cultural area
✦	obsidian source
✧	copper source
·······	southern limit of dry farming
------	modern coastline and drainage where altered

0   300 km
0   200 mi

Mediterranean Sea

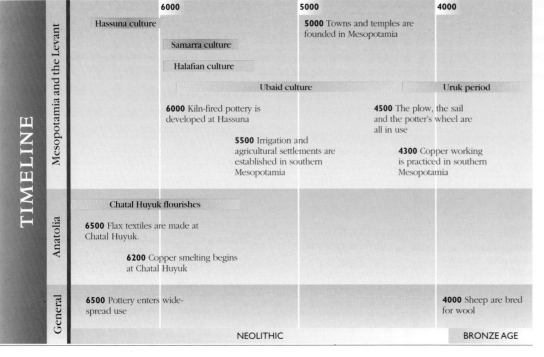
1 Chatal Huyuk had a population of about 6000 people, mainly farmers, between 6700-5700 BC.

2 Tell Umm Dabaghiyeh was a permanent hunter settlement c.6000, trading hides for grain with the northern farmers.

3 Choga Mami is the site of the earliest known irrigation canals; 5500 BC.

4 The fertile but rainless south Mesopotamia plain was colonized by farmers after the development of irrigation c.5500 BC.

5 Kilns were first used for firing pottery in Hassuna c.6000 BC.

6 The Ubaid settlement of Tell Awayli had a grain storehouse with a total area of 200 square meters.

7 Eridu was the oldest town in southern Mesopotamia. It had a large temple and a population of five thousand by the end of the Ubaid period.

8 Ubaid pottery from Ur found here indicates trade links between Mesopotamia and Arabia.

CLAY stamps with incised decoration were found in Chatal Huyuk in Anatolia. They were probably used to print textiles.

Samarran culture which developed around 6000 to the south of the Hassunan area. The most significant achievement of this culture was the development of large-scale irrigation techniques such as canal-building. This boosted yields within the dry farming zone but, more importantly, allowed Samarran farmers to settle on the arid plains of central Mesopotamia.

The earliest known culture of the floodplain of the Tigris and Euphrates rivers in southern Mesopotamia, the Ubaid, developed around 5900 and in its early stages showed clear affinities with the Samarran culture to the north. The Ubaid culture lasted over fifteen centuries and laid the foundations of the later Sumerian civilization of southern Mesopotamia. The first inhabitants of this almost rainless region depended mainly on fishing, hunting and herding, but the introduction of irrigation techniques from the north transformed the settlement pattern. Irrigation allowed the enormously productive potential of southern Mesopotamia's fertile alluvial soils to be realized. Productivity received another boost in the 5th millennium with the invention of the plow. Intensive agriculture meant that the population rose rapidly and many new farming villages were founded. Some of these, like Eridu, the

best known Ubaid site, had grown into small towns by the 5th millennium. A simple shrine established at Eridu in early Ubaid times already displayed the distinctive features of later Mesopotamian temples: an ornamental facade, an offering table and an altar for the statue of the god. This temple was rebuilt several times and by the end of the Ubaid period it had become a multi-roomed complex built on top of a one-meter high platform. Over the centuries the platforms of such temples grew ever taller until, by about 2100 BC, they evolved into ziggurats. Eridu functioned as a religious center for a number of surrounding hamlets, which it may have controlled through the spiritual power of a priesthood or by control of irrigation or trade.

Southern Mesopotamia lacks many essential raw materials, including building timber, metals and stone for toolmaking (and, later for building and sculpture) and semi-precious stone: as a result trade links were of vital importance to – and helped to spread the influence of – the Ubaid culture. By 5400 the Ubaid culture had replaced the Halafian culture in northern Mesopotamia while Ubaid pottery manufactured around Ur has been found throughout the Persian Gulf region.

An important innovation of the Ubaid culture

was to introduce an accounting system, based on clay tokens, a precursor of the first writing system. Although some form of social organization was needed for irrigation works and temple building, burial practices of the Ubaid period suggest that society was still basically egalitarian. When the Ubaid period came to a close in about 4300 BC, the population of southern Mesopotamia was still on the increase and the succeeding Uruk period saw the development of a far more complex and hierarchical society.

See also 1.03 (the rise of agriculture), 1.10 (earliest cities), 1.20 (southeast Europe)

The world's first cities and states emerged in the region of Sumeria in southern Mesopotamia in the Uruk period (4300–3100), named for the oldest and largest Sumerian city. States, with their social classes, centralized government and well-organized trade, became important mechanisms for coordinating flood control (important in this region) and other public works. Early Sumerian cities were dominated by temple complexes, and the priesthood probably took the lead in this organization. The Tigris and Euphrates rivers are subject to violent floods and unpredictable changes of course, events which must have seemed like the acts of capricious gods (the biblical story of the flood is of Sumerian origin). The priests claimed to be able to propitiate the gods, and this may have given them the authority to be accepted as rulers of their cities.

Most Sumerian cities of the Uruk period had a population between two and eight thousand people, although Uruk itself, the largest, had over 10,000; by 2700 BC this had risen to about 50,000. Most of these were farmers who traveled out each day to the surrounding fields. However, the food surpluses they produced were great and Sumerian society became the first to have the resources to support large numbers of people in specialist occupations: sculptors, potters, bronze-casters, stonemasons, bakers, brewers and weavers.

The temples became centers of redistribution where the surplus food of the countryside and craft products were gathered to be given out as rations, or traded abroad for raw materials that could not be found locally. These trade links ranged from India and Afghanistan to Egypt, and played an important part in spreading the influence of Sumerian civilization throughout the Middle East. It was a complex task to manage the redistribution of produce. Keeping track of all the transactions was beyond the ability of unaided memory and by around 3400 a system of pictographic writing, probably derived

area of strongest Sumerian cultural influence

kingdom of Lugalzagesi, c.2350

city named in the Sumerian King List (compiled c.2100)

other city

Mari site of major temple

Kish site of palace

origins of writing

➤ hollow clay spheres and impressed tablets (token system)

➤ inscribed clay tablets (Sumerian pictographic script), 3400–2900

➤ inscribed clay tablets (proto-Elamite script), 3100–2900

— trade route

copper imports to Mesopotamia

grain exports from Mesopotamia

▦ area of alluvial soils

— modern coastline and drainage where altered

| 0 | 300 km |
| 0 | 200 mi |

from an earlier token system, had been developed.

Sumerian civilization entered a new and troubled phase in the Early Dynastic period (2900–2334 BC). Massive defensive walls were built around the cities, bronze weapons were produced in increasing quantities and war begins to feature prominently as a subject of official art with rulers often being shown trampling on their enemies. This period also saw writing applied to purposes other than administration, as rulers began to record their glorious deeds to ensure their posthumous reputations. The gap between rich and poor widened and slavery appears in the records for the first time. Secular leaders now appear alongside the priest-kings. Some had the title *sangu* (accountant), suggesting that bureaucrats had achieved equal status with the priests. Others were called *lugal* (literally "big man"): these may have been war leaders, elected in times of emergency in the past, who had succeeded in making their power permanent. To show that their rule had divine approval these secular rulers built palaces next to the temple precincts, where they lived in opulence. In death they were given rich burials, such as those excavated at the Royal Cemetery at Ur, accompanied by the luxuries of their everyday lives and even their sacrificed retainers. Lacking the spiritual authority of the priesthood, the new secular rulers established their authority through law codes,

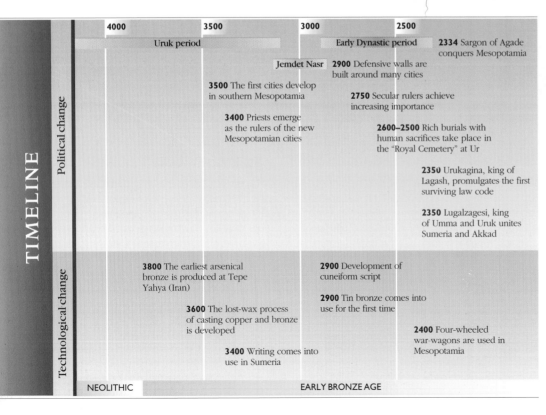

TIMELINE

	4000	3500	3000	2500

Political change

Uruk period

Early Dynastic period

2334 Sargon of Agade conquers Mesopotamia

Jemdet Nasr

2900 Defensive walls are built around many cities

3500 The first cities develop in southern Mesopotamia

2750 Secular rulers achieve increasing importance

3400 Priests emerge as the rulers of the new Mesopotamian cities

2600–2500 Rich burials with human sacrifices take place in the "Royal Cemetery" at Ur

2350 Urukagina, king of Lagash, promulgates the first surviving law code

2350 Lugalzagesi, king of Umma and Uruk unites Sumeria and Akkad

Technological change

3800 The earliest arsenical bronze is produced at Tepe Yahya (Iran)

2900 Development of cuneiform script

2900 Tin bronze comes into use for the first time

3600 The lost-wax process of casting copper and bronze is developed

2400 Four-wheeled war-wagons are used in Mesopotamia

3400 Writing comes into use in Sumeria

NEOLITHIC

EARLY BRONZE AGE

Caspian Sea

obsidian

Murat

Lake
Van

copper
tin
turquoise

Hassek Huyuk

silver
tin

Hasanlu

Great Zab

Lake
Urmia

Tell Brak

Tepe Gawra

Nineveh

M E S O P O T A M I A

Z A G R O S   M O U N T A I N S

Ashur

Euphrates

5

Nuzi

Hamazi

Gutians

Godin Tepe

Tepe Sialk

7

Diyala

Mari

Tigris

5

Tell Gubba

Kassites

E L A M

carnelian
lapis lazuli
from Afghanistan

Desert

bitumen

Hit

6

textiles

Eshnunna

Tutub
(Khafaje)

Tell Agrab

Der

Akshak

Karkheh

Sippar

Awan

Tell Uqair

Jemdet Nasr

A K K A D

Susa

Choga Mish

Kish

8

Abu Salabikh

S U M E R

grain
textiles

3

Nippur

Adab

Shuruppak

Umma

Girsu

Bad-tibira

Lagash

grain

Uruk

Larsa

Nina

Anshan

2

Tell al-Ubaid

Ur

Eridu

9

chlorite
from Tepe Yahya
(southern Iran)

1

Persian Gulf

RULERS and other citizens
in Early Dynastic
Mesopotamia often
erected statues of them-
selves in the temples. This
late 4th-millennium stone
statuette is from Uruk.

pearls
shells

Dilmun

carnelian
ivory
steatite
timber
from Meluhha
(Indus valley)

such as that of Urukagina of Lagash around 2350 BC.
Compared with later Mesopotamian law codes,
Sumerian law codes were remarkably humane and
rarely had resort to the death penalty.

The new martial spirit of Early Dynastic Sumeria
was due in part to inroads by Elamite peoples from
the Zagros mountains and nomads from the Syrian
desert. Mainly, however, it was a result of intense
competition between the various city-states to dominate their neighbors as the population density on the
plains reached saturation point. The Sumerian King
List names nearly a dozen Mesopotamian city-states
in the Early Dynastic period while others, such as
Lagash and Umma, are known from other sources.
Other cities had already lost their former independence: Girsu and Nina, for instance, were ruled by
Lagash by this date.

The early Early Dynastic was dominated by
rivalry between Kish, Uruk and Ur. This was ended
when Sumeria was conquered first by the Elamites
and then, after a brief revival by Kish, by Hamazi.
Hamazi was itself overthrown by Uruk after which
the city of Adab rose to a dominant position. By 2500
Mesilim of Kish seems to have been the nominal
overlord of Sumeria. The dominance of Kish was
ended around 2400 by Eannatum of Lagash, who
fought successfully against Kish, Akshak, Mari and
the Elamites. A dispute between Lagash and Umma

was resolved finally when Lagash was conquered by
Lugalzagesi of Umma, who went on to carve out a
kingdom in Sumeria and Akkad to the north. His
kingdom lasted only about 16 years, but it effectively
ended the period of independent city-states.

1 According to Mesopotamian tradition, Eridu was
the first Sumerian city to be ruled by a king.

2 Uruk was probably the world's first city, with a
population of around fifty thousand by 2900.

3 According to Mesopotamian tradition, Kish was the
first city to be refounded after the Flood.

4 Habuba Kabira was a Sumerian merchant colony
established around 3400, highlighting the growing
importance of long-distance trade.

5 The Tigris and Euphrates were the main transport
routes of Mesopotamia.

6 Hit was the main source of bitumen in
Mesopotamia, used for bonding courses of bricks.

7 The Gutians and Kassites were hill tribes who often
raided the Sumerian heartlands.

8 Susa was capital of Elam. Sumerians and Elamites
were frequently at war.

9 The "Royal Cemetery" at Ur revealed the existence
of a wealthy and powerful dynasty 2600–2500 BC.

See also 1.03, 1.08 and 1.09 (agricultural
revolution), 1.17 (Egypt)

1.11 The first empires • 2334 – 1595 BC •

By the end of the Early Dynastic period Sumeria, though still wealthy and populous, was being overtaken by Akkad as the leading center of Mesopotamian civilization. The rise of Akkad is reflected in the career of the first great conqueror known to history, Sargon "the Great" of Agade (r.2334–2279). Sargon's origins are obscure. He claimed that his father had been a date-grower and that he himself had been an official to the king of the Akkadian city of Kish. How he came to power is unknown but he may have staged a coup against his employer to become king of Kish. Sargon's first task was to eliminate the most powerful ruler in Mesopotamia, Lugalzagesi of Umma and Uruk, which he did in three hard-fought battles. He went on to conquer the rest of Sumeria, Akkad and Elam before pushing west to the Mediterranean and Anatolia. The island of Dilmun (Bahrain) and parts of Iran may also have been conquered. Sargon united peoples of many different ethnic and cultural identities to create an entirely new kind of state, an empire. To celebrate his conquests he founded the city of Agade, which has yet to be located. His empire reached its peak of power under his grandson Naram-Sin (r.2254–2218) but thereafter declined and collapsed about 2193, probably as a result of invasions by the Gutians and Amorites. For eighty years the old pattern of competing city-states returned until a Sumerian revival occurred.

Using diplomacy as much as force, Ur-Nammu (r.2112–2095), the first king of the Third Dynasty of Ur, built a new empire stretching as far north as Assyria. Ur-Nammu's reign saw the construction of the first ziggurats, the high temple platforms that are Mesopotamia's most distinctive monuments. About 2034 the empire of the Third Dynasty came under pressure from the nomadic Amorites of the Syrian desert but it was a knockout blow from the Elamites, who sacked Ur in 2004, that led to the fall of the empire. Sumeria never regained its preeminence.

The two centuries following the fall of the Third Dynasty are a confusion of minor states and of inroads by the Amorites. The Amorites were a strong influence in the rise of the two states that were to dominate the next one and a half millennia of Mesopotamian history: Assyria and Babylon. Assyria emerged as an important trading power in the 19th century BC but it was only after the Amorite Shamshi-Adad took the capital Ashur, along with most of northern Mesopotamia, in about 1813 that it became a major territorial power. An Amorite dynasty had also set up at Babylon around 1894 and when Hammurabi came to the throne in 1792 Babylon controlled most of Akkad (subsequently known as Babylonia). Five years later Hammurabi marched south and conquered Sumeria. In 1781 Shamshi-Adad died and, weakened by attacks from Eshnunna and the Elamites, most of his kingdom was under Hammurabi's control by 1757. Two years later Hammurabi conquered the last Mesopotamian power, Eshnunna. Babylon now became the religious and cultural center of Mesopotamia.

In the 17th century BC new and threatening powers began to gather on the borders of Mesopotamia. The most important of these were the Hurrians and the Hittites. The Hurrians were a tribal people from Armenia who overran Assyria around 1680. The Hittites were an Indo-European people who had invaded Anatolia from Thrace about 1800 and had emerged as a powerful kingdom by 1650.

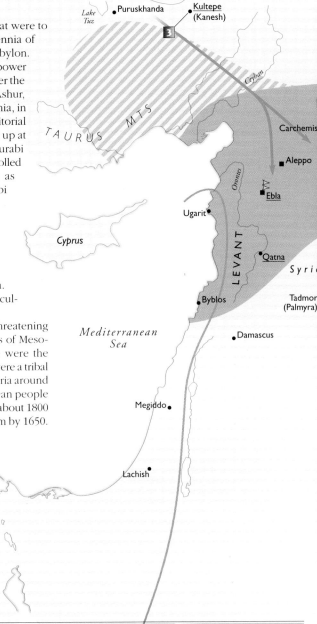

Lake Tuz · Puruskhanda · Kultepe (Kanesh) · 3 · Carchemish · Aleppo · TAURUS MTS · Ceyhan · Orontes · Ebla · Ugarit · LEVANT · Qatna · Syria · Cyprus · Mediterranean Sea · Byblos · Tadmor (Palmyra) · Damascus · Megiddo · Lachish · EGYPT · Heliopolis · Memphis · Nile

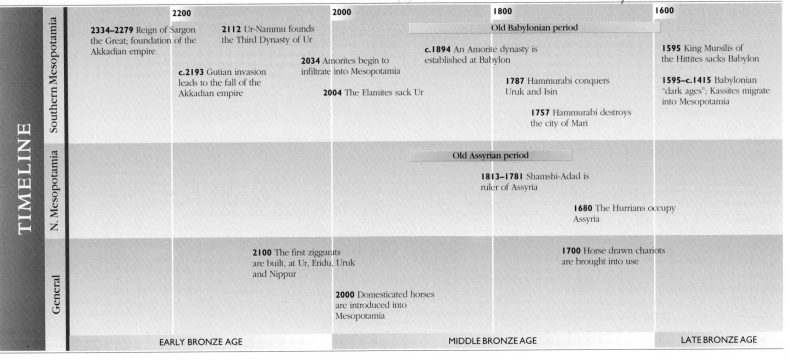

TIMELINE		2200	2000	1800	1600
Southern Mesopotamia		**2334–2279** Reign of Sargon the Great; foundation of the Akkadian empire	**2112** Ur-Nammu founds the Third Dynasty of Ur	Old Babylonian period	**1595** King Mursilis of the Hittites sacks Babylon
		c.2193 Gutian invasion leads to the fall of the Akkadian empire	**2034** Amorites begin to infiltrate into Mesopotamia	**c.1894** An Amorite dynasty is established at Babylon	**1595–c.1415** Babylonian "dark ages"; Kassites migrate into Mesopotamia
			2004 The Elamites sack Ur	**1787** Hammurabi conquers Uruk and Isin	
				1757 Hammurabi destroys the city of Mari	
N. Mesopotamia				Old Assyrian period	
				1813–1781 Shamshi-Adad is ruler of Assyria	
				1680 The Hurrians occupy Assyria	
General			**2100** The first ziggurats are built, at Ur, Eridu, Uruk and Nippur		**1700** Horse drawn chariots are brought into use
			2000 Domesticated horses are introduced into Mesopotamia		
		EARLY BRONZE AGE		MIDDLE BRONZE AGE	LATE BRONZE AGE

Murat

Lake Van

Lake Urmia

Hurrians

SUBARTU

Harran

Chagar Bazar (Ashnakkum) 5 **Shubat-Enlil**

Tell Brak

Tuttul

Nineveh

Shusharra

Qatara (Tell al-Rimah)

Ekallatum

Nuzi

Ashur 2

Terqa

MESOPOTAMIA

ASSYRIA

Mari 8

Hit

Mu-ti 4

Eshnunna

Der

Dur-Apilsin (Dur-Kurigalzu)

Sippar 1

Agade? Babylon

Kish

Abu Salabikh

Borsippa

Nippur 9

Isin

Adab

Shuruppak

Uruk

Larsa

Eridu 7

SUMER

Ur

AKKAD

EMUTBAL

Tell Wilaya

Lagash

Susa

ELAM

ZAGROS

Gutians

Kassites

Lullubians

MOUNTAINS

MARHASHI

Amorites

Persian Gulf

DILMUN 6

HEAD of an Akkadian king, cast in copper. It probably portrays Naram-Sin (the grandson of Sargon) who called himself "god of Agade".

	empire of Sargon "the Great" of Agade, c.2279
	territories possibly part of Sargon's empire
	empire of the Third Dynasty of Ur, 2112–2004
	Babylonian empire under Hammurabi, c.1750
	kingdom of Shamshi-Adad, c.1813–1781
	limit of Egyptian influence, c.1850
■	city
Kish	royal palace
	preserved palace archive of clay tablets
Ur	capital of empire

ziggurat

◆ Ur III, 2112–2004

◆ old Babylonian, 1900–1700

→ campaign of Hammurabi, with date

→ Hittite campaign against Babylon, c.1595

〰 defensive barrier

— modern coastline and drainage where altered

0 ___ 300 km
0 ___ 200 mi

When the Hittite king Mursilis invaded and sacked Babylon in 1595, Mesopotamia entered a dark age that lasted almost two centuries. The Kassites migrated into the region from the east and by 1415 Babylonia had reemerged as a Kassite kingdom.

The most notable characteristic of the early Mesopotamian empires was instability. The success of a state was very dependent on the abilities of its ruler. Government was an expression of the king's will: a strong ruler could carve out an empire for himself but if his successor were indolent or weak the empire would decline. Part of the reason for this was the mechanism of government of the empires themselves. Conquered states were not occupied, garrisoned or subjected to a centrally controlled provincial government; instead, tribute was imposed and native rulers were given the duty of collecting and delivering it to the imperial power. This system worked well under strong emperors, but if imperial power was weakened, a vassal state could assert its independence simply by stopping payment of the tribute. Also, Mesopotamia lacked defensible frontiers and was vulnerable to invasions and infiltration from the Syrian desert or the Zagros mountains. The inhabitants of these regions were eager to share in the wealth and fertility of the plains. They might overthrow states, but were not seeking to destroy Mesopotamian civilization itself; indeed, those – like the Kassites and Amorites – who did succeed in settling on the plains quickly adopted Mesopotamian customs and became assimilated with the native population.

1 Sargon's capital Agade has not been located but is believed to have been near Babylon.

2 Ashur developed as a major trading power in the 19th century BC with links with Iran, Anatolia and the Persian Gulf.

3 An Assyrian merchant colony was founded at Kultepe in the 19th century BC, part of a network that extended as far as the Black Sea.

4 The Mu-ti defensive wall was built between the Tigris and Euphrates by King Shu-Sin of Ur (r.2037–2029) to protect Akkad and Sumer from invasion.

5 Shubat-Enlil was the capital of Shamshi-Adad, the Amorite king of Assyria c.1813–1781.

6 Later traditions held that Sargon the Great led a fleet against Dilmun; if true, this was the first recorded naval campaign in history.

7 After the sack of Ur by the Elamites in 2004, Sumeria never regained its former influence.

8 More than 20,000 inscribed clay tablets have been recovered from the royal archives at Mari.

9 The temple of the god Enlil at Nippur was the most important Sumerian religious center; control of Nippur conferred the right to rule all Sumer and Akkad.

See also 1.03 (rise of agriculture); 1.09 (Mesopotamia); 1.16 (early Africa)

In the two centuries following the Hittite sack of Babylon in 1595, the kingdom of Mittani controlled most of northern Mesopotamia and, at its peak, southern Anatolia. Mittani was founded about 1550 by the Hurrians, who had begun to encroach on northern Mesopotamia early in the previous century. As its power spread west into the Levant (the part of the Fertile Crescent bordering the Mediterranean), Mittani came into conflict with the Egyptians. Under Tuthmosis I (r.1504–1492), Egypt controlled all of the Levant and established a frontier on the Euphrates.

The Egyptians were unable to maintain this frontier and over the next century Mittani regained control over the northern Levant and pushed the Egyptians south of the Orontes river. Then, during the reign of Tuthmosis IV (r.1401–1391) Egypt and Mittani formed an alliance. The peace initiative probably came from Mittani which was faced with a revival of Hittite power in the north, while in the east the Assyrians had won back their independence. When Egypt became preoccupied with internal affairs during the reign of Akhenaten (r.1353–1335), Mittani was left exposed.

The Hittite king Suppiluliumas (r.1344–1322) spent the early part of his reign establishing Hittite dominance in Anatolia, and then in about 1340 sacked Washukanni, Mittani's capital, before sweeping on into the Levant. Mittani began to crumble and when he launched a second campaign around 1328 (or 1323) the western half of the kingdom fell. Suppiluliumas established a puppet ruler at Washukanni, intending western Mittani to become a buffer state against Assyria. As such it was a failure, and fell to the Assyrians by 1300.

The Hittites, who now held the same commanding position in the Levant that Mittani had held in the 15th century, incurred the enmity of Egypt, where a new dynasty had come to power in 1307, eager to reestablish Egypt's position in the Levant. By 1290 the Egyptians had recovered Canaan, which had become independent under Akhenaten, and in 1285 pharaoh Ramesses II (r.1290–1224) launched a major invasion of Hittite territory. The Hittite king

Muwatallis II (r.1295–1271) was prepared and, in a battle between two fleets of chariots at Qadesh, Ramesses was defeated (though he claimed a great victory). The Egyptians withdrew and Hittite control was extended as far south as Damascus. Relations between the two empires remained difficult until 1258 when they agreed an alliance, as the Hittites were alarmed at the growth of Assyrian power.

Assyrian expansion had begun under Ashur-uballit I (r.1363–1328), who seized Nineveh from the crumbling Mittanian kingdom in about 1330, and was continued in the 13th century. Tukulti-Ninurta I (r.1243–1207) waged campaigns against the Hittites and the Kassite kingdom of Babylonia and built an empire that stretched from the upper Euphrates to the Persian Gulf. However, the empire fell apart after he was murdered by discontented nobles.

		1400		1200		1000	
Mesopotamia	**1595** Babylon is sacked by the Hittites and enters a "dark age"			Middle Assyrian empire		**1076** Fall of the Middle Assyrian empire	
		c.1415 The first recorded Kassite king of Babylon		**c.1220** Babylon is under Assyrian control		**1000** Chaldeans occupy Ur	
	c.1550 Foundation of the kingdom of Mittani	**1400** Assyria regains independence			**1160–1130** Babylon is occupied by the Elamites	**950** Assyria and Babylon begin to recover from the Aramaean invasions	
		c.1472 Mittani annexes Assyria	**c.1328** Western Mittani is conquered by the Hittites		**1115** The Assyrians repel a Mushki invasion		
			c.1300 Eastern Mittani is conquered by the Assyrians		**c.1080** The Aramaeans invade Mesopotamia		
Levant and Anatolia	**1600** The Canaanites invent the first alphabetic script			**1285** Peak of Hittite power: battle of Qadesh between Hittites and the Egyptians	**1180** The "Sea Peoples" are driven from Egypt and settle in Canaan five years later		
		c.1500 The Egyptian empire is extended as far as the Euphrates		**1220–1100** The Hebrews settle Canaan			
		1500 Ironworking emerges in the Hittite empire		**c.1200** The Phrygians invade Anatolia; fall of the Hittite empire			
			LATE BRONZE AGE			IRON AGE	

TIMELINE

Caspian Sea

### Map labels

Kaskas

Mushki
(Mysians)

1

ttusas
oghazkoy)

HATTI

Kizil Irmak

Kanesh

c.1340

Hurrians

Murat

Malatya

c.1328

Ceyhan

KIZZUWATNA

Tarsus

Carchemish

Washukanni
(Tell al-Fakhariyeh)

2

MITTANI

Aleppo

Orontes

Ugarit

LEVANT

Syrian Desert

Euphrates

Arvad

Qadesh
1285

6

4

Byblos

Tadmor
(Palmyra)

Aramaeans

Damascus

Tyre

CANAAN

Jerusalem

Hebrews

Urartians

Lake
Van

Lake
Urmia

5

1115

Tigris

Great Zab

Nineveh

Arbil

Kalhu

ASSYRIA

Kar-Tukulti-Ninurta

Ashur

Nuzi

Diyala

Gutians

MESOPOTAMIA

Hit

Dur-Kurigalzu

Der

Sippar

Babylon

3

BABYLONIA

Nippur

Isin

Uruk

Ur

Susa

ELAM

Al-Untash-Napirisha

ZAGROS MTS

Persian Gulf

Chaldeans

Legend

major kingdom, c.1400

- Hittite
- Hurrian kingdom of Mittani
- Assyria
- Kassite kingdom of Babylon
- New Kingdom of Egypt

- maximum extent of Hittite empire, c.1322
- Mycenaean civilization, c.1300
- maximum extent of the Middle Assyrian empire, 1243–1207
- maximum northern expansion of Egyptian kingdom of Tuthmosis I, 1504–1492
- capital city
- campaign of Suppululiumas, 1344–1323

campaign of Assyrian king

- Adad-nirari, 1305–1274
- Shalmaneser I, 1273–1244
- Tukulti-Ninurta I, 1243–1207
- Tiglath-pileser I, 1115–1076

- migration, 12th and 11th centuries
- modern coastline and drainage where altered

0 — 300 km
0 — 200 mi

HITTITE metalworkers of around 1200 BC demonstrate their skill with this silver ceremonial drinking cup in the shape of a stag.

Main text

Around 1200 new waves of migrations brought chaos to the region. Shortly after 1205 the Hittite kingdom collapsed, destroyed by the Phrygians, who had entered Anatolia from Thrace. At the same time Egypt came under attack from a group known to the Egyptians as the Sea Peoples. Their origin is uncertain. Some may have come from the Aegean islands and Anatolian coast but they were joined by others already settled in the Levant and Libya. The Sea Peoples were driven from Egypt in 1180 but settled in Canaan where they became known as the Philistines. Nomadic Hebrew tribes, related to the Aramaeans, were also moving into Canaan.

At the end of the 12th century Assyria was attacked by a confederation of Mushki (probably Mysians – relatives of the Phrygians) and native Anatolian peoples including the Kaskas and Hurrians. The new Assyrian king Tiglath-pileser I (r.1115–1076), forced the invaders to retreat into Anatolia, but he had less success against the nomadic Aramaeans who, despite 28 campaigns against them, had made considerable settlements in Assyria before his death. Tiglath-pileser's successors failed

to contain the Aramaeans and by 1000 Assyria was reduced to its heartland around Ashur and Nineveh.

Babylonia's main problem from the 14th to 12th centuries was the kingdom of Elam. Devastating Elamite invasions of Babylon in the mid 12th century led to the fall of the Kassite dynasty. Babylon recovered under a native dynasty around 1130 and defeated the Elamites so thoroughly that they disappeared from history for 300 years. Then, in the 11th century Babylonia, like Assyria, had problems with migrating nomads – Aramaeans in the north, Chaldeans in the south – and, also like Assyria, was unable to do much about them. The nomads' tribal structures provided no central authority to destroy or negotiate with, and they had no cities that could be taken nor crops to be burned. The powerful Assyrian and Babylonian armies had no target to attack.

The period saw key technological advances, glass, glazed pottery and bricks and iron-smelting all appearing for the first time. Iron did not supplant bronze as the main metal for tools and weapons until around 900, but its use was widespread by 1200, the date accepted as the start of the Iron Age.

1 Hattusas became the Hittite capital in about 1650, and was destroyed about 1200, probably by Phrygian invaders.

2 Tell al-Fakhariyeh is the likely site of Washukanni, capital of Mittani, sacked by the Hittites in 1340 and the Assyrians c.1304–1274.

3 Babylon was sacked by the Hittites in 1595, and was under Kassite rule by 1415, held by the Assyrians 1220–1213 and the Elamites 1160–1130.

4 The Egyptians and Hittites clashed at Qadesh over control of Syria; this is the first battle in history well enough recorded for historians to reconstruct its course.

5 Tiglath-pileser I defeated an invading army of 20,000 Mushki in the upper Tigris valley.

6 On reaching the Mediterranean, Tiglath-pileser I went sailing and claimed to have harpooned a whale.

See also 1.13 (later Assyria); 1.14 (Bible lands); 1.18 (Egypt)

By the 10th century the Aramaeans had begun to abandon their nomadic lifestyle and to settle in city-states across a wide area of the Levant and northern Mesopotamia. Simultaneously the Chaldeans were undergoing the same process in southern Mesopotamia. By settling down, the Aramaeans and Chaldeans lost most of the advantages that their loose nomadic organization had given them over the old military powers, and these now began to revive.

Like the Amorites a millennium earlier, the Aramaeans and Chaldeans adopted Mesopotamian culture but the Aramaeans, at least, kept their identity; their language and alphabet was the common tongue of the region by 500 BC. Mesopotamia experienced no further immigrations in this period but Anatolia and Iran saw the arrival of several waves of Iranian peoples, including the Medes and the Persians, who had both formed powerful kingdoms by the 6th century.

Of the Hittites, Assyria and Babylon, the three powers who had dominated the region before 1200, the Hittites made the least impressive recovery. With their heartland lost to the Phrygians, the Neo-Hittites (as they are now called) formed a number of small states in southern Anatolia, of which the most successful were Carchemish, Kummukhu (Commagene) and Khilakku (Cilicia). The Neo-Hittites were conquered by Assyria in the 8th century after which their identity became lost.

The Assyrian heartland around Ashur and Nineveh had survived the Aramaean invasions relatively unscathed and formed a strong base for recovery. The old pattern, established during the Middle Assyrian period, of expansion under able warrior kings followed by contraction under weak kings was continued in the new Assyrian empire.

Expansion began again in the reign of Adad-nirari II (r.911–891) and by the reign of Ashurnasirpal II (r.883–859) the empire dominated northern Mesopotamia and received tribute from the Levant as far south as Tyre. During Ashurnasirpal's reign Ashur, Assyria's ancient capital, declined in importance and was superseded by a new purpose-built capital at Kalhu.

In 854 a coalition of Levantine states tried to halt the expansion of Assyrian power in the region. The coalition met Shalmaneser III (r.858–824) in battle at Qarqar on the Orontes and, though Shalmaneser claimed complete victory, Assyrian power in the Levant did suffer a setback. Relations between Assyria and Babylon had been good since about 911 when the two states became allies. Shalmaneser gave military support to the Babylonians against the Chaldeans and also gave them assistance against internal enemies.

After Shalmaneser's reign Assyria was crippled by internal problems and went into decline for sixty years. Recovery and expansion began again in the reign of Tiglath-pileser III (r.744–727), who assumed overlordship over Babylon, reconquered the Levant and exacted tribute from Israel and Judah. Tiglath-pileser was responsible for a complete overhaul of the administration of the empire to assert central power. Hereditary provincial governors in the Assyrian heartlands were replaced by a hierarchy of officials under direct royal control. Traveling inspectors were sent out to examine the performance of local officials. A post system was introduced and officials were required to send regular reports to the capital. Representatives were appointed to the courts of vassal states to safeguard the interests of Assyria. Large numbers of subject peoples were resettled to prevent local opposition. Finally, in

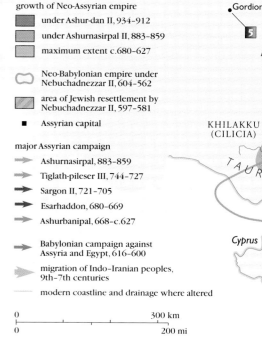

growth of Neo-Assyrian empire

- under Ashur-dan II, 934–912
- under Ashurnasirpal II, 883–859
- maximum extent c.680–627

Neo-Babylonian empire under Nebuchadnezzar II, 604–562

area of Jewish resettlement by Nebuchadnezzar II, 597–581

■ Assyrian capital

major Assyrian campaign

- Ashurnasirpal, 883–859
- Tiglath-pileser III, 744–727
- Sargon II, 721–705
- Esarhaddon, 680–669
- Ashurbanipal, 668–c.627

Babylonian campaign against Assyria and Egypt, 616–600

migration of Indo-Iranian peoples, 9th–7th centuries

modern coastline and drainage where altered

0 — 300 km
0 — 200 mi

perhaps the greatest break with the imperial traditions of the past, rebellious vassal states lost their nominal independence and were reorganized as provinces of Assyria, directly ruled by officials appointed by the king.

Under Sargon II (r.721–705) Assyrian power reached its zenith. Sargon broke the power of the Armenian kingdom of Urartu and expanded Assyrian dominions with campaigns against the Chaldeans (who had seized Babylon), Elamites and Hebrews. Sargon's last campaign ended in defeat, however, and he was killed in battle in Anatolia in 705. Sargon's successor Sennacherib (r.704–681) was preoccupied with rebellions in Judah, with Babylon

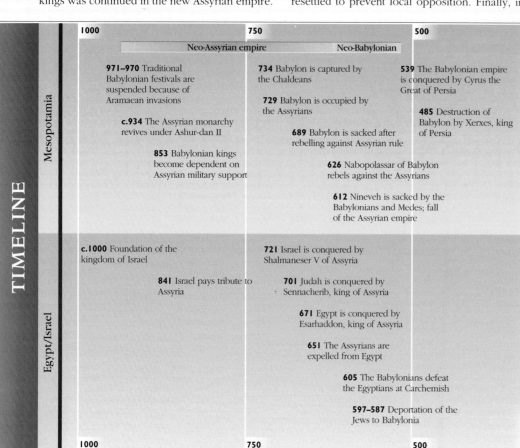

TIMELINE

	1000	750	500
		Neo-Assyrian empire	Neo-Babylonian

Mesopotamia

971–970 Traditional Babylonian festivals are suspended because of Aramaean invasions

c.934 The Assyrian monarchy revives under Ashur-dan II

853 Babylonian kings become dependent on Assyrian military support

734 Babylon is captured by the Chaldeans

729 Babylon is occupied by the Assyrians

689 Babylon is sacked after rebelling against Assyrian rule

626 Nabopolassar of Babylon rebels against the Assyrians

612 Nineveh is sacked by the Babylonians and Medes; fall of the Assyrian empire

539 The Babylonian empire is conquered by Cyrus the Great of Persia

485 Destruction of Babylon by Xerxes, king of Persia

Egypt/Israel

c.1000 Foundation of the kingdom of Israel

841 Israel pays tribute to Assyria

721 Israel is conquered by Shalmaneser V of Assyria

701 Judah is conquered by Sennacherib, king of Assyria

671 Egypt is conquered by Esarhaddon, king of Assyria

651 The Assyrians are expelled from Egypt

605 The Babylonians defeat the Egyptians at Carchemish

597–587 Deportation of the Jews to Babylonia

| 1000 | 750 | 500 |

Phrygians

ANATOLIA

Cimmerians, c.705-c.695

Scythians, late 7th century

Caspian Sea

Lake Van

Tushpa

Lake Urmia ✕ 714

Murat

KUMMUKHU (COMMAGENE)

URARTU 4

MANNEA

Tigris

Neo-Hittites

Ceyhan

CARCHEMISH

Nisibis

Great Zab

Medes, 9th century

Medes, 614-612

Carchemish ✕ 605

Harran

608

Dur-Sharrukin

1

714

Hamadan (Ecbatana) 8

Aramaeans

Nineveh

Arbil

7

Kalhu

Aleppo

605

ASSYRIA

Ashur

Arrapha

Z A G R O S

Orontes

Qarqar ✕ 854

605 601

Euphrates

M E S O P O T A M I A

710-707

Ugarit

Aramaeans

Aleppo

605

Syrian Desert

SYRIA

Tadmor (Palmyra)

Mari

729

615-612

Diyala

653 648-647

M O U N T A I N S

Arvad

Riblah

Karkheh

Susa

Byblos

ARAM

Damascus

Der

Sidon

600

Dur-Kurigalzu

ELAM

Tyre

Sippar

Babylon

Karkheh

3

601

Borsippa 2

BABYLONIA

Nippur

PHILISTIA

ISRAEL

Uruk

Ur

Jerusalem

Chaldeans

Lachish

Persians 8th century

JUDAH

MOAB

EDOM

Persian Gulf

A r a b s

LION hunting was symbolic to the Assyrians of royal power and only kings (Ashurbanipal in this bas-relief) were shown killing the animals.

Taima

Red Sea

supported by the Medes, took Nineveh in 612. A rump kingdom held out at Harran until 609, but after that Assyrian resistance ended. The pharaoh Necho II (r.610–595) seized the opportunity offered by the collapse of Assyrian power to reoccupy the Levant but was defeated by the Babylonian crown prince Nebuchadnezzar at Carchemish in 605. The Babylonians followed up their victory by occupying virtually all of the territory previously held by Assyria. Nebuchadnezzar came to the throne in the following year and spent his reign (r.604–562) consolidating his empire, rebuilding the city of Babylon in imperial splendor and ruling very much within the Assyrian tradition.

Nebuchadnezzar's dynasty lasted only until 556 when it was overthrown in a palace coup. An official, Nabonidus (r.555–539), was chosen as king but his religious unorthodoxy soon made him unpopular in the Babylonian heartland. When the Persian king Cyrus the Great invaded in 539, Babylon surrendered without a fight, bringing to a quiet end an imperial tradition that was almost two thousand years old. Mesopotamian civilization survived for some centuries but gradually declined under the influence of Persian, and subsequently Hellenistic, culture, and had died out by the beginning of the Christian era.

and with Chaldean and Elamite attacks in the south. Assyrian expansion was renewed under Esarhaddon (r.680–669), who began the conquest of Egypt, and Ashurbanipal (r.668–c.627), who completed it and took great stores of booty back to Nineveh. This last conquest, however, succeeded only in overextending the empire while Ashurbanipal's increasingly tyrannical rule spread discontent everywhere. Egypt regained its independence by 651 and, despite his subsequent conquest of Elam in 648, Ashurbanipal's reign ended in chaos. The Babylonian king Nabopolassar (626–605) rebelled against Assyrian rule and after ten years of fighting drove the Assyrians from Babylon.

In 615 Nabopolassar took the offensive and,

1 The Assyrian capital moved: Ashur (c.1363–c.878); Kalhu (c.878–707); Dur-Sharrukin (707–705); Nineveh (705–612, when it was sacked by the Babylonians and Medes).

2 Though overshadowed militarily by Assyria before 626, Babylon was the dominant religious and cultural center of Mesopotamia.

3 Tyre was the leading Phoenician city; in the 9th century the Phoenicians established trade routes to the western Mediterranean.

4 Urartu developed as a rival to Assyria in the 8th century; its power was broken by Sargon II in 714.

5 Gordion was the capital of the Phrygians; its last king Mitas (Midas) killed himself after being conquered by the Cimmerians around 695.

6 Thebes, the most southerly point reached by the Assyrians, was sacked by Ashurbanipal in 663.

7 Pharaoh Necho II's attempt to seize the Levant was ended by the Babylonians at Carchemish.

8 Hamadan became the capital of a powerful Median empire after the fall of Assyria.

See also 1.12 (Early Assyria and Babylon); 1.14 (Bible lands); 1.15 (Persians); 1.18 (Egypt)

The Hebrew kingdoms of the Bible lands were dwarfed in scale and longevity by the great empires of the Middle East, yet their significance in world history is at least as great. The period of the independent monarchy, from the time of David to the Babylonian conquest in 587, was a formative time for Judaism and gave Jews a sense of historical destiny, driving them to preserve their religion and identity through centuries of foreign rule, exile and worldwide dispersal. Christianity and Islam both owe so much to Judaism that neither religion would have its present form had Judaism not survived.

The Hebrews migrated into Canaan in the early 12th century BC, a time when the great powers of the region were neutralized by troubles of various kinds. In their initial attacks under Joshua, the Hebrews occupied most of Canaan, which they settled in tribal units under chieftains (the "judges" of the biblical Book of Judges). However, many Canaanite enclaves remained and Hebrew expansion to the southwest was blocked by the Philistines who had settled in the area after being repulsed from Egypt in 1180. Most of the Canaanite enclaves were mopped up in the 11th century, but the Hebrews began to lose ground in the southwest to the Philistines.

The need for effective defense against the Philistines led the Hebrew tribes to unite under a monarchy. According to the Bible, the first king of the Hebrews was Saul (r.c.1020–c.1006), but it was his successor David who was responsible for consolidating the monarchy and creating the first Hebrew state. David conquered the Philistines, Ammonites, Moabites and Edomites and forced several of the Aramaean tribes of the Levant to accept his overlordship. These were great achievements, but he was aided by the temporary impotence of the powers who might otherwise have intervened. It was also to his advantage that the Aramaeans of the Levant (who had moved into the area after the fall of the Hittite empire) had settled in urban communities by 1000, and so were more vulnerable to attack than the still-nomadic Mesopotamian Aramaeans. Perhaps the most important event of David's reign was his capture of Jerusalem from the Canaanite Jebusites. By making Jerusalem his capital David ensured its lasting importance as a religious center.

David was succeeded by his son Solomon. Solomon's reign was largely peaceful, but maintaining his splendid court life and ambitious building projects, including the temple at Jerusalem, proved burdensome to his people. Some Hebrews were used as forced labor and territory was ceded to Tyre in return for supplying craftsmen and materials. He was criticized for tolerating the pagan religious practices of the many non-Hebrew wives he had acquired from diplomatic marriages. When his successor Rehoboam (r.928–911) dealt tactlessly with the economic complaints of the northern tribes, the kingdom split in two halves, Israel and Judah, and most of the non-Hebrew provinces fell away.

probable border of the kingdom of Saul, c.1006

kingdom of David and Solomon
- border, 1006–928
- under direct rule
- vassal states and tributaries
- campaigns of David, c.1006–965
- Canaanite enclaves conquered by David
- area ceded to Tyre by Solomon
- fortress built by Solomon
- other major building project by Solomon

0 ____ 200 km
0 ____ 150 mi

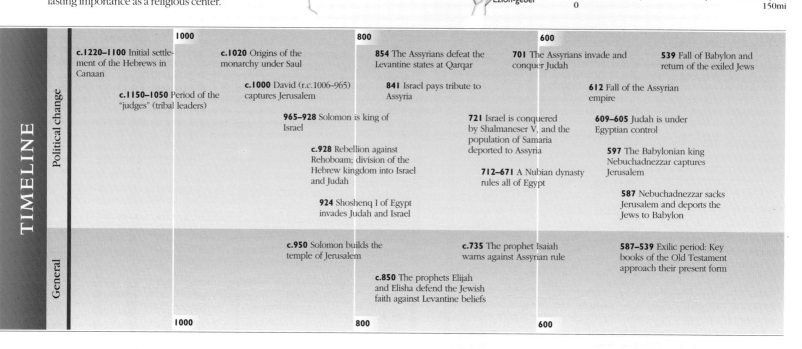

	1000	800	600	
Political change	**c.1220–1100** Initial settlement of the Hebrews in Canaan	**c.1020** Origins of the monarchy under Saul	**854** The Assyrians defeat the Levantine states at Qarqar	**701** The Assyrians invade and conquer Judah	**539** Fall of Babylon and return of the exiled Jews
	c.1150–1050 Period of the "judges" (tribal leaders)	**c.1000** David (r.c.1006–965) captures Jerusalem	**841** Israel pays tribute to Assyria	**612** Fall of the Assyrian empire	
		965–928 Solomon is king of Israel	**721** Israel is conquered by Shalmaneser V, and the population of Samaria deported to Assyria	**609–605** Judah is under Egyptian control	
		c.928 Rebellion against Rehoboam; division of the Hebrew kingdom into Israel and Judah		**597** The Babylonian king Nebuchadnezzar captures Jerusalem	
			712–671 A Nubian dynasty rules all of Egypt	**587** Nebuchadnezzar sacks Jerusalem and deports the Jews to Babylon	
		924 Shoshenq I of Egypt invades Judah and Israel			
General		**c.950** Solomon builds the temple of Jerusalem	**c.735** The prophet Isaiah warns against Assyrian rule	**587–539** Exilic period: Key books of the Old Testament approach their present form	
			c.850 The prophets Elijah and Elisha defend the Jewish faith against Levantine beliefs		
	1000	800	600	

**Map labels:**

Aleppo

Orontes

Euphrates

6

Ugarit

×Qarqar
854

Hamath

Syrian   Desert

Arvad

ARAM

Tadmor

Riblah

L
E
V
A
N
T

Byblos

Cyprus

A
R
A
M
–
Z
O
B
A
H

Sidon

Damascus

Tyre

Dan

A
R
A
M
–
D
A
M
A
S
C
U
S

7

*Mediterranean
Sea*

Acco

Hazor

Megiddo

*Sea of Chinnereth
(Sea of Galilee)*

P
H
O
E
N
I
C
I
A

Beth-shean

8

Samaria   Shechem

Joppa

KINGDOM OF ISRAEL

5

AMMON
Rabbah

Eltekeh
701

Gezer

9

Ashkelon

×Jerusalem

Bethlehem

MOAB
independent of
Israel, 843 BC

Gaza   Lachish

*Salt Sea
(Dead Sea)*

Arad

P
H
I
L
I
S
T
I
A

KINGDOM
OF JUDAH

EGYPT

EDOM
independent of
Judah, 843 BC

•Ezion-geber

Legend:

— border of former kingdom of Solomon

▨ greatest extent of kingdom of Israel

▨ greatest extent of kingdom of Judah

— border of state gaining independence
from kingdoms of Israel or Judah

▨ kingdom of Egypt, 924

▨ Assyrian empire, 722

▨ Babylonian empire, 597

campaigns in Israel and Judah

→ pharaoh Shoshenq I, 924

→ Sennacherib, 701

0   150 km
├──────────────────┤
0   100 mi

Disunity was a luxury the Hebrews could ill afford, as the power of both Egypt and Assyria was reviving. In 924 the pharaoh Shoshenq I (r.945–924) led a campaign through Philistia, Judah and Israel, sacking many cities and imposing tribute, although both kingdoms survived. In the 9th century relations between Israel and Judah was usually hostile and Israel often suffered attacks from Aram–Damascus, which was frequently allied to Judah. Under Omri and Ahab Israel became the most powerful kingdom in the region and played a leading role in attempts by the Levantine states to check the growing power of Assyria under Shalmaneser III. However, under Ahab's successor Jehu, Israel was forced to pay tribute to Assyria. In the early 8th century the kingdoms enjoyed relative peace and prosperity with Assyria in a period of decline, until Tiglath-pileser III (r.744–727) overran the Levant and forced vassal status on Israel and Judah. When Hoshea, king of Israel, rebelled against Assyria in 724 his capital Samaria was taken after a three-year siege and its population deported to Assyria. Despite receiving Egyptian support, a rebellion by Hezekiah, the king of Judah, was also put down by the Assyrians. As Assyrian power entered terminal decline in the 630s, Judah briefly regained independence under Josiah (r.640–609) who extended his authority over the old kingdom of Israel until he was killed in battle with the Egyptians at Megiddo. The Egyptians occupied the Levant but were defeated by the Babylonians at Carchemish in 605, after which Judah became a vassal state of Babylon.

In 597 Judah rebelled against Babylonian rule and was crushed by Nebuchadnezzar. Jerusalem was captured, the temple plundered and many of its citizens were deported to Babylonia. Ten years later Judah rebelled again but Jerusalem was taken after an eighteen-month siege. This was the end for independent Judah. Its last king Zedekiah was blinded and imprisoned with most of his nobles and more Hebrews were deported. Many others fled into exile in Egypt. Though a disaster in political terms, the Babylonian captivity was a creative period in Jewish history. Exile caused a great deal of religious reflection and it was the period when much of the Old Testament was written up in something close to its present form. Nor perhaps were the conditions of the exile extremely harsh. When Cyrus of Persia destroyed the Babylonian empire in 539 and gave the Jews leave to return home, thousands chose to remain where they were. Many others remained in Egypt. It was the beginning of the Diaspora.

HEBREW captives march into exile after the fall of Lachish in 701. Sennacherib commissioned this relief to record his triumph.

1 Saul was killed in battle against the Philistines at Gilboa c.1006.

2 Hebron was David's capital before his capture of Jerusalem from the Jebusite Canaanites c.1000.

3 The Aramaeans of Hamath submitted after David defeated the Aramaeans of Zobah and Damascus.

4 Solomon built a fleet at Ezion-geber to trade on the Red Sea with east Africa and Arabia.

5 Northern tribes rebelled against Rehoboam and formed the breakaway kingdom of Israel.

6 A coalition of Levantine states including Israel briefly checked Assyrian expansion at Qarqar, 854 BC.

7 Aram–Damascus emerged as a major rival to Israel in the 850s, but was conquered by Assyria in 732.

8 Samaria, the capital of Israel, was taken by the Assyrians in 721 after a three-year siege.

9 Jerusalem, capital of Judah, was sacked after the rebellion of 587, and its population deported to Babylon; they stayed until 539 when the victorious Achemenid Persians allowed them to return.

See also 1.07 (writing), 1.13 (Assyrians and Babylonians) , 1.23 (eastern Mediterranean)

The Persians who took Babylon in 539 were comparative newcomers to the region. An Indo-Iranian people, the Persians had followed their close relations the Medes from central Asia to Iran in the 8th century. The founder of the Persian monarchy was Achemenes, who gave his name to the dynasty, but it is uncertain when he ruled. In 648, when Ashurbanipal destroyed the Elamite kingdom and occupied western Elam, the Persians seized the opportunity to take its eastern territories. Despite this Persia was overshadowed by, and often subject to, the powerful Median kingdom. It was in the reign of Cyrus the Great that Persia rose to empire.

Cyrus' career as a great conqueror started when his nominal overlord, the Median king Astyages, invaded Persia around 550 following a rebellion. Astyages was deserted by his army and captured when he met Cyrus in battle at Pasargadae. Cyrus followed up this easy victory by taking the Median capital at Hamadan (Ecbatana). Cyrus was now the most powerful ruler in the region. In 547 he repulsed an invasion of Media by King Croesus of Lydia, who withdrew to his capital Sardis and disbanded his army for the winter. Cyrus, however, had nothing against winter campaigns and, when he arrived unexpectedly, Sardis fell after a siege of only fourteen days. Leaving his generals to complete the conquest of Lydia and the Ionian Greeks, Cyrus marched east to push deep into central Asia. In 539 he crowned his career by conquering Babylonia. Discontent over the religious unorthodoxy of its king Nabonidus was rife and, by posing as a servant of the god Marduk and restorer of orthodoxy, he was even welcomed in Babylon.

In little more than a decade Cyrus had built the largest empire the world had yet seen, with remarkably little hard campaigning. Clearly the close relationship between the Medes and Persians aided in what was more of a dynastic takeover than a conquest, and in Mesopotamia the experience of incorporation in the Assyrian and Babylonian empires had long-since mixed cultures, weakened local identities and accustomed people to imperial rule. As a result there was little spirit of resistance to what amounted, in practice, to no more than the advent of

a new imperial dynasty. Cyrus was diplomat as well as soldier and the consolidation of his empire owed much to his moderation. Demands for tribute were modest, he did not interfere with local customs, upheld the rights of the local priesthood and left local institutions of government intact.

Cyrus was killed in 530 on campaign against the Sakas in central Asia and was succeeded by his son Cambyses. Cambyses added Egypt and Libya to the empire before dying in mysterious circumstances,

Legend

Persia at the accession of Cyrus, 559
conquered by Cyrus, 559-550
conquered by Cyrus, 550-530
conquered by Cambyses, 530-522
conquered by Darius, 521-486
tributary region or vassal state
border of pre-Achemenid state
uncertain border of pre-Achemenid state
border of Persian empire, 496
royal road
capital of Persian empire
Susa major royal palace
LYDIA conquered state
Caria region paying tribute to Persia in 500
modern coastline and drainage where altered

major Persian campaign
Cyrus
Cyrus, conjectural
Cambyses
Darius
Darius, conjectural
Xerxes

### Map labels

Scythia
Scythians
513 513
THRACE
Black Sea
Skudra — horses, weapons
Bosporus
Sinope
480
MACEDON
480
6
Hellespont
Cappadocia — 300 talents of silver, clothing, horses
GREEK CITY STATES
LYDIA
547–546
547
Pteria
2
Plataea 479
Marathon 490
Salamis 480
Athens
547–546 Sardis
Lydia — 500 talents of silver, vessels
Lake Tuz
Kizil Irmak
Sparta
7
Ionia — clothing, vessels
Cilician Gates
TAURUS MTS
Crete
Rhodes
Xanthus
Aleppo
Caria — 400 talents of silver with Ionia, chariots, weapons
Cilicia — 360 white horses
Sy char jewe vess
Cyprus — 350 talents of silver with Palestine and Phoenicia
Sidon
Tyre
Phoenicia
Syri
Mediterranean Sea
Cyrene
Barca
Libya — chariots, goats
525
Jerusalem
Pelusium
525
Palestine
4
525
5
Memphis
Siwa Oasis
KINGDOM OF EGYPT
Arabia — camels, cloth, frankincense
Ta
Egypt — 700 talents of silver, bulls, cloth
526
El Kharga Oasis
Thebes
523
Nile
Red Sea
Kingdom of Meroë (Nubia) — elephant tusks, giraffe, vessels

TIMELINE

Persian empire

c.850 The Medes migrate into Iran from central Asia.

c.750 The Persians migrate into southern Iran from central Asia.

c.640 Persia becomes a vassal state of Media.

c.630–553 Life of Zoroaster, the prophet of Iran and founder of the Parsee religion

559 Accession of Cyrus, who seizes the Median throne in 550

547–546 Cyrus captures Lydia

539 Cyrus takes Babylon

525–523 Cambyses (r.530–522) conquers Egypt

520 Darius (r.521–486) campaigns against the pointed-hat Scythians

518 Conquest of the Indus valley by the Persians

513 Darius invades southeast Europe

499 The Ionian Greeks rebel against Persian rule

490 The Greeks defeat the Persians at Marathon

480 The Greeks halt Xerxes (r.486–465) at Salamis

General

612 Fall of Nineveh and collapse of Assyria's empire

562 Decline of Babylon after the death of Nebuchadnezzar

520 Darius links the Nile and Red Sea by a canal

507 Kleisthenes lays the basis for democracy in Athens

0 — 600 km
0 — 400 mi

GOLD bracelets like this were shown as part of the Lydians' tribute, depicted on reliefs at Persepolis

**Map labels:**

Aral Sea

Sakas

Sogdiana
horses, jewelry, weapons

Kyreskhata [3]

Marakanda (Samarkand)

Bactria
360 talents of silver, camels, vessels

Syr Darya

Caspian Sea

Pointed-hat Scythians
250 talents of silver, clothing, jewelry, horses

Pointed-hat Scythians

CAUCASUS MTS

Colchis
25 boys, 25 girls

Araks

Armenia
400 talents of silver, clothing, horses, vessels

Lake Van
• Van

Lake Urmia

Murat

MEDIAN

Media
450 talents of silver, animal hides, clothing, jewelry, vessels, weapons

ZAGROS MOUNTAINS

547

Assyria
animal hides, cloth, eunuchs, metals, rams, vessels

• Nineveh
• Arbil

Diyala

EMPIRE

Hamadan

Turan Lowland

Amu Darya

Chorasmia
300 talents of silver with Parthia and Aria, horses, jewelry, weapons

546–539

Parthia
camels, vessels

520

Aria
camels, lionskin cloaks, vessels

• Herat

Hindu Kush

Bactra

Capisa

Kabul

Gandhara
170 talents of silver, bulls, weapons

Indus

Peshawar (Caspatyrus?)
• Taxila

Jhelum
Chenab

Helmand

BABYLONIAN EMPIRE

Tigris

539

Elam
300 talents of silver, lioness & cubs, weapons

539
• Opis

Sippar

Babylon
Nippur

Susa

550

Euphrates

Babylonia
1000 talents of silver with Assyria, bulls, cloth, eunuchs, vessels

Dasht-e Lut

Drangiana
camels, lionskin cloaks, vessels

Kandahar

Sagartia
600 talents of silver, cloth, horses

Arachosia
animal hides, camels, vessels

Sind
360 talents of gold dust, axes, weapons

c.518

HINDU KINGDOMS

Indus

550
Pasargadae [1]

Persepolis

PERSIA

Persian Gulf

Maka

Gulf of Oman

Arabian Sea

---

possibly murdered by his brother Smerdis. Smerdis was quickly overthrown and killed by Darius (r. 521–486), a member of a junior Achemenid house. Darius faced rebellions from one end of the empire to the other but suppressed them all within a year. By 520 he was secure enough to campaign against the Caspian Scythians. In 518 he extended Persian control as far as, and possibly a little beyond, the Indus and in 513 he crossed into Europe; though he conquered Thrace, the expedition failed in its main objective of subduing the Black Sea Scythians. This failure encouraged a rebellion by the Ionian Greeks in 499. This was put down in 494 and Darius dispatched an expedition to punish the mainland Greeks for supporting the rebels. When this force was defeated by the Athenians at Marathon in 490, Darius began to plan for the conquest of Greece. The expedition was finally launched by his son Xerxes, but the decisive defeat of his fleet at Salamis in 480 and of his army at Plataea the following year brought the expansion of the empire to a halt.

Darius reorganized the empire into about twenty provinces under governors, or satraps, often relatives or close friends of the king. The system of taxation was regularized and fixed tributes, based on the wealth of each province, were introduced. Only Persia, which was not a conquered province, was exempt. The Assyrian imperial post system was expanded and the roads improved. Local garrison commanders remained directly responsible to the king. The official capital of the empire under Cyrus had been Pasargadae, but Hamadan was effectively the administrative capital. Darius moved the administrative capital to Susa and founded a new official capital at Persepolis. Under Darius the imperial administration used various local languages transcribed into cuneiform and written on clay tablets for documents, but his successors abandoned this system in favor of writing on parchment using the widespread Aramaic language and alphabet.

The Persian empire was a thoroughly cosmopolitan state which united elements of all the major civilizations of its time except the Chinese. By throwing together peoples from so many backgrounds, the empire promoted the diffusion and mixing of cultures and ended the isolation of the old civilizations.

[1] Astyages, king of Media, was defeated by Cyrus at Pasargadae; Cyrus then took Hamadan and seized the Median throne.

[2] Cyrus repulsed a Lydian invasion at Pteria, then captured the Lydian capital Sardis and King Croesus.

[3] Kyreskhata was the strongest of a chain of forts built by Cyrus to protect the northern frontier.

[4] After a hard-fought battle at Pelusium Cambyses captured Memphis (525) and took pharaoh Psammeticus III to Susa in chains.

[5] A Persian force sent by Cambyses to capture Siwa vanished in the desert.

[6] Darius built a bridge of boats over the Bosporus (513) to invade Europe; Xerxes did the same over the Hellespont in 480.

[7] Persian expansion to the west was decisively halted by the Greeks at the naval battle of Salamis.

See also 1.14 (Babylon); 1.24 (Greece)

The end of the Ice Age, about 10,000 years ago, brought major climatic changes. Africa had been an arid continent during the last glaciation: rainforests were small and the Sahara desert formed a virtually impenetrable barrier between central and northern Africa. When the last glaciation ended rainfall increased over the whole continent, with most of the Sahara now able to support semi-arid grassland, diverse wildlife and large permanent lakes. Some 9,000 years ago hunter–gatherer bands lived in most of the area, exploiting game, lake-fish and wild plants of all kinds. Most groups became sedentary around favored watercourses or lakes and produced pottery decorated with a wavy-line motif while they exploited wild plants and hunted over the semi-arid neighborhood. They have yielded bone fishing harpoons, small stone tools and a pottery style decorated with wavy line patterns.

Some of Africa's earliest farming communities developed among these Saharan groups, perhaps as early as 6000 BC. Even though wetter than today, the Sahara suffered long drought cycles that affected the availability of both game and wild plant foods. One survival strategy was to supplement cereal grass yields by planting small gardens in areas where these wild grasses flourished. Over many centuries this resulted in a permanent dependence on crops such as bulrush millet, sorghum and African rice.

In the eastern Sahara, farming based on barley and wheat and domesticated indigenous wild cattle was established by 6500 BC. Farming probably began in the Nile valley soon after. A period of low Nile floods around this time probably reduced supplies of fish and other aquatic animals on which the local hunter–gatherers depended, and forced them to adopt farming. The fertile soils and reliable water supply of the Nile valley made it the richest and most densely populated farming area in Africa by the 4th millennium BC. Wheat and barley spread from Egypt throughout north Africa and to the Ethiopian highlands by about 500 BC, but they were unsuited to the climate of tropical Africa.

Another early center of agriculture in Africa was the Ethiopian highlands, where farming may have begun by 5000 BC based on teff, an indigenous Ethiopian cereal, and finger millet, a cereal of unknown origin. Other Ethiopian domesticates included noog, an oil plant, and ensete, a relative of the banana grown for its starchy root. Of these, only finger millet became important outside Ethiopia. Ethiopia's relative isolation meant that many food plants, including barley, flax, emmer wheat, peas and lentils, developed strains unique to the area.

Farming along the margins of the west African forest zone had begun by the 2nd millennium with indigenous plants such as yams, cowpeas and the oil palm. African rice, adapted to grow in flooded savanna waterholes, became a staple west of the Bandama river. Farmers spread using a technique of shifting agriculture in clearings cut or burned out of the forest.

The introduction of cattle, sheep and goats about 5000 BC revolutionized farming in the central Sahara. By the 4th millennium cattle- and sheep-herding and limited cultivation of cereals were widespread. The herders were seminomadic, and drove their animals between seasonal pastures. The Saharan herders left a vivid record of their way of life in thousands of naturalistic rock paintings found widely across the central Sahara. By about 3000 BC desertification intensified, perhaps in part because of overgrazing. The herders' response was to move out to the Sahel region of semi-arid savanna at its southern margins. South of the Sahara, cattle-herding was restricted by areas of dense rainforest and by the widespread tsetse fly. However, herder groups spread onto the east African highlands by 2000 BC and moved south.

Copper was worked in the southern Sahara in the 2nd millennium, but sub-Saharan Africa moved straight from the Stone Age to the Iron Age. Knowledge of iron working may have developed indigenously in the southern Sahara; alternatively it may have been introduced either down the Nile valley or from the Phoenician colonies in north Africa. Iron was being worked in the Nubian kingdom of Kush by about 600 BC, while it is attested in northern Nigeria at about the same time, where the Nok culture developed by the late 6th century.

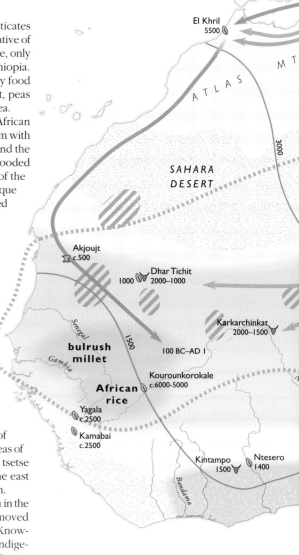

ATLANTIC
OCEAN

TIMELINE

North Africa

	7000	5000	3000	1000
	c.7500 Wavy line pottery is made by hunter–gatherer groups in southern Sudan	**c.5500** Sheep and goats are being raised in Africa	**c.4000** Sailing boats are used in Egypt	**c.2550** The Great Pyramid is built at Giza, Egypt
		c.6500 Cattle are domesticated in the eastern Sahara	**c.4000** Copper working begins in Egypt	**1700** The horse is introduced into Egypt
		c.6000 Wheat and barley are cultivated in Egypt	**c.3500** Desertification of the Sahara begins	**c.1500** Copper working starts in the Sahara; bronze is introduced to Morocco from Iberia
		c.6000 Millet is cultivated in the Sahara	**c.3300** The first Egyptian towns develop	**800–500** Phoenician settlements flourish in north Africa
			c.3000 Foundation of the kingdom of Egypt	**c.700** The Nubian kingdom of Kush flourishes

EPIPALEOLITHIC	NEOLITHIC	BRONZE AGE	IRON AGE

Sub-Saharan Africa

	5000–4000 Eleusine, teff and ensete domesticated in Ethiopia	**c.2750** Farming begins in the west African forest zone; yams possibly domesticated	**600** Iron working is known in the Nok region of Nigeria
	4000 Sorghum cultivated in southern Sudan	**c.2000** Cattle are introduced to the east African highlands	

LATE STONE AGE			EARLY IRON AGE

distribution of bone harpoon points and wavy line pottery, 8000–3000

Saharan rock art, 6000–1000

Nok Early Iron Age culture, c.600 BC–AD 400

teff earliest domestication of African cereal

African cereals domesticated c.5000–1000, combined with cattle, goat and sheep rearing.

domestication of yams

tropical forest

Sahara desert, c.6000

route of introduction

Middle Eastern cereals, c.6000–500

sheep and goats, c.6000–500

horse, c.1700

iron working, c.600 BC–AD 400

mixed farming, c.500 BC–AD 500

500 southern limit of cattle by date shown

early farming site, with date

farming site with cattle, with date

early copper-working site, with date

early iron-working site, with date

modern shoreline and drainage of Lake Chad

CARTHAGE
c.600–500

Mediterranean Sea

LEVANT

Hapeletti Cave
4000 ?

Haua Fteah
5650

Merimda
4200

Faiyum
5300 4300

Upper Egypt
c.3500

KINGDOM
OF EGYPT
c.3000

SAHARA DESERT

Wadi Kubbaniya
18,000

Nabta Playa
6000

TASSILI MASSIF

Jabbaren
3500

Ouan Muhaggiag
4000

Amekni
6100

OGGAR MASSIF

TIBESTI
MASSIF

Adrar Bous
c.4000–3000

3000

Red Sea

Do Dimmi
c.700–600

Agadez
2000–1000

KINGDOM
OF KUSH
c.1700

Meroë
600

Shaheinab
6500   3200

Nile

SAHEL

bulrush millet

sorghum

Kadero
4000   3000

Godebra
c.3000–2000

*Lake
Chad
c.4000*

1500

Daima
600

500

White Nile

Blue Nile

Lalibela
500

E T H I O P I A N
H I G H L A N D S

**teff
finger
millet**

Benue

Taruga
c.800

Iwo Eleru
4000–3000

ADAMAWA HIGHLANDS

1500

Shabelle

Ileret
c.2000–1000

Uele

C O N G O
B A S I N

Congo

North Horr
c.2000–1000

Juba

400–300

*Lake
Turkana*

Lualaba

500–400

Njoro River
Cave
1000

Long's Drift
1000

Narosura
900

Narosura
500

500

R I F T   V A L L E Y

*Lake
Victoria*

I N D I A N
O C E A N

possible route

possible route from the Middle East or India

*Lake
Tanganyika*

R I F T   V A L L E Y

AD 400–500

*Lake
Malawi*

R I F T   V A L L E Y

Zambezi

AD 400–500

ROCK paintings from the Tassili plateau depict a pastoral way of life in the then fertile Sahara.

herding reaches
southern Africa
around AD 1

Limpopo

1 The Sahara had many lakes in the post-glacial period; Lake Chad was 40 times its present size.

2 Amekni is one of the earliest farming sites; the population hunted, fished and grew millet c.6100 BC.

3 Linguistic evidence suggests that teff and finger millet were cultivated in the Ethiopian highlands c.5000 BC.

4 Eastern Sahara was an early center of wheat and barley cultivation, and domestication of cattle c.6500.

5 Hunter–gatherers harvested wild cereals in Wadi Kubbaniya c.18,000 BC; agriculture began c.6500 BC.

6 Do-Dimmi is the earliest identified iron-working site in sub-Saharan Africa.

7 The Nok culture of modern Nigeria is one of the earliest west African Iron Age cultures.

8 Kush, the first African state outside Egypt, developed 1700–1500 BC under Egyptian influence.

0   1000 km
0   800 mi

See also 1.03 (agriculture); 1.08 (Mesopotamia); 1.17 (Egypt)

Ancient Egypt was totally dependent on the Nile. Below the First Cataract, the Nile flows through a narrow valley and, except where it broadens out into the Delta, its flood plain is nowhere more than a few kilometers wide, often less. The flood plain was probably the most favorable area for agriculture anywhere in the ancient world. The Nile flooded annually in the late summer, falling in the autumn and leaving the fields moist and fertilized with fresh silt ready for sowing. The crops grew through the warm Egyptian winter and were harvested in the spring before the next cycle of flooding. Egypt had little need of the complex irrigation systems and flood defenses of Mesopotamia, where the rivers flooded in spring, after the start of the growing season. Canals, however, were used to spread the floodwaters and increase the cultivable area. High yields were possible year after year: the farmers' surpluses were taken to state storehouses for distribution to administrators, craftsmen and priests, for trade or to build up reserves against the famine that would follow if the Nile flood failed. The Nile was also Egypt's main highway. The prevailing winds in Egypt blow north to south, enabling boats to travel upstream under sail and return downstream with the flow. Few settlements were far from the river, making it relatively easy to transport heavy loads of grain or stone over long distances. On either side of the narrow 800-kilometer (500-mile) fertile strip was the desert which isolated Egypt from the influence of other civilizations and protected it from invaders: Egyptian civilization was over 1,300 years old before it suffered its first major invasion.

Farming began in the Nile valley before 6000 BC and by 4000 BC it was densely populated by subsistence farmers. Chiefdoms and towns appeared by 3300. In the narrow confines of the valley competition was probably intense. Eventually, the chiefdoms amalgamated into two coalitions or kingdoms, centered respectively in Upper and Lower Egypt, which fought each other for supremacy. The first king known to have ruled all Egypt was Narmer, king of Upper Egypt who conquered Lower Egypt about 3000. This unification was consolidated by the foundation of Memphis as a new capital.

By the same date the hieroglyphic system of writing had appeared. The system worked on similar principles to the Sumerian pictographic script, but hieroglyphs were developed from symbolic motifs used to decorate pottery in Egypt's Predynastic period. Early hieroglyphs appear on slate palettes which Narmer had carved to commemorate his victories. These palettes show that the principle of theocratic kingship that would be the basis of the ancient Egyptian state was already well established. During the ensuing Early Dynastic period (2920–2575) the kings developed an efficient administration which made possible a dramatic increase in royal power at the beginning of the Old Kingdom (2575–2134), named for the kingdom ruled from Memphis by a succession of four dynasties.

The annual Nile flood was seen as a gift from the gods. The king claimed to be able to control the flood, but if the flood failed, his authority could be called into question. He was believed to be of divine descent and was held to be immortal. At his death immense effort was put into preserving his body and to providing it with a suitably regal tomb furnished with the luxuries of everyday life. Early royal tombs were built on platforms known as *mastabas*, but these were superseded by pyramids in the reign of King Djoser (r.2630–2611). Pyramid building climaxed in about 2550 with the 146-meter-high Great Pyramid, built for Khufu, and the slightly smaller pyramid of his son Khephren. These enormous buildings are impressive evidence of the power the kings exercised over their subjects. However the large pyramids strained the resources of the kingdom: later ones were more modest and none were built after the 17th century BC, by which time ideas of the afterlife had changed.

Egypt was governed by an efficient central and local bureaucracy. The kingdom was treated as the personal property of the king and the central bureaucracy was an extension of the royal household. The highest official was the vizier, who supervised the administration of justice and taxation. Below the vizier were chancellors, controllers of stores and other officials, supported by a staff of scribes trained in mathematics and writing. For the purposes of local government, Egypt was divided into provinces, or *nomes*, under governors selected from the royal or noble families.

During the 5th Dynasty (2465–2323) the monarchy was weakened by granting out lands as rewards and favors to the nobility. The provincial governorships became hereditary and drifted out of the control of the king. A period of low Nile floods then began around 2150, bringing famine and starvation, and the remaining royal authority crumbled. The Old Kingdom state collapsed and Egypt was divided between rival dynasties in Upper and Lower Egypt in what is known as the First Intermediate period.

THIS pottery lion, with a stylized mane resembling a headcloth, was found in the temple at Hierakonpolis. It dates from about the 3rd Dynasty.

Mediterranean Sea

to Libya

1 The First Cataract was the traditional southern frontier of Egypt through most of its history.

2 Hierakonpolis and Naqada were the first towns to develop in Egypt, c.3300. Narmer was probably king of Hierakonpolis.

3 Saqqara is the site of the oldest pyramid, the Step Pyramid, c.2630.

4 Giza is the site of the largest pyramids, including the Great Pyramid of Khufu.

5 The mountains of the Eastern Desert were the chief source of minerals.

6 Graffiti show that the Egyptians were exploiting Sinai's mineral wealth as early as the 3rd Dynasty (2649–2575).

7 The Egyptians maintained a trading post at Buhen in Nubia during the Old Kingdom.

8 Memphis was capital of Egypt for most of the Early Dynastic and Old Kingdom.

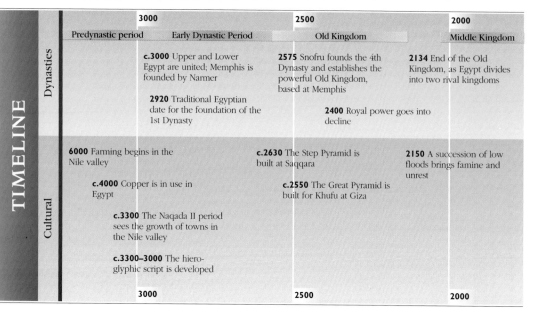

TIMELINE

		3000		2500		2000
		Predynastic period	Early Dynastic Period	Old Kingdom		Middle Kingdom
Dynasties		**c.3000** Upper and Lower Egypt are united; Memphis is founded by Narmer		**2575** Snofru founds the 4th Dynasty and establishes the powerful Old Kingdom, based at Memphis	**2134** End of the Old Kingdom, as Egypt divides into two rival kingdoms	
			2920 Traditional Egyptian date for the foundation of the 1st Dynasty		**2400** Royal power goes into decline	
Cultural		**6000** Farming begins in the Nile valley		**c.2630** The Step Pyramid is built at Saqqara	**2150** A succession of low floods brings famine and unrest	
		c.4000 Copper is in use in Egypt		**c.2550** The Great Pyramid is built for Khufu at Giza		
			c.3300 The Naqada II period sees the growth of towns in the Nile valley			
			c.3300–3000 The hieroglyphic script is developed			
		3000		2500		2000

to the Levant

timber
from Lebanon

SINAI

Tell el-Rub'a

Buto

Nile River Delta

LOWER
EGYPT

natron

Great Bitter
Lake

natron

Wadi
Natrun

Heliopolis

quartzite
limestone

4

Abu Rawash

Giza

Zawyet el-Aryan

Abusir

Saqqara

Memphis

3

8

Dahshur

basalt
dolerite
gypsum

Maidum

Seila

Birket Qarun
(ancient shoreline)

Faiyum

Nile

Herakleopolis

Abu Rawash

Dishasha

flint

Sawaris

Gebel el-Teir

Tihna

Zawyet el-Amwat

Beni Hasan

limestone

Deir el-Malik

Sheik Sa'id

alabaster

Sheik Atiya

Quseir el-Amarna

Deir el-Gabrawi

Meir

Dara

Asyut

Hammamiya

Qaw el-Kebir

Akhmim

Nag el-Deir

Hagarsa

Dendara

Abydos

Nag el-Gaziriyah

Koptos

Naqada

Tukh

Thebes

Gebelan

El-Mo'alla

El-Kab

El-Kula

Edfu

Hierakonpolis

2

2

Bahariya
Oasis

MIDDLE EGYPT

Bahr Yusuf

Western
Desert

Farafra
Oasis

Eastern
Desert

Gulf of Suez

copper
turquoise

6

copper

Red Sea

copper

porphyry
granite
jasper

copper

lead

5

copper

granite

UPPER EGYPT

limestone

limestone

gold
feldspar
emeralds
to the Red Sea

alum

El-Kharga
Oasis

Kurkur
Oasis

Qubbet el-
Hawa

Elephantine
1st Cataract

amethyst

lead
granite
diorite
steatite
quartzite

1

7

to Buhen

ebony
gold
ivory
from Nubia

El-Dakhla
Oasis

Balat

TERRACOTTA figure of a
dancing woman from the
Predynastic Naqada I
culture.

fertile area

conjectural borders of Kingdom
of Upper Egypt, c.3000

southern border of Old Kingdom

border of Kingdoms of Upper and
Lower Egypt, 2134–2040

Old Kingdom pyramids, 2650–2040

single

multiple

non-royal

capital of Old Kingdom

Predynastic and Early Dynastic
royal tomb, c.3250–2650

later Old Kingdom tomb, c.2500-2100

military expansion of Upper Egypt, c.3000

campaign in the Early Dynastic and
Old Kingdom

lead source of commodity

desert route

modern coastline and drainage where altered

0   300 km

0   200 mi

See also 1.07 (writing); 1.10 (Mesopotamia);
1.18 (Middle and New Kingdoms)

The reunification of Egypt in 2040 BC by Men-tuhotpe (r.2061–2010), of the Theban dynasty of Upper Egypt, marks the start of the Middle Kingdom. A few decades later royal authority and political stability had been restored and the power of the provincial governors reduced. To rebuild a loyal administration, the Middle Kingdom rulers promoted propagandist literature, while statuary presented the king as the care-worn "good shepherd" of his people. Pyramid building was revived, though more modestly than in the Old Kingdom.

Egypt's neighbors were now becoming organized in chiefdoms and petty kingdoms, and the Middle Kingdom rulers had to pursue a more aggressive foreign policy than their predecessors. Under Amenemhet I (r.1991–1962), Lower Nubia was conquered; the frontier at the Second Cataract was garrisoned and heavily fortified by his successors. Egyptian influence was extended over the Levant during the reign of Senwosret III (r.1878–1841) and local rulers were forced to become vassals of Egypt. During the 18th century the bureaucracy began to grow out of control and for much of the time the effective rulers of Egypt were the viziers. In the 17th century there was considerable immigration from the Levant into the Delta. Most immigrants were absorbed into the lower classes of Egyptian society but one, Khendjer, became king around 1745 BC.

Around 1640 Egypt was invaded by the Hyksos, a Semitic people from the Levant, who overran Lower Egypt, which they ruled from their capital at Avaris in the Delta. Upper Egypt remained independent under a vassal Theban dynasty but control over Lower Nubia was lost to the nascent kingdom of Kush. Hyksos rule, in what is known as the Second Intermediate period, made Egypt more open to foreign influences. Bronze came into widespread use, war chariots were introduced, as were weapons such as the composite bow and scale armor. New fashions in dress, musical instruments, domestic animals and crops were adopted through Hyksos influence. Otherwise, the Hyksos accepted Egyptian traditions and historical continuity was unbroken.

Under the Theban king Seqenenre II (died c.1555) the Egyptians began a long struggle to expel the Hyksos which was finally completed by Ahmose in 1532. This victory marks the beginning of the New Kingdom, under which the power and influence of ancient Egypt reached its peak. The Hyksos invasion had shown the Egyptians that their borders were no longer secure, and the New Kingdom was overtly militaristic and expansionist, reaching its greatest extent around 1500 under the warrior king Tuthmosis I. Tuthmosis conquered the entire Levant and established a frontier on the Euphrates. Lower Nubia was reconquered and Kush was overrun to beyond the Fourth Cataract. The primary motive of expansion into the Levant was to establish a buffer zone between Egypt and the aggressive powers of the Middle East; in Nubia, which had rich gold deposits, the motive was economic. In the Levant, local rulers were kept under the supervision of Egyptian officials and key cities were garrisoned. Nubia was subjected to full colonial government under a viceroy directly responsible to the king. Nubia was a great source of wealth to the New Kingdom, but the Egyptians faced a constant struggle to control the Levant, against local rebellions and expansionist powers such as the Hittite empire.

The power of Egypt declined after the reign of Amenophis IV (r.1353–1335). Amenophis, who changed his name to Akhenaten, was a radical religious reformer who attempted to replace Egypt's traditional polytheism with the monotheistic cult of the Aten, or sun disk. Akhenaten founded a new capital and promoted radically new art styles to symbolize the break with the past, but there was little popular enthusiasm for the new religion, which was abandoned after his death. In the ensuing period of political instability, Egypt lost control of the Levant to the Hittites. Campaigns by the kings (or pharaohs as they were now known) Sethos I (r.1305–1290) and Ramesses II "the Great" (r.1290–1224) to restore the Egyptian position were only partially successful and Ramesses eventually made peace with the Hittites.

Around 1200 the entire region was disrupted by

Middle Kingdom (12th Dynasty, 1991–1783)

- zone of direct control
- zone of dominance

Second Intermediate period

- Hyksos Kingdom (15th Dynasty, 1640–1532)
- Theban (17th Dynasty, 1646–1550)
- Kingdom of Kush
- maximum extent of New Kingdom under Tuthmosis I, 1504–1492

- royal capital, with dynasty
- ■ city

royal tomb
- Middle Kingdom
- New Kingdom

fort or garrison
- ◆ Middle Kingdom
- ◇ New Kingdom

- sacked c.1200, probably by Sea Peoples
- Giza temple
- desert route used for communication between the Hyksos and Kushite allies
- gold deposit
- major migration
- modern coastline and drainage where altered

Libyan

0   300 km
0   200 mi

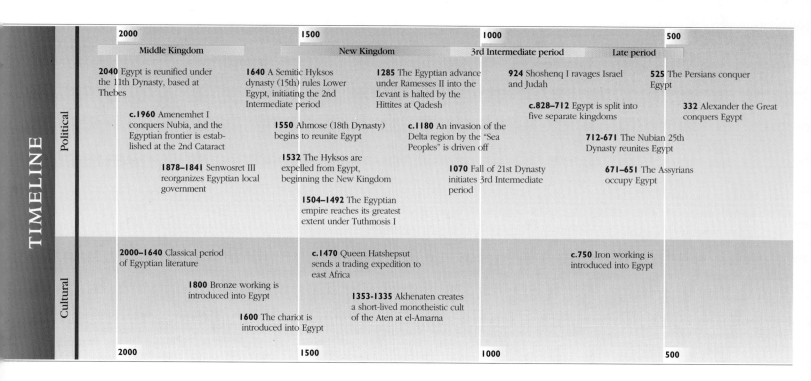

	2000	1500	1000	500
	Middle Kingdom	New Kingdom	3rd Intermediate period	Late period
Political	**2040** Egypt is reunified under the 11th Dynasty, based at Thebes	**1640** A Semitic Hyksos dynasty (15th) rules Lower Egypt, initiating the 2nd Intermediate period	**1285** The Egyptian advance under Ramesses II into the Levant is halted by the Hittites at Qadesh	**924** Shoshenq I ravages Israel and Judah	**525** The Persians conquer Egypt
	c.1960 Amenemhet I conquers Nubia, and the Egyptian frontier is established at the 2nd Cataract	**1550** Ahmose (18th Dynasty) begins to reunite Egypt	**c.1180** An invasion of the Delta region by the "Sea Peoples" is driven off	**c.828–712** Egypt is split into five separate kingdoms	**332** Alexander the Great conquers Egypt
	1878–1841 Senwosret III reorganizes Egyptian local government	**1532** The Hyksos are expelled from Egypt, beginning the New Kingdom		**712–671** The Nubian 25th Dynasty reunites Egypt	
		1504–1492 The Egyptian empire reaches its greatest extent under Tuthmosis I	**1070** Fall of 21st Dynasty initiates 3rd Intermediate period	**671–651** The Assyrians occupy Egypt	
Cultural	**2000–1640** Classical period of Egyptian literature	**c.1470** Queen Hatshepsut sends a trading expedition to east Africa		**c.750** Iron working is introduced into Egypt	
	1800 Bronze working is introduced into Egypt	**1353–1335** Akhenaten creates a short-lived monotheistic cult of the Aten at el-Amarna			
	1600 The chariot is introduced into Egypt				
	2000	1500	1000	500	

Sea peoples c.1180

HITTITE EMPIRE

MITTANI

Carchemish

Aleppo

Alalakh

Orontes

Euphrates

Ugarit

Hamath

Syrian Desert

Arvad

Qadesh
1285

Byblos

LEVANT

Sidon

Tyre

Hazor

Acco

Megiddo
c.1456

Beth-shean

5

Cyprus

Jerusalem

Joppa

Amman

Gaza

Mediterranean Sea

Damascus

Hyksos
17th century

Hebrews
late 13th century

1180

6

Raqote

Buto

Sakha

Tanis

Sile

Kom el-Hisn

Sais

Athribis

Bubastis

Avaris
15, 19, 20

LOWER EGYPT

Heliopolis

Giza

Memphis
12, 13, 18, 19

Dahshur

El-Lisht
12, 13

Hawara

El-Lahun

Kom Medinet Ghurab

Herakleopolis

SINAI

Serabit

Bahariya Oasis

El-Ashmunein

El-Amarna
18

Farafra Oasis

7

Asyut

Nile

Eastern Desert

Mersa Gawasis

Akhmim

Western Desert

Abydos

8

Karnak

El-Dakhla Oasis

Balat

El-Kharga Oasis

Valley of the Kings

Armant

Luxor

2

Thebes
11, 17, 18

El-Kab

Hierakonpolis

Edfu

UPPER EGYPT

Elephantine

1st Cataract

Kurkur Oasis

Beit el-Wali

Dunqul Oasis

Gerf Hussein

Ikkur

Quban

3

Aniba

LOWER NUBIA

Abu Simbel

Red Sea

Salima Oasis

Buhen

Kot

Faras

Meinarti

Mirgissa

Dorginarti
2nd Cataract

Uronati

Semna

1

Kumma

Sai

Amara West

Amara East

UPPER NUBIA

Soleb

Sesebi

Tombos
3rd Cataract
Kerma

Kawa

4

KUSH

Nile

Napata

4th Cataract

5th Cataract

WAR chariots and the powerful bow were introduced to Egypt by the Hyksos. This painting of the boy-king Tutankhamun portrays him using both.

waves of migrations. In the 1180s Egypt was invaded by the Sea Peoples, a coalition of Aegean, Anatolian and Levantine peoples. They were driven off after a naval battle in the Delta by Ramesses III but he could not prevent them settling around Gaza.

During the New Kingdom large tracts of land were granted to the temples, and by the 11th century they controlled a third of Egyptian land: the temple of Amun at Karnak effectively controlled all Upper Egypt. By now the priesthood had become hereditary and was largely out of the king's direct control.

The Third Intermediate period (1070–712) was a complex period of weak monarchies and decentralized power. The empire of the New Kingdom was completely lost by 1000. Although the petty kingdoms of the Levant posed no threat to Egypt, the Nubian kingdom of Kush developed into a powerful Egyptianate state which eventually conquered Egypt in 712. The Nubian conquest marked the beginning of the Late period (712–332) which saw foreign influence in, and over, Egypt increase. Spells of Nubian, Assyrian and Persian rule were followed by revivals under native dynasties, but after the conquest by Alexander the Great in 332, Egypt was permanently under foreign rule.

1 The 2nd Cataract, long unnavigable rapids, was heavily fortified by the 12th Dynasty 1991-1783.

2 Thebes became capital of Egypt at the start of the Middle Kingdom; by the New Kingdom it was Egypt's most important religious center.

3 The fort at Aniba was the administrative capital of the Nubian province during the Middle Kingdom.

4 The strongly fortified Kerma was the capital of the kingdom of Kush in the 2nd Intermediate period.

5 The rebellious king of Qadesh was defeated by Tuthmosis III at Megiddo in c.1456, and the city fell after a seven-month siege.

6 Ramesses III defeated the Sea Peoples in a naval battle in 1180, after which they settled near Gaza.

7 El-Amarna was founded as a new capital by the "heretic" pharaoh Akhenaten c.1350 and was abandoned after his death.

8 The Valley of the Kings contains 62 tombs, mostly of members of the royal family of the 18th-20th Dynasties, including Tutankhamun's (r.1333-1323).

See also 1.12 (Hittites and Assyrians); 1.14 (Bible lands); 1.15 (Persia); 1.17 (Old Kingdom Egypt)

Anatomically modern humans from Africa reached what is now the Middle East some 90,000 years ago, but it was not until the beginning of the Upper Paleolithic period, about 40,000 years ago, that they were able to move into Europe. Unlike the indigenous Neanderthals, who were physically adapted to the harsh Ice Age climate, the early anatomically modern humans were poorly equipped to survive in Europe until, some 50,000–40,000 years ago, they also acquired a fully modern human mental capacity. This enabled them to adapt to the cold climate through technological and social innovation, and compete on more than equal terms with the Neanderthals. The Neanderthals became extinct about 28,000 years ago. Whether it was as a result of a war of extermination or because superior modern human hunting techniques drove them into marginal environments is a subject of debate: current archeological opinion favors the latter.

Two parallel toolmaking traditions, the Châtelperronian and the Aurignacian, are found in Europe during the 10–12,000 years that modern humans and Neanderthals shared the continent. The Châtelperronian is apparently a development of the Mousterian tool culture and is thought to have been used by the Neanderthals. The Aurignacian has similarities with contemporary tool cultures in the Middle East and is therefore thought to have been introduced to Europe by anatomically modern humans. The Aurignacian and the succeeding Gravettian tool cultures both are fairly uniform over wide areas but later Upper Paleolithic tool cultures show greater variety between different regions. These variations are often in style rather than function and probably served as a way of expressing emerging ethnic identities. Typical Upper Paleolithic stone tools include scrapers, sharpened blades, burins – engraving tools used for antler harpoons – and bone points and needles were also used. The Solutrean culture introduced a sophisticated technique of pressure flaking which produced beautiful leaf shaped spear heads.

The most impressive characteristics of the Upper Paleolithic cultures are their art traditions, both decorated artifacts and cave-wall painting. The earliest Upper Paleolithic art dates from around 31,000 years ago but the traditions reached their peak in the Magdalenian (17,000–11,000 years ago), in the cave paintings of sites such as Lascaux and Altamira. The greatest concentration of Upper Paleolithic cave art is to be found in southwest France and northern Spain, an area with a particularly dense population at the time. The function of cave art is unknown but it is thought to have played a religious role. The most distinctive decorated artifacts are female "Venus" figurines made around 25,000 years ago. These have been found across Europe – evidence, perhaps, of a widespread religious cult.

Despite the cold, the tundras and steppes of Ice Age Europe were a very favorable environment for hunters, being filled with easily tracked herds of large grazing mammals. Upper Paleolithic hunters used a combination of semi-permanent base-camps – often sited at bottlenecks on animal migration routes, such as river crossings – and seasonal camps where particular game species were intensively exploited. Caves and south-facing rock shelters were favored camp sites, but in more exposed areas tents and huts were built.

The end of the last glaciation, around 10,000 years ago (8000 BC) marks the end of the Upper Paleolithic and the beginning of the Mesolithic

Legend

Upper Paleolithic, 40,000–10,000 years ago
- Levantine Aurignacian culture
- Aurignacian culture
- ◆ cave site
- ✋ cave site with painting
- ● open site
- ▲ open site with structure
- ⚱ "Venus" figurine find

Mesolithic, 10,000–6000 ya (8000–4000 BC)
- major site
- site with shell midden

- maximum extent of ice sheet during last glaciation, c.18,000 ya
- extent of ice sheet, 7000 BC
- northern limit of deciduous woodland, c.18,000 ya
- northern limit of deciduous woodland, 7000 BC
- migration of anatomically modern humans from Middle East, c.40,000 ya
- ancient course of Thames/Rhine, 7000 BC
- modern coastline and drainage where altered

0 ———— 800 km
0 ———— 600 mi

"VENUS" figurines with exaggerated sexual characteristics were a feature of the Gravettian culture and probably symbolized fertility. This example is from Willendorf in Austria.

Map labels: Oronsay, Oban, Mount Sandel, Star Carr, Creswell C, Paviland, Pincevent, ATLANTIC OCEAN, Loire, PYRENEES, Douro, Tagus, Cabeço da Arruda, 8, 1, 7

TIMELINE

	40,000 years ago (ya)	30,000	20,000	10,000 ya (8000 BC)
	Mousterian / Châtelperronian			
	Aurignacian	Gravettian	Solutrean / Magdalenian	
Cultural	c.41,000 Blade tool technology introduced to Europe	c.30,000 The earliest cave paintings in southwest France and northern Spain	c.20,000 The pressure-flaking technique of tool manufacture is adopted	14,000 Production of cave paintings at Altamira, Spain
		25,000–22,000 "Venus" figurines are found widely from Spain to Russia	17,000 The cave paintings at Lascaux, France, are made	8000 (6000 BC) Beginning of the transition to a farming way of life in southeast Europe
			16,000 Microlithic tools are developed	
Physical	c.40,000 The first anatomically modern humans enter Europe	c.28,000 The last remaining Neanderthals become extinct in Spain	18,000–15,000 The Ice Age is in its coldest phase	10,000 End of the last glaciation
	MID PALEOLITHIC	UPPER PALEOLITHIC		MESOLITHIC

period. As the climate became warmer, sea levels rose and dense forests advanced over most of Europe, bringing the big-game hunting way of life to an end. Large mammals were now fewer and more elusive, but a far greater diversity of plant foods, shellfish, fish, birds and small mammals was available. Mesolithic hunter–gatherers introduced many new devices to exploit these new food sources. The most important technological change was a reliance on microliths – small stone blades or flakes – used in combination to make composite tools such as knives, harpoons, fish spears and lightweight arrow heads. Nets, fish traps, shellfish scoops and dug-out canoes also came into widespread use for the first time in the Mesolithic.

Many areas of northern Europe which had previously been uninhabitable because of extreme cold or ice sheets received their first modern human inhabitants during the Mesolithic, while some which had been relatively densely populated, such as southwest France and the southwest steppes, became comparatively depopulated. The densest population moved to areas such as the Atlantic coast and southern Scandinavia. Hunter–gatherers here were able to adopt an increasingly sedentary way of life, making fewer and shorter migrations between camps. In southern Scandinavia and eastern Europe there were even permanent settlements occupied all year round. Task groups set out from these settlements to spend short periods at temporary seasonal camps to exploit locally abundant food resources.

The Mesolithic period came to an end with the adoption of the Neolithic farming way of life, a process which began about 6000 BC in southeast Europe and about two thousand years later in the British Isles and Scandinavia. In extreme northerly areas, an essentially Mesolithic way of life continued until the domestication of the reindeer early in the Christian era.

1 In the Upper Paleolithic, southwest France had light woodland for fuel, sheltered valleys with many caves, and lay across major animal migration routes; it was therefore Europe's most densely populated area.

2 Upper Paleolithic hunters used temporary camps to exploit particular game species. Solutré was a base for horse hunters, Predmosti for mammoth.

3 Cave paintings of woolly rhinoceros, horses and buffalo found at Vallon Pont d'Arc in 1994 are, at 30,000 years old, the oldest yet found.

4 On the treeless steppes, mammoth bones were used to build huts; a well-known example, c.18,000 years old, was found at Mezhirich.

5 The well-preserved Mesolithic settlement of Lepenski Vir includes many fish-head sculptures, perhaps indicating worship of a fish-deity.

6 Denmark, with marine, freshwater and terrestrial food sources in close proximity, was densely populated in the Mesolithic.

7 The first cemeteries, such as those at Cabeço da Arruda and Oleneostravski (about 170 burials each) date from the late Mesolithic (c.4250 BC).

8 Late Mesolithic hunter-gatherers (c.4000-3400 BC) visited Oronsay island several times a year for fish and shellfish.

See also 1.02 (peopling the earth);
1.08 (Middle East); 1.20 (Neolithic Europe)

The spread of agriculture through Europe was a complex process of small-scale migrations by farming peoples and the adoption of farming techniques by Mesolithic hunter–gatherers. It took time to develop crop strains suited to the colder and wetter climates of central, western and northern Europe. Hunter–gatherers readily adopted some aspects of the material culture of neighboring farmers, such as pottery and polished stone axes, but only adopted food production when natural food sources were in short supply. In many areas, Mesolithic hunter–gatherers were already semi-sedentary, so the transition to a settled farming way of life was probably easily made when it became necessary.

Farming, based on cereals, legumes, sheep, goats and cattle, first began in Europe in Greece and the Balkans around 6500 BC. This pattern of farming spread from the Balkans around the Mediterranean coasts to southern France and Spain by 5000. Whether the adoption of farming in Europe was an indigenous development or was influenced by the farming societies of the Middle East is doubtful. Southeastern Europe was within the range of wild einkorn wheat, cattle, pigs and sheep and farming may have developed as a result of experimentation with cultivation and animal husbandry by indigenous hunter–gatherers. Cattle may have been domesticated independently in southeast Europe but some crops, such as emmer wheat and barley, were certainly introduced from the Middle East.

The earliest farming culture of central Europe is the Bandkeramik or Linear Pottery culture. This originated in the northern Balkans around 5400 BC and over a few centuries spread north and west across the band of fertile and easily worked loess soils that extends across Europe from Romania to the Rhineland. When the population of a village became too large, a daughter settlement was simply founded a few kilometers away. The indigenous Mesolithic hunter–gatherer bands were not displaced by the Bandkeramik people, who settled on vacant lands between them, usually along rivers. However, the steady encroachment by the farmers placed pressure on the hunter–gatherers' resources and they were gradually forced to adopt farming too: gradually the two populations became assimilated. After a delay of several centuries, the farming way of life spread

from central Europe into western Europe, then Britain and Scandinavia and the southwest steppes.

Farming in central and northern Europe was very different from that in the south. The cold winters led to spring sowing of crops (autumn sowing prevailed in southern Europe, the Middle East and north Africa) and there was greater emphasis on cattle and pigs, which were better suited to grazing in woodland than sheep and goats.

Neolithic settlements were generally small, with populations of only forty to sixty. The most common type of building was the wooden longhouse that accommodated both people and livestock. Except in treeless areas such as the Orkney Islands, where stone houses were built, settlements have left few traces; burials and ritual structures provide most evidence of the nature of Neolithic societies. In most of Europe the dead were buried in individual graves in cemeteries with offerings of stone tools, pottery and ornaments. There is little variation in the quantity and quality of grave goods, indicating that these communities were not divded between rich and poor. In many areas the dead were buried communally in megalithic tombs which remained in use for many generations. The tombs were usually covered with mounds of earth, and may have served as territorial markers as well as burial places, the presence of the community's ancestors legitimizing the ownership of the present generation. The Atlantic coast of western Europe, where the earliest megalithic tombs were built, was already relatively densely populated in Mesolithic times. Population pressure may have been felt after the introduction of agriculture, leading to a new concern with territoriality.

In the later Neolithic and the early Bronze Age, northwest Europe saw the construction of megalithic stone circles and circular earth structures known as henges. Some circles have astronomical alignments or form part of a complex ritual landscape but their exact functions are unknown. Some monuments are so large that they must have been built by chiefdoms able to command the resources

	6000	5000	4000	3000	2000
South, east & central Europe	**c.6500** Farming starts to appear in the Balkans	**c.5400** The Bandkeramik farming culture of central Europe begins	**c.4000** The horse is domesticated on the southwestern steppes		**c.2500** Bronze is made in central Europe
	c.6500 Cattle are domesticated in the Balkans				**c.2300** Bronze is in use in southeast Europe
		c.5000 Hierarchical societies emerge in southeast Europe		**c.3300** Copper smelting begins in central Europe	
	c.6000 Farming spreads to Italy		**c.4500** Copper smelting begins in the Balkans	**c.3200** Wheeled vehicles are in use in the Balkans and the southwestern steppes	**c.2000** The Minoan palace civilization emerges in Crete
			c.4500 The plow is in use in southeast Europe		
West and north Europe			**c.4500** Farming begins in western Europe	**c.2900** Cord Impressed Pottery cultures appear in northern Europe	**c.2000** The main stage of Stonehenge is completed in southern Britain
			c.4300 The first megalithic tombs are built, in Brittany	**c.2500** Bell Beaker cultures appear in western Europe	
			c.4000 Farming is introduced into Britain and Scandinavia	**c.2400** Copper is first in use in western Europe	

NEOLITHIC   BRONZE AGE

TIMELINE

earliest farming cultures

- early Aegean and Anatolian Painted Ware cultures, 7000–6000
- Balkan Painted and Impressed Pottery cultures, 6500–4000
- Impressed Pottery cultures, 6000–4000
- Bandkeramik or Linear Pottery culture, 5400–4500
- Bowl cultures, 4500–3300
- Tripolye–Cucuteni cultures, 4200–3800
- Funnel-necked Beaker cultures, 4200–2800

- megalithic monument building, 4300–2000
- stone circle or alignment
- megalithic tomb
- excavation of early farming village
- other site
- spread of copper working by 4500
- spread of copper working by 3000
- general direction of the spread of farming, 6000–3000

```
0                    600 km
0              400 mi
```

BELL-BEAKER drinking cups with incised decoration have been found in graves all over western Europe. Pollen grains found in the bottom of some indicate that they had contained a mead-like drink.

and populations of wide areas. The emergence of more hierarchical societies in the later Neolithic is also reflected in burial practices. In cultures such as the Cord Impressed Ware culture of eastern Europe and the Bell Beaker cultures in western Europe, variations in the quality and quantity of grave goods in burials indicate differences of wealth and status in farming societies. In many areas these changes are associated with the introduction of copper and gold metallurgy.

Metallurgy developed separately in the northern Balkans around 4800 BC and in southern Spain about fifteen centuries later. Both copper and gold were used to make small tools and ornaments. At first only native metals were used, cold-hammered into shape, but by 4500 copper ores were being mined in the Balkans for smelting. Copper was smelted in Spain, Italy and probably Britain by 2400. Copper tools had few advantages over stone ones, but the elites valued metal for display objects. Only in the Bronze Age did metal tools begin to replace stone tools in everyday use.

1 Starcevo was one of the earliest farming settlements in the Balkans, 6000–4000 BC. Hunting and gathering, cereals and cattle were all important.

2 Horses were domesticated in the Tripolye–Cucuteni cultures in the 4th millennium BC.

3 Incised clay tablets from Tartaria show that a simple system of notation had developed in the Balkans by 5000.

4 Copper ores were being mined at Rudna Glava in 4500 BC, the earliest known in the world.

5 A major stone temple complex was built at Tarxien c.3500–2400 BC.

6 Some three thousand standing stones aligned in multiple rows make Carnac one of the largest megalithic sites. Its purpose is unknown.

7 The stone circle at Stonehenge was built in several phases spanning the Neolithic and Bronze Age (c.3000–1500 BC).

8 An "ice man", whose body was found in 1991, froze to death in the Otztaler Alps c.3350–3120 BC.

See also 1.03 (spread of agriculture); 1.08 (Middle East); 1.19 (Mesolithic Europe)

The Bronze Age saw chiefdoms and warrior elites established across most of Europe. Beyond the Aegean, states were not formed until the Iron Age was well advanced and in northern and eastern Europe not until the early Middle Ages. The chiefdoms were competitive communities: fortifications were built in great numbers and new weapons such as swords and halberds were invented. Superb crafted display objects – ornaments, weapons, "parade-ground" armor, tableware, cult objects – made of bronze and precious metals, express the competitiveness of the period. Long-distance trade , particularly in tin and amber, arose to satisfy the demand for metals and other precious objects in areas where such resources were lacking. The increase in trade aided the spread of ideas and fashions and led to a high degree of cultural uniformity.

The earliest known use of bronze in Europe, in the Unetice culture in central Europe about 2500 BC, was probably an independent development and not the result of influence from the Middle East. Bronze came into use in southeast Europe, the Aegean and Italy two hundred years later, followed by Spain and, finally, the British Isles in about 1800. Scandinavia, with no workable deposits of copper or tin, continued in the Stone Age until the middle of the 2nd millennium BC. By this time bronze had entered Scandinavia, brought by traders in exchange for amber and, probably, furs.

Bronze technology led to a rapid increase in the use of metals. Bronze weapons and tools kept an edge better than stone or copper, could easily be resharpened and when broken could be melted down and recast. It was expensive, however, and its use was largely confined to the social elites in the early Bronze Age. Stone tools, sometimes copying the style of prestigious bronze tools, continued in everyday use. Large quantities of bronze artifacts, often of the highest quality, were buried or sunk in bogs as offerings to the gods.

The social distinctions of Bronze Age society are apparent in burial practices: a minority of burials being richly furnished with grave goods and the majority with few offerings. In the earlier Bronze

early Bronze Age cultures, c.2300–1800

- late megalithic cultures
- Bell Beaker cultures
- Nordic late Neolithic cultures
- Cord Impressed Pottery cultures
- Catacomb Grave cultures
- Unetice culture
- Danubian–Carpathian Bronze Age cultures
- Balkan Bronze Age cultures
- early Aegean Bronze Age cultures
- North Italian Bronze Age cultures
- South Italian Bronze Age cultures

spread of Urnfield cultures in late Bronze Age

- by 14th century
- by 12th century
- by 9th century

- early Bronze Age barrow burial
- fortified site
- late Bronze Age urnfield
- metal hoard
- shipwreck
- settlement
- other site
- source of tin
- source of copper
- source of gold
- source of amber
- Mycenaean trade route
- main amber trade route

0 ————————————— 600 km
0 ————————————— 400 mi

Age three distinct burial practices are found. In southeast Europe the normal practice was burial of rich and poor alike in flat grave cemeteries. In most of eastern, northern and western Europe, the poor were buried in flat graves but the rich were buried under earth mounds known as barrows. Barrows required a communal effort to build and are evidence of the power of the elites. In some parts of western Europe Neolithic-style communal burials in megalithic tombs continued until about 1200 BC.

In southern and central Europe, large villages, often fortified, developed but in northern and western Europe the settlement pattern was one of dispersed homesteads. Population rose across Europe and agricultural settlers moved into many marginal upland areas. These were abandoned late in the Bronze Age, perhaps because of climatic deterioration or because the poor soils had been exhausted. As agricultural land rose in value, clear boundaries were laid out between communities in

TIMELINE

		2000	1500	1000
South and east Europe		**c.2500–1800** The Unetice culture appears in central Europe	**c.1650** The Mycenaean civilization develops and traders are active in south Italy	**c.1350** The Urnfield culture appears in central Europe
		c.2300 Bronze working begins in southeast Europe		**c.1200** Fall of the Mycenaean civilization
		c.2000 Hillforts are built in central Europe		**c.1000** Iron comes into widespread use in Greece
		c.2000 The first European state emerges, in Crete		**c.750** Beginning of the Hallstatt ("Celtic") Iron Age
		c.2000 Trade routes across Europe appear for amber and metals		
West and north Europe		**c.2000** The Wessex culture flourishes in Britain, with rich barrow burials		**1100** Hillforts are built in western Europe
		c.2000 The main stage of Stonehenge, in southern Britain, is completed		**1000** Urnfield cultures spread to western Europe
				c.700 Iron in widespread use throughout Europe
		NEOLITHIC	BRONZE AGE	IRON AGE

sub-Neolithic forest
hunters and gatherers

Rickeby

Tromøy
Vänern
Hallunda
Vättern
Kvarnby

Bulbjerg

Lake
Peipus

Rezne

Western Dvina

VOTIVE offerings, thrown
into the bogs, include this
bronze and gold "chariot of
the sun" from Trundholm
(Denmark).

Trundholm
Brudevaelte
Egtved
Kivik
Voldtofte

4
Drenthe
Barger-Oosterveld

Perleberg

Biskupin
Jankowo
Kamieniec

Pustinka

3
Nieder-Neundorf
Schweinert
Miejsce

Donec group

Toterfout
Court St Etienne
Leubingen
Grossenheim
Iwanowice

Ivanja

Moska
Dnieper

Bad Nauheim
Helmsdorf
Gedinne
Flörsheim
Postoloprty
Spissky Stvrtok
Havré
Heidesheim
Unetice
Velatice
Barca
Rostov

Hagenam
Mannheim
Blucina
Veterov

Usatove

Danube
Kelheim
5
Wasserburg
Ettins
Unter-Radl
Malé Kosihy

Mohi
ixheim
Baldegg
Volders
Nitriansky Hrádok
Caka
Fuzesabony
Suciu du Sus
Tudoromo

Kamenka

1
Wittnauer Horn
Hölting
Vál
Ptuj
Monteoru

Cortaillod
Kisapostag
Tószeg
Crestaulta
Ledro
Bled
Czorvas
Periam
Angarano
Polada
Dobova
Sava
Gomalova
Vattina
Canegrate
Fontanella
Gîrla Mare
Cîrna

A L P S

C A R P A T H I A N   M T S

Black Sea

Bismantora
Danube
Tarnava
Ezerovo

Ezero

Corsica
Luni
Ezero
Filitosa
Allumiere
Narce

Danja Slatina

Nuraghe
Albucci
Phlegraean
Fields
Scoglio del
Tonno

Barumini
A N A T O L I A

Sardinia
6
Troy

Hittites

Lipara
Millazzo

Sicily

Mycenae

Cyprus

Borg in-Nadur

M e d i t e r r a n e a n   S e a

Malta

Crete
Knossos
Minoan
civilization

many areas, especially northwest Europe, and farm-
land was enclosed into small fields that could be
managed more intensively. Farmers benefited from
the introduction of heavier plows, wheeled vehicles
and horses. European wild oats were domesticated
at this time, probably as horse fodder.

Around 1350 the Urnfield culture, named for its
distinctive burial practices, appeared in Hungary.
Bodies were cremated and the ashes buried in funerary urns in flat grave cemeteries of hundreds, even
thousands, of graves. As with earlier Bronze Age
burial customs, a minority of graves included rich
offerings, weapons and armor. Some of these graves
were covered with barrows, demonstrating a degree
of continuity with the past, but this was by no means
universal: the powers enjoyed by chieftains in the
early Bronze Age may have been undermined to an
extent by the emergence of a warrior class. By the
9th century Urnfield customs had spread over most
of continental Europe. Except in the west where it

was probably taken by migrating Celtic peoples,
the Urnfield culture spread mainly as a result of
the wide-ranging contacts on trade links. The later
Bronze Age saw increased militarization, with extensive fortress building in western Europe and the
introduction of the bronze slashing sword. Bronze
armor was introduced, but probably for display
only: it offers less protection than leather.

Small numbers of iron artifacts appeared in many
areas about 1200. However, iron tools first became
common only around 1000 in Greece and two
hundred and fifty years later in northern Europe.

1 Bronze Age settlements along the northern fringes
of the Alps were often built on islands in lakes for
defense.

2 One of the last megalithic tombs to be used was at
Island, in Ireland; it was still in use about 1200 BC
about a millennium later than most megalithic tombs.

3 At Leubingen, an early Bronze Age barrow contains
the remains of an elderly man accompanied by a girl,
pottery, stone and bronze tools and weapons, and
gold jewelry.

4 A late Bronze Age dismantled wooden "temple" was
deliberately sunk into a peat bog at Barger-Oosterveld.

5 The Urnfield cemetery at Kelheim of 900–800 BC
had more than 10,000 burials.

6 Defensive towers called *nuraghe* were built about
1800 BC in Sardinia; similar structures are found in
Corsica and the Balearic islands.

7 A shipwreck from 800 BC off the southwest coast
of Spain included more than 200 bronze weapons
made in the Loire region.

See also 1.20 (Neolithic Europe);
1.22 (Minoans and Mycenaeans)

Europe's first cities and states developed on the Aegean island of Crete around 2000 BC, where the Minoans developed a system of intensive agriculture based on wheat, olives and vines. Olives and vines grew well on rough hillsides and produced valuable commodities for long-distance trade, allowing good plowland to be kept for wheat production. Sheep were kept on Crete's mountain pastures and their wool supplied a textile industry that exported cloth to Egypt. Minoan pottery and metalwork was in demand throughout the eastern Mediterranean.

By 2000 BC Minoan society was controlled from palaces at Knossos, Phaistos, Mallia and Khania, probably the capitals of small kingdoms. A number of smaller palaces were probably subordinate centers. The palaces, which incorporated vast storehouses for grain, oil and other products, were centers for redistributing produce collected as taxes or tribute for rations to support administrators, craftsmen or traders. The Minoans had a hieroglyphic script by 2000, but this was superseded by a syllabic script three centuries later. Neither script has been deciphered so the ethnic identity of the Minoans is unknown, but they did not speak an Indo-European language and were therefore not Greeks.

Around 1700 most of the Minoan palaces were destroyed by fire, probably as a result of warfare between the palace states; they were subsequently rebuilt, but only Knossos regained its former splendor, taking control of the whole island and reducing the other palaces to tributary status. In 1626 the palaces were damaged by ash falls and earthquakes resulting from a volcanic eruption on the nearby island of Thera. The palaces were rebuilt and the Minoan civilization endured until it collapsed in about 1450 after conquest by the Mycenaeans.

The Mycenaeans, or Achaeans as they probably called themselves, were a Greek-speaking people who had moved to the Greek peninsula from the Balkans around 2000 BC. By around 1600 small kingdoms based on fortified towns were beginning to develop and a system of writing, based on the Cretan syllabic script, had been adopted. The earliest

MINOAN CRETE

Sea

Crete

Khania
Knossos
Mallia
Arkhanes
Monastiraki
Palaikastro
Gournia
Hagia Triadha
Phaistos
Myrtos
Kato Zakro

0   60 km
0   40 mi

	Minoan civilization, c.1600
	Minoan influence, c.1600
	Mycenaean civilization, c.1300
	Mycenaean colonization, late 13th century BC
	Minoan city, with palace
	other Minoan settlement
	Mycenaean city, with palace
	other Mycenaean settlement
Knossos	capital city
Troy	fortified settlement
	site damaged or destroyed by Mycenaeans, c.1450

	site damaged or destroyed by invaders from the north, or "Sea Peoples", c.1200
	mountain-top shrine on Crete
	sacred cave on Crete
	shipwreck
	probable trading route of the Ulu Burun ship
ivory	source of objects in the cargo of the Ulu Burun wreck, 14th century BC
	major migration, c.2000
	major migration, c.1200
	area affected by ash falls from the eruption of Thera, 1626

HITTITE EMPIRE

Sea Peoples
Mersin
Tarsus
Carchemish

tin ingots

Alalakh
Aleppo

Sea Peoples

6
Cape Gelidonya
as

Orontes

Ugarit

Sea Peoples

Hamath

Lapethos
Chytroi
Soloi
Enkomi
8
Idalion
Tamassos
Kition
Paphos
Amathous
Kourion

Mycenaeans

amphoras, bronze, dye, glass, ivory, olives, resin, weapons

*Cyprus
copper ingots,
pottery*

Sea Peoples

EVIDENCE of a wealthy and powerful kingdom is offered by this gold death mask from Mycenae, c.1500 BC.

*cylinder seals
from Mesopotamia*

P
A
L
E
S
T
I
N
E

1180 ✕

*bronze weapons, ebony,
scarab brooches*

Gaza

Avaris
3

EGYPT

Memphis

0   300 km
0   200 mi

Nile

---

evidence of Mycenaean civilization is a series of richly furnished shaft graves at Mycenae, dating to between 1650 and 1550. The grave goods reveal a wealthy warrior society and include hoards of bronze weapons, gold, silver and electrum tableware, jewelry and gold deathmasks. Mycenaean warriors rode to battle in horse-drawn chariots, but fought on foot with spear, sword and dagger. The towns were well defended, especially after the 14th century, by strong walls, built with massive blocks of stone and bastioned gateways. From the 15th century, Mycenaean rulers were buried in vaulted *tholos* (beehive shaped) tombs in which rituals related to a cult of kingship could be performed.

Each Mycenaean stronghold was ruled over by a king with a warrior aristocracy. The kings controlled many craftsmen – the king of Pylos employed about four hundred bronzesmiths – and hundreds of mainly female slaves. The royal palaces were smaller than those on Crete. According to a survey preserved in Homer's *Iliad*, known as the Catalog of Ships, there were some twenty kingdoms theoretically acknowledging the leadership of Mycenae.

Around 1450 the Mycenaeans expanded in the Aegean, conquering Crete and founding Miletos on the Anatolian coast: they may also have raided Egypt and the Hittite empire and, perhaps, they sacked Troy. They traded throughout the eastern Mediterranean and as far west as Malta, Sicily and Italy.

The Mycenaean civilization came to a violent end around 1200. Most of the major centers were sacked, town life came to an end and writing fell out of use. The whole Aegean entered a dark age which lasted about four centuries. The attackers were probably the Sea Peoples who also brought chaos to Egypt and the Levant. Some Mycenaeans sought refuge on Cyprus and on the coast of Anatolia; others may have joined with the Sea Peoples – Mycenaean influence is evident in Palestine where some of them settled. A power vacuum developed in Greece into which another Greek-speaking people, the Dorians, migrated around 1100, overrunning the Peloponnese, Crete and Rhodes: of the old Mycenaean centers only Athens retained its independence.

---

1 Knossos, the greatest of the Cretan palaces, was first built around 2000 and was rebuilt several times after earthquake damage or war.

2 The Minoan city of Akrotiri was preserved by ashfalls after the volcanic eruption on Thera in 1626.

3 Avaris was an Egyptian city which contained a Minoan colony founded in about 1550.

4 Mycenae had rich tombs and massive defenses built between 1600 and 1200. According to Homer, its king Agamemnon led the Greeks in the Trojan War.

5 A defensive wall was built across the Isthmus of Corinth in the late 13th century to protect the Peloponnese from invasion from the north.

6 A 14th-century shipwreck found at Ulu Burun near Kas had a cargo from around the east Mediterranean.

7 Troy was sacked twice in the 13th century, and again in 1100.

8 Mycenaeans reached Cyprus in the 15th century but the main settlement was 300 years later.

See also 1.12 (Sea Peoples); 1.18 (Egypt);
1.24 (Greek city-states)

As the eastern Mediterranean recovered from the disruptions of the late second millennium, the Phoenicians and Greeks began to establish trade routes and colonies throughout the western Mediterranean and, in the case of the Greeks, the Black Sea.

The first to extend their trade routes into the western Mediterranean were the Phoenicians, a Levantine people culturally and linguistically closely related to the Canaanites. The Phoenician homeland had the best natural harbors on the coastline of the Levant, where small ports had grown up as early as the third millennium BC, trading cedar wood, purple dye and other commodities with Egypt. The leading Phoenician ports had developed into independent city-states by 1500 BC. In the earliest records the Phoenician cities were ruled by hereditary kings, but by the 6th century monarchy had been replaced by elected officials. The Phoenician cities never exercised control far inland and for the greater part of their history they were dominated by one or other of the region's great powers.

The earliest evidence of Phoenician expansion overseas is at Kition, originally a Mycenaean colony, on Cyprus about 1000 BC. Cyprus was an important source of copper and had had close trade links with Phoenicia for centuries before this. The main period of Phoenician expansion, however, extended from the late 9th century to the mid 7th century. The main concentration of Phoenician colonies were in Tunisia, Sicily and Sardinia, which gave them control over the main approaches to the western Mediterranean. By the 7th century Carthage, a Tyrian colony, had become the leading Phoenician city in the west. By the 8th century Phoenician trade routes extended through the Straits of Gibraltar and some way along the Atlantic coasts of Spain and Morocco. At first the Phoenicians maintained only seasonal trading posts in this area, but permanent colonies, such as Tingis and Gades, were established in the 7th century. Phoenician colonies technically remained subject to their parent cities, but they were forced to become independent when Phoenicia was conquered by the Babylonians in the 6th century.

Legend

- Phoenicia
- coast under Phoenician influence, 6th century
- Phoenician colony, founded 900–600
- ☆ Phoenician trading post
- Phoenician trade route
- Greeks, c.900
- coast under Greek influence, 6th century

Greek colonies
- ○ Achaean
- △ Aeolian
- ▽ Dorian
- □ Ionian
- ◇ other

foundation date of Greek colony
- ● 9th century
- ● 8th century
- ● 7th century
- ● 6th century
- ☆ Greek trading post, 6th century
- ▽ Greek objects (c.700–500) found
- Sparta Greek parent state or region
- subdivisions of Greek peoples
- Greek trade route
- → tin route

0 ____ 600 km
0 ____ 400 mi

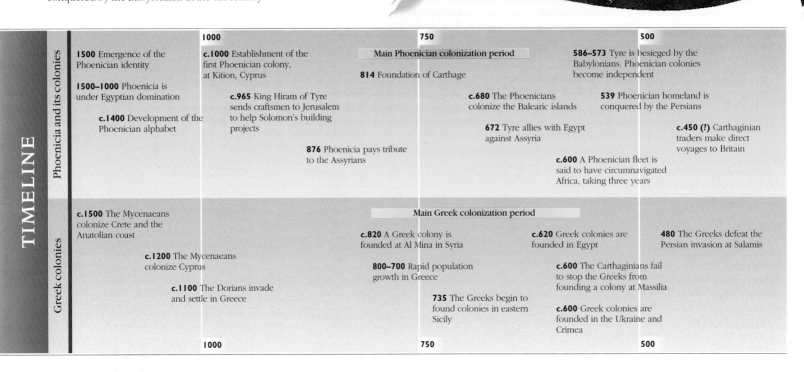

GORGON'S head handles and a frieze of soldiers and chariots embellish this head-height bronze *krater* (a vessel for mixing wine and water). Of 6th-century Greek manufacture, it was found at Vix, France

SHIPBUILDING and navigation were essential skills. This detail of a vase painting c.540 shows the god Dionysus at sea (having escaped capture by pirates).

**Map labels:**

Rhine · Elbe · Danube · Dnieper · Don · Sava · Po · Tigris · Euphrates · Nile

Celts · Scythians **3** · Tanais · Olbia · Berezean Island · Tyras · Pantikapaion · Phanagoria · Theodosia · Kimmerikon · Dioskurias · Istros · Kallatis · Black Sea · Phasis · COLCHI · Odessos · Mesembria · Apollonia · Sinope · Trapezus · Kytoros · Sesamos · Kerasous · Herakleia · Byzantium · Chalcedon · Phrygians

ALPS · Spina · Etruscan city states · Illyrians · Thracians · Macedonians · Volaterrae · Volci · Graisca · Italics · Alalia · Corsica · Epidamnos · Apollonia · Stageiros · Thasos · Ainos · Kardia · Methone · Sestos · Cyzicus · Abydos · Ilium · Lydians · Tigris · Kymai · Neapolis · Pithekoussai · Taras · Satyrion · Poseidonia · Elea · Metapontum · Skidros · Sybaris · Terina · Kroton · Mende · Torone · Aeolians · Lesbos · Phokaia · Chalcis · Eretria · Smyrna · Locris · Athens · Samos · Megara · Corinth · Miletos · Sardinia · Tharros · Caralis · Nora · ulcis · Himera · Soleis · Metauros · Hipponion · Lokroi · Panormus · Mylai · Rhegion · Motya · Katana · Naxos · Leontinoi · Minoa · Akragas · Gela · Syracuse · Kamarina · Epirotes · EPIROTES · Achaeans · ACHAEA · Sparta · Ionians · Phaselis · Side · Kelenderis · Soloi · Al Mina · Nagidos · Ugarit · ASSYRIA · Lycians · Arvad · LEVANT · Cyprus · Kition · Berytus · Byblos · Tyre · Sidon · Thera · Rhodes · Dorians · Crete · Jerusalem · Utica · Hippo Regius · Carthage **1** · Melite · Malta · Mediterranean Sea · Hebrew kingdoms · Hadrumetum · Girba · Oea · Sabrata · Leptis Magna · Kinyps · Cyrene · Apollonia · Platea Island · Ptolemais · Aziris · Taucheira · Barca · Euesperides · CYRENAICA · Naukratis · Daphnai · Memphis **7** · EGYPT

For almost three centuries after the collapse of the Mycenaean civilization, Greece remained impoverished and isolated. Recovery began around 900 as the Greeks reestablished trade links with the Levant and Italy. By the 8th century prosperity had returned, urban life was restored and the Greek population was rising rapidly. The earliest Greek overseas colonies, such as Al Mina in Syria and Pithekoussai and Kymai in Italy, were motivated by trade. The earliest long-distance trade was in iron ore, slaves and luxury goods; in return the Greeks offered wine and acted as middlemen. Even before the end of the 8th century, colonies had also become a way for the Greek cities to resettle surplus population. Often colonists were chosen by lot. Most active as colonizers were the Ionian Greeks, descendants of the Mycenaeans, and the Dorians. The Greek colonies, unlike Phoenician colonies, were founded from the outset to be independent states in their own right, although relations with the parent states often remained close.

The Greeks initially looked west. The first major colonizing efforts in the 8th century were in southern Italy and Sicily, where there were many good harbors and fertile agricultural land to support the colonists. Relations with the native peoples were poor, but that did not prevent Greek culture from having a great impact in Italy, especially on the Etruscans in the north. The Italian colonies were initially highly successful – Syracuse, for example, was the most populous Greek city in the 5th century – but the constant hostility of the natives sapped their strength and by the 3rd century they were in decline. Further west in the Mediterranean, the Greeks faced the opposition of the Phoenicians but Massilia was founded around 600. The Celtic chiefs of Gaul prospered greatly from trade with the Greeks, as the superb quality of Greek artifacts found in burials, such as that at Vix, shows.

In the 7th and 6th centuries the effort of colonization shifted to the coasts of Thrace and the Black Sea. The Greek colonies here traded luxury goods with the steppe peoples for wheat to feed the cities of the Greek homeland. The same period also saw colonies founded in Cyrenaica and Egypt. The Greek colonies in Egypt became politically influential and through them the Greeks gained a deep knowledge of Egyptian art and architecture.

1 Carthage was the most important Phoenician colony, founded in 814. It became a powerful independent state in the 6th century.

2 Phoenician trading posts on the African coast, such as Mogador, were occupied for only part of the year.

3 The Scythians traded grain with the Greek Black Sea colonies in return for luxury goods

4 The burial mound at Vix of a 6th-century Celtic princess has yielded some of the finest Greek bronze-work yet found.

5 Syracuse, founded by Corinth around 733, became the wealthiest and most powerful of the western Greek colonies.

6 Massilia, founded around 600 to exploit the tin trade, declined after 500 when the trade routes shifted to the Atlantic and the Alpine passes.

7 Greek mercenaries played a key role in Egyptian armies around 600.

See also 1.14 (Bible lands), 1.22 (Mycenaeans), 1.24 (Mainland Greece), 1.25 (Carthage)

During the dark ages (1200–800 BC), the Greeks lived in tribal communities under chiefs or kings who combined the roles of warleader and chief priest but who had to consult a council of elders and the warrior aristocracy. Their subjects sometimes paid tribute to the kings, but there was no regular system of taxation. There were no palaces, and kings lived in houses distinguished from those of their subjects only by their greater size. Town life almost ceased and such long-distance trade as survived was controlled by the Phoenicians. War, hunting and lavish displays of hospitality were the hallmarks of dark-age Greek culture. One of the most important developments of the period was that iron replaced bronze.

By the 9th century power began to pass to the hereditary aristocracy, and by the end of the 7th century only Sparta, Argos and Thera still had monarchies. Little is known about the institutions of aristocratic government but it was under their rule that trade and city life revived in Greece and that Greek colonization overseas began. The *polis* (city-state) became the dominant form of political organization. The cities dominated the countryside and became the main centers of political power, commerce and cultural life. The revival of trade made it necessary to re-invent writing in the 8th century, as the Mycenaean script had been entirely forgotten. The Greeks adopted the Phoenician consonantal alphabet and by adding separate signs for vowels turned it into a far more flexible and simple writing system. As a result writing became a common accomplishment in Greece. This was to be a major factor in the brilliant flowering of Greek civilization in the 6th and 5th century.

In the 7th century aristocratic government became unpopular. New military tactics, involving large numbers of heavily armed infantry, deprived them of their status as a warrior elite. There was discontent also among the newly rich who, not having aristocratic birth, were excluded from political power. In many Greek city-states these discontents led, between 660 and 485, to revolutions under popular leaders known as "tyrants" (a term describing rulers who had gained power through their own efforts, rather than by virtue of birth). Most tyrannies endured only a few decades before they were overthrown and replaced with "oligarchies", in which the aristocracy was influential but had no monopoly on power. Other Greek city-states reformed their constitutions without revolutions and by the 6th century most were ruled by oligarchies: the remaining strongholds of aristocratic power were in the north of Greece, where there were few cities, and in Sicily.

The most far-reaching political upheavals took place in Athens. Faced with mounting internal problems, the Athenians sought to avoid revolution by

	area of Greek settlement, 6th century BC
	Greek territory under royal or aristocratic rulers, c.600
	Spartan territory, 505
	allies of Sparta, 505
🏛	major city-state, 6th century BC
Athens	tyranny at some time between 660–485
—	Persian conquests by 513
▲	site of pan-Hellenic festival
▣	Amphictonic shrine, with associated god named
▢	other major temple or shrine, with associated god named

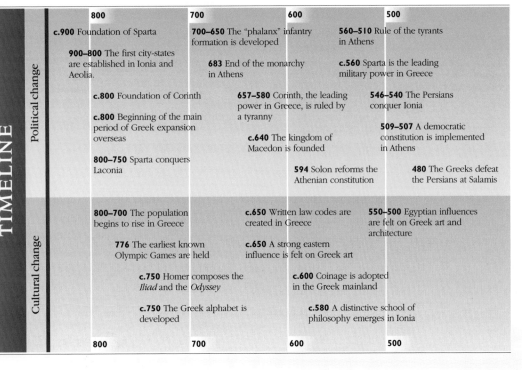

		800	700	600	500
Political change		c.900 Foundation of Sparta	700–650 The "phalanx" infantry formation is developed		560–510 Rule of the tyrants in Athens
		900–800 The first city-states are established in Ionia and Aeolia.	683 End of the monarchy in Athens		c.560 Sparta is the leading military power in Greece
		c.800 Foundation of Corinth	657–580 Corinth, the leading power in Greece, is ruled by a tyranny		546–540 The Persians conquer Ionia
		c.800 Beginning of the main period of Greek expansion overseas			509–507 A democratic constitution is implemented in Athens
			c.640 The kingdom of Macedon is founded		
		800–750 Sparta conquers Laconia		594 Solon reforms the Athenian constitution	480 The Greeks defeat the Persians at Salamis
Cultural change		800–700 The population begins to rise in Greece	c.650 Written law codes are created in Greece		550–500 Egyptian influences are felt on Greek art and architecture
		776 The earliest known Olympic Games are held	c.650 A strong eastern influence is felt on Greek art		
		c.750 Homer composes the *Iliad* and the *Odyssey*		c.600 Coinage is adopted in the Greek mainland	
		c.750 The Greek alphabet is developed		c.580 A distinctive school of philosophy emerges in Ionia	
		800	700	600	500

1 A century of far-reaching political reforms transformed Athens from a backwater in 600 into a leading state in 500.

2 Regarded by the Greeks as a barbarian kingdom, Macedon had a mixed population of Illyrians, Thracians and Dorian Greeks.

3 Olympia was the wealthiest religious center in Greece; pan-Hellenic games were held in honor of Zeus every four years from 776 BC to AD 393.

4 The oracle of Apollo at Delphi was widely consulted by the Greek states on important political matters; it was famous for its ambiguous answers.

5 Corinth benefited from its strategic position on the isthmus between the Gulf of Corinth and the Aegean Sea to become a major trading power.

6 The Ionians were the most culturally sophisticated Greeks in the 7th and 6th centuries, taking advantage of close links with the Middle Eastern civilizations.

7 Argos was a bitter rival of Sparta for control of the Peloponnese from the 7th to the 5th century.

8 Coinage was introduced by Lydian kings in about 700; its use had spread to Greece by about 600.

BURIED under the ruins of the Acropolis when the Persians attacked Athens in 480, this marble *kore* (maiden) would once have been brightly painted.

Black Sea

Thracians

Danube

Oit

Marista

Herakleia

Byzantium
Chalcedon

Strymon

Abdera
Thasos
Thasos

Samothrace

Sestos
Lampsakos
Cyzicus
Abydos

Imroz

Lemnos

MACEDON
2

Lake Prespa

Aliakmon

Axios

Mt Olympos
(Zeus)

EPIRUS

Pinios

Vijose

Corcyra
Dodona
(Zeus)

Corfu

THESSALY

Achelöos

Ambracia

ACARNANIA

AETOLIA

Kephallenia

Anthela
(Apollo)

Alacomenae
(Apollo)

PHOCIS
Delphi
(Apollo)

Kephisos

BOEOTIA

Thebes

ACHAEA

Sikyon

Nemea
(Zeus)

Megara

Corinth
(Poseidon)

ATTICA

Eleusis (Demeter)

Athens

4

5

Chalcis
Eretria

Euboea

Northern Sporades

Aegina

1

Argos
(Hera)

Epidauros (Asclepios)

Calauria
(Poseidon)

ELIS

ARCADIA

Olympia
(Zeus)

Mantineia

Tegea

3

7

MESSENIA

Sparta

LACONIA

KYNOURIA

Aegean Sea

Andros

Ikaria

Delos
(Apollo)

Paros

Naxos

Naxos

Melos

Thera

KYTHERA
(Aphrodite)

AEOLIA

Lesbos

Mytilene

Phokaia

Chios

Chios

Klasomenai
Kolophon
Ephesos
(Artemis)

Gediz

Menderes

LYDIA
conquered by Persians
547–546

8

Samos

6

Miletos
Didyma
(Apollo)

Halikarnassos

IONIA

Kos
Kos

Knidos
(Aphrodite)

Ialysos

Kameiros
Rhodes

Lindos

LYCIA

Carpathos

Mediterranean Sea

Kydonia

Crete

Knossos

Itanos

Gortyn

Mt Olympos

Menderes

---

appointing Solon to reform the constitution in 594. The result was a compromise that satisfied nobody and in 546 the tyrant Peisistratus seized power. Peisistratus was an effective and popular ruler who broke the aristocratic hold on power and did much to address the problems of the peasantry. Peisistratos was succeeded by his less able son Hippias who was overthrown by an aristocratic faction in 510. After three years of internal strife the aristocratic party was defeated. The reformer Kleisthenes "took the people into partnership" and introduced a democratic constitution which gave all 45,000 male citizens the right to attend the assembly and vote on all major decisions and appointments.

By actively involving its citizens in government, Athens had become a self-confident and assertive state by 500, but for most of the 6th century the most powerful state was Sparta, which had taken the lead in developing new infantry tactics in which armored spearmen fought in a close-packed phalanx, presenting an impenetrable hedge of spears to the enemy. Sparta formed a league of similar cities based on a hoplite franchise, through which it dominated the Peloponnese.

The first Greeks to fall under Persian power were the Ionians on the Anatolian coast. Since about 600 the Ionians had paid tribute to the kings of Lydia but relations were good: the Greeks adopted coinage as a result of Lydian influences and the Lydians themselves became increasingly Hellenized. Persian rule was not particularly oppressive but it was more unpopular than the loose control of the Lydians.

Despite their rivalries, Greeks had a strong sense of common identity by the 8th century, expressed through the name they gave themselves – Hellenes – and by religion. All Greeks worshiped the same gods and celebrated pan-Hellenic festivals, such as the Olympic Games, during which hostilities had to cease. The neutrality of shrines of pan-Hellenic importance was protected and supported by leagues (*amphictonies*) of neighboring states, such as the Amphictony of Delphi. A cultural heritage had also emerged, epitomized by the epic poems of Homer, which were composed in the 8th century.

See also 1.15 (Persia), 1.22 (Minoans and Mycenaeans), 1.25 (western Mediterranean)

The first cities and states in the western Mediterranean developed in the early Iron Age. The first were the Etruscan city-states of northern Italy, which had emerged by 800 BC. Then in the 8th century many cities were founded on the coasts of southern Italy, France, Spain and north Africa by Phoenician and Greek colonists. The Greeks had a strong impact on the Etruscan civilization while the Phoenician colonies in Spain influenced the growth of cities and states among the native Tartessian, Turdetanian and Iberian peoples by 500 BC.

The origin of the Etruscans is uncertain. Their language was unrelated to any other European language, suggesting that the Etruscans may have migrated into Italy from the Middle East. There is no convincing evidence of this, however, and it is more likely that the Etruscans were an indigenous people. The forerunner of the Etruscan civilization was the Villanova culture – the first iron-using culture in Italy – which developed in Tuscany around 900 and later spread north into the Po valley. This culture itself seems to have developed out of local Urnfield cultures. In Tuscany the Villanova culture was replaced by the Etruscan civilization in the 8th century BC but it survived in the Po valley until the 6th century, when the area was overrun by the Etruscans.

Etruria was rich in iron and copper ores, had good agricultural land and a coastline with many natural harbors, which encouraged the Etruscans to become active seafarers and traders. Most early Etruscan cities were sited a few kilometers from the coast, close enough for convenience but not vulnerable to pirate raids. Each city was an independent state ruled by a king but the twelve most important cities were loosely united in the Etruscan league. From the 8th century the Etruscans faced competition from Greek and Phoenician colonies in the western Mediterranean. The foundation of the Greek colony at Massilia around 600 was a particularly serious development as it shut the Etruscans out of the important trans-Gallic tin routes. To some extent this was offset by Etruscan expansion into the Po valley in the 6th century, which brought them control of the transalpine and Adriatic trade routes

and diverted some trade away from the Greek colonies. With Carthaginian help, the Etruscans succeeded in driving the Greeks out of Corsica in 535 but attacks on the Greeks at Kymai (Cumae) in southern Italy were repulsed in 524, 505 and 474. Despite these hostilities, Etruscan culture had become very Hellenized by the 6th century.

The other major group of peoples in Italy were the Italic speakers who had probably migrated into Italy from central Europe during Urnfield times. Though most of the Italic peoples were still organized into tribes in 500 BC, city-states had developed among the Latins as a result of Etruscan influence. The leading Latin city was Rome. The Romans expelled their Etruscan king in 509 and founded a republic but Rome was still little more than a market town.

Carthage was not the earliest Phoenician colony in north Africa but its fine harbor and strategic position had made it into the most important by the mid 7th century.

- Villanova early Iron Age culture, c.900
- Etruria, c.600
- area under Etruscan domination, c.500
- Carthaginian empire, c.500
- area settled and controlled by Greeks, c.500
- Iberian peoples
- Tartessian–Turdetanian peoples
- Italic peoples
- Illyrian peoples
- Celtic and related peoples, c.500
- Hallstatt heartland, c.700
- Etruscan city
- Greek city
- other city
- trans-Gallic tin route
- transalpine trade route
- major migration

0 ———— 400 km
0 ———— 300 mi

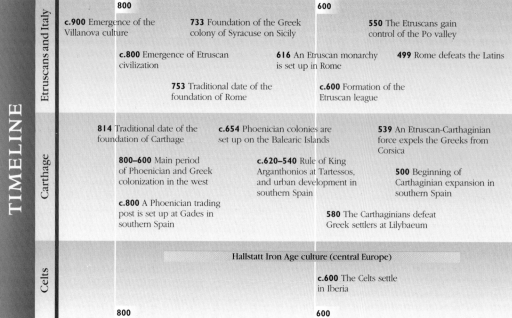

1 By 600 BC, Tartessos was the capital of a wealthy kingdom, and the region saw rapid urban growth under Phoenician and Carthaginian influence in the 6th century.

2 The Hallstatt Iron Age culture (c.750–450) is named for a rich cemetery at an ancient salt-mining center in the Austrian Alps.

3 The stone defenses of the 6th-century Celtic fort at Heuneburg show the influence of Greek architecture.

4 Until the end of the 6th century, the main importance of the small market town of Rome was its control of the main crossing point of the river Tiber.

5 The Lipari Islands were the base for Greek pirates in the 6th and 5th centuries.

6 A joint Carthaginian–Etruscan force defeated the Greeks off Corsica in 539, halting Greek colonization in the western Mediterranean.

7 Populonia was the main iron-working center of Italy from the 6th century; around 10,000 tonnes of iron ore were imported from Elba and smelted there annually.

Seine

Rhine

• Hochdorf

Hohenasperg •

Hirschlanden •

Hallstatt early Iron Age culture (Celts)

Danube

☐3

• Heuneburg

Hallstatt •

☐2 **I t a l i c s**

Loire

• Mont Lassois

• La Tène

A L P S

Rhône

Rhaetians

Veneti c.1000

Sava

Danube

Po

Mantua ☐

Adria ☐

Spina ☐

L i g u r i a n s

Bologna ☐ Villanova •

I l l y r i a n s

Adriatic Sea

c.1000

T h r a c i a n s

• Entremont

Volaterrae ☐ ☐7 Arretium ☐

Cortona ☐

Nicaea •

Populonia ☐ Rusellae ☐ Perusia ☐

Vetulonia ☐

Umbrians

PERSIAN
EMPIRE

• Agathe

Massilia ☐ Athenopolis ☐

Telamun ☐ Volsinii ☐

Volci ☐ ☐4

Clusium ☐

Veii ☐

Sabines

MACEDON

E S

Alalia ☐

Casa ☐

Tarquinii ☐

Gravisca ☐

Rome ☐

L a t i n s

Terracina •

Samnites

Messapians

Thessaly

Ullastret • Emporion ☐

• Kese

Corsica

Caere ☐

LATIN CITY
STATES

Kymai ☐

524, 505, 474

Pompeii ☐

O s c a n s

Taras ☐

Epirus

Chalcis ☐

Eretria ☐
Athens ☐

✕539

Sybaris ☐

Corinth ☐
Argos ☐

• Mago

L i g u r i a n s

☐6

Palma ☐

Sardinia

☐5

Lipari ☐

Rhegion ☐

Sparta ☐

Ebusus

*Balearic
Islands*

Tharros ☐

Caralis ☐

Sulcis ☐ Nora ☐

Himera ☐

Panormus ☐

Soleis ☐ ✕480

S i c a n i

S i c u l i

Melite •

Motya ☐

Malta

Lilybaeum ✕
580

Selinus ☐

Akragas ☐

Syracuse ☐

Sicily

Crete

• Rusucurru

Utica ☐

Carthage ☐

M e d i t e r r a n e a n   S e a

Hippo Regius ☐

Cartenna ☐

Hadrumetum ☐

Cyrene •

Girba ☐

Sabrata ☐ Oea ☐

Leptis Magna ☐

Kinyps ☐

7th–6th century BC

RICH deposits of copper and
tin in Etruria enabled the
development of skilled
bronzeworking as in this
Chimera from Arretium.

Although technically still subject to its parent city Tyre, Carthage had by this time begun its own independent colonization of the Balearic Islands. In 580 Carthage intervened in Sicily to protect Motya against the Greek city of Selinus and shortly after to support the Phoenician colonies in Sardinia against the natives. These actions established Carthage as the protector of the Phoenician colonies in the west, and by 500 it had become the capital of a loose-knit maritime empire which dominated the western Mediterranean trade routes. The Greeks, however, succeeded in gaining control of most of Sicily in 480.

The area most influenced by the Phoenicians and Carthaginians was southern Spain. Gades (Cadiz) was an important Phoenician trading post from at least the 8th century, if not earlier, and Huelva –

almost certainly the ancient city of Tartessos – was a port with trading links with the Greeks, Phoenicians and Atlantic Europe by around 800. Excavations at Huelva have yielded huge quantities of imported pottery. Huelva's prosperity was based on exports of silver and other metals from southern Spain and of tin from Galicia, Brittany and Cornwall. By the 6th century a Tartessian kingdom had developed and fortified towns were being founded in the Guadalquivir valley. Phoenician techniques were incorporated into local metalworking and sculpture and a script based on the Phoenician alphabet was adopted. Urban development was also beginning in the Iberian area on the east coast of Spain by 500. Here too a Phoenician-based script was adopted.

The dominant influence in west and central

Europe in the 7th and 6th centuries was the Hallstatt culture, which is generally identified with the Celts. The Hallstatt culture began to develop in the 12th century BC from the Urnfield cultures of the upper Danube region. Bronze-using in its earlier stages, the Hallstatt culture adopted iron working in about 750. In the early 7th century the Celts spread west across Germany and France and by the early 6th century they had crossed the Pyrenees and occupied over half of the Iberian peninsula. The Celts there were quickly assimilated with the native peoples to produce a distinctive Celtiberian culture.

See also 1.21 (Bronze Age Europe), 1.23 (Greek
and Phoenician colonization)

The first civilization of south Asia emerged in the Indus river valley around 2600 BC. The Indus civilization covered the greatest geographical extent of the Bronze Age civilizations. In its origins it resembled the Mesopotamian civilization, arising on the arid flood plain of a great and unpredictable river where the need for large-scale irrigation and flood defense schemes led to the development of a well-organized hierarchical society.

The first farming communities in south Asia developed at sites such as Mehrgarh in the mountains of Baluchistan as early as 6000 BC and spread from there into the Indus valley in the 4th millennium. There was considerable interaction between the valley settlements and those in the highlands. Highland peoples took their flocks to winter in the valley and traded metals, semiprecious stones and timber for grain and other foodstuffs. The early farming communities of the Indus valley showed no signs of social ranking, but the transition to a hierarchical society occurred very rapidly in about 2600 BC. This may have been a result of the establishment of trading contacts with Mesopotamia. Towns grew up in the Indus valley as a result of this trade. The metals and other products of the highlands were gathered in the towns and sent on to Mesopotamia: a shipment of 5,900 kilograms of copper was recorded on one occasion. The growth of trade also led to the development of small towns, such as Nindowari, in the highlands.

Most of the cities and towns in the Indus valley were small but two, Mohenjo-Daro and Harappa (from which the Indus civilization gets its alternative name, "Harappan"), had populations of around 30,000–40,000, placing them among the largest Bronze Age cities anywhere. Both Mohenjo-Daro and Harappa, as well as several of the smaller cities such as Kalibangan, had impressive mud-brick city walls, a citadel with public buildings and granaries and streets laid out on a grid pattern. The civilization was literate but its pictographic script has not been deciphered. As a result, the identity of the Indus people is unknown: they may have been related to the modern Dravidian peoples of southern India.

By 1800 BC the Indus cities were in decline and a century later they had been abandoned. Writing fell

farming settlement, c.6000
spread of farming, c.4000–3000
Kulli complex, c.4000–3000
Banas culture, c.2200–1500
major settlement of Indus valley civilization, 2600–1700
minor settlement of Indus valley civilization, 2600–1700
Harappa possible capital
ancient river course
desert

0   400 km
0   300 mi

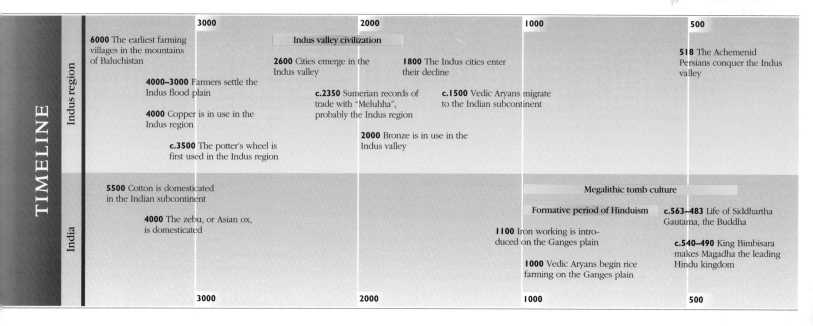

TIMELINE

		3000	2000	1000	500
Indus region		**6000** The earliest farming villages in the mountains of Baluchistan	*Indus valley civilization*		**518** The Achemenid Persians conquer the Indus valley
			2600 Cities emerge in the Indus valley	**1800** The Indus cities enter their decline	
		4000–3000 Farmers settle the Indus flood plain	**c.2350** Sumerian records of trade with "Meluhha", probably the Indus region	**c.1500** Vedic Aryans migrate to the Indian subcontinent	
		4000 Copper is in use in the Indus region			
		c.3500 The potter's wheel is first used in the Indus region	**2000** Bronze is in use in the Indus valley		
India		**5500** Cotton is domesticated in the Indian subcontinent		*Megalithic tomb culture*	
				Formative period of Hinduism	**c.563–483** Life of Siddhartha Gautama, the Buddha
		4000 The zebu, or Asian ox, is domesticated		**1100** Iron working is introduced on the Ganges plain	**c.540–490** King Bimbisara makes Magadha the leading Hindu kingdom
				1000 Vedic Aryans begin rice farming on the Ganges plain	

## Map labels

Taxila

GANDARA

Indus

HIMALAYAS

Aryans
from central Asia,
mid 2nd millennium

KURU

Sutlej

PANCHALA

Hastinapura

Ahichhattra

SURASENA

Atranjikhera

KOSALA   **6**

Bairat

Sravasti   Lumbini

Thar Desert

Mathura

Yamuna

Ganges

MALLA

Tilaura-kot   Kusinagara

VRIJJI

Vaisali

VATSA

MATSYA

Campa

CHEDI

Pataliputra   KASI   Rajgir   ANGA

Ahar

Kausambi   MAGADHA   **7**

AVANTI   **9**

Arabian Sea

Vidisha

Ujjain

Mahismati   Narmada

Tamluk

Tapti

Mahanadi

ASSAKA   Bay of Bengal

Deccan   Godavari

WESTERN GHATS

Krishna

EASTERN GHATS

8

Brahmagiri

Kaveri

Sinhalese
settlement of Ceylon,
c.500 BC

Ceylon

Veddas

Legend

- Indus valley civilization
- Banas culture
- distribution of Painted Grey ware pottery, 1000–500
- distribution of Black-and-Red ware pottery, 2nd and 1st millennium BC
- area of early Iron Age megalithic tombs
- Persian empire, 518
- city, c.500
- other important site
- KASI   *mahajanapada* ("great realm"), c.550
- major migration
- Persian conquest of Indus valley, c.518
- ancient river course
- desert

0   600 km
0   400 mi

ALOOF and solemn, the "priest-king" statuette from Mohenjo-Daro wears a decorated robe with one shoulder bare, a way of showing reverence.

out of use. To date, no entirely convincing explanation has been found for the abandonment of these cities. Life in the countryside continued unchanged for several centuries, suggesting at least that the civilization did not fall as a result of outside invasion. Sometime around 1500 BC the Aryans, a semi-nomadic Indo-European pastoralist people, migrated into the Indian subcontinent from central Asia and occupied the northern half of the territory once covered by the Indus civilization. Some aspects of Indus culture were absorbed by the Aryans and the pottery styles of the late Indus Banas culture survived, then slowly spread across most of southern India, but all memory of the civilization itself was lost; it was rediscovered only in the 1920s.

For five centuries, the semi-nomadic Aryans left little physical trace of their presence, but a mythic record of their migrations and wars with the indigenous peoples has been preserved in the *Vedic Hymns*. These, the holiest books of the Hindu religion, were transmitted orally for centuries until they were written down in the 6th century BC. Around 1100 BC the Aryans adopted iron working, possibly independently of outside influence, and soon afterward they moved east and began to settle down in villages on the Ganges plain as rice farmers. The

appearance, round 1000–800 BC, across the Ganges plain, of the Painted Grey ware pottery style has been linked to the Aryan settlement of the area. By 900 small tribal kingdoms and aristocratic tribal republics, known collectively as *janapadas*, were developing across the Ganges plain. By 700 they had coalesced to form 16 *mahajanapadas* ("great realms"). By 500 BC Magadha, under its energetic king Bimbisara, had emerged as the most powerful. Hand in hand with the process of state formation was the growth of cities, many which, like Ujjain and Kausambi, had mud-brick defensive walls. This was a period of great developments in religion: it was the formative period of the Hindu religion and the late 6th century witnessed the lives and teachings of Mahavira, the founder of Jainism, and of Siddhartha Gautama, the Buddha.

By 500 BC the Gangetic civilization extended as far south as the River Godavari. South of this were iron-using, tribally organized farming peoples, many of whom buried their dead in megalithic cists (box-shaped tombs). Only towards the end of the 1st millennium did state formation and urban development start in this area.

1 Mohenjo-Daro is the first known planned city, built on a massive brick platform to protect it from floods.

2 Lothal was a port with a brick-lined artificial harbor; it had trading links with Mesopotamia.

3 Shorthugai was a colony possibly founded to exploit the trade in lapis lazuli from the Hindu Kush.

4 Mehrgarh was one of the earliest farming settlements in south Asia, flourishing about 6000.

5 The Kulli complex of towns centered on Nindowari had close trade links with the Indus valley.

6 Lumbini was the birthplace of Siddhartha Gautama, the Buddha; he died at Kusinagara.

7 Magadha was the leading Hindu kingdom in 500 BC, later forming the center of the Mauryan empire.

8 Brahmagiri is a major site of the south Indian Iron Age megalithic, with 300 tombs and stone circles.

9 Black-and-Red ware pottery appeared in the Banas region in late Indus times and spread across southern India after 1800 BC.

See also 1.10 (Mesopotamia), 1.15 (Persia)

The first civilization of east Asia developed in the Yellow river valley in the 18th century BC from indigenous Neolithic cultures. Farming began as early as 5800 BC on the broad band of loess soils that stretches across the Yellow river basin. By 5000 millet farming villages of the Yangshao culture were spread across much of the region. At the same time rice farming communities were spreading among the wetlands of the Yangtze valley. Rice farming spread to the Yellow river valley in the late 4th millennium and the Longshan cultures emerged. In favorable areas, the Longshan cultures practiced intensive rice cultivation using irrigation. The population rose, copper came into use, regional trading networks developed and a warrior class emerged. There is evidence of warfare, such as rammed earth fortifications and massacres of prisoners. A system of divination based on the use of "oracle bones" was developed.

According to Chinese traditions, civilization was founded by the emperor Huang Di around 2698 BC while the first dynasty, the Xia, was founded by Yu the Great in about 2205. However, there is no evidence for states in China in the 3rd millennium BC.

The first historically and archeologically attested Chinese dynasty is the Shang. This was founded about 1766 BC by King Tang, around the time of the appearance of the Erlitou culture. Cities with monumental buildings began to develop craft specialization and advanced bronze-casting techniques were adopted. The appearance of rich burials points to the emergence of a powerful ruling elite. A pictographic script came into use: the modern Chinese script is its direct descendant. Shang cultural influence extended across most of northern China and as far south as the Yangtze river. Like many early states, the Shang kingdom combined directly run provinces and vassal states.

Around 1122 the Shang king Di-xin was defeated and overthrown by his vassal king Wu of Zhou. The dynasty established by Wu became the longest lived of Chinese history and the early centuries of its rule were looked back on as a golden age. To legitimize their rule after their usurpation of the Shang, the Zhou rulers introduced the theory of the "Mandate

rice farming, 6500–3000

Yangshao Neolithic culture, 5000–3200

Longshan Neolithic cultures, 3200–1800

Erlitou culture, c.1800–1650

Shang bronze working

Shang city

PI   administrative subdivision of Shang kingdom

Anyang rich burial of the Shang period

spread of rice farming

source of copper

source of tin

area of loess soils

modern coastline and drainage where altered

0   800 km

0   600 mi

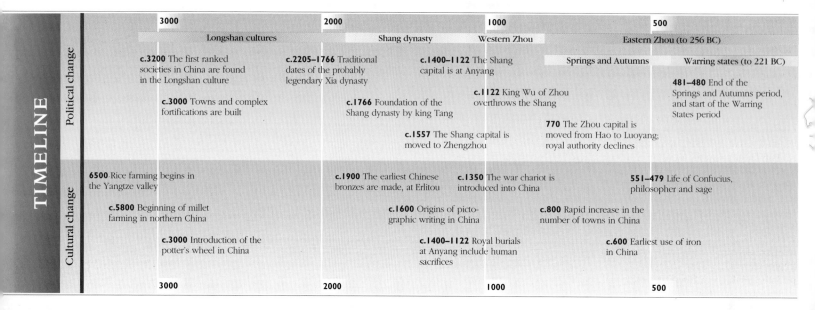

TIMELINE		3000	2000	1000	500
Political change		Longshan cultures	Shang dynasty	Western Zhou	Eastern Zhou (to 256 BC)
					Springs and Autumns — Warring states (to 221 BC)
		c.3200 The first ranked societies in China are found in the Longshan culture	**c.2205–1766** Traditional dates of the probably legendary Xia dynasty	**c.1400–1122** The Shang capital is at Anyang	
		c.3000 Towns and complex fortifications are built	**c.1766** Foundation of the Shang dynasty by king Tang	**c.1122** King Wu of Zhou overthrows the Shang	**481–480** End of the Springs and Autumns period, and start of the Warring States period
			c.1557 The Shang capital is moved to Zhengzhou	**770** The Zhou capital is moved from Hao to Luoyang; royal authority declines	
Cultural change		**6500** Rice farming begins in the Yangtze valley	**c.1900** The earliest Chinese bronzes are made, at Erlitou	**c.1350** The war chariot is introduced into China	**551–479** Life of Confucius, philosopher and sage
		c.5800 Beginning of millet farming in northern China	**c.1600** Origins of pictographic writing in China	**c.800** Rapid increase in the number of towns in China	
		c.3000 Introduction of the potter's wheel in China	**c.1400–1122** Royal burials at Anyang include human sacrifices	**c.600** Earliest use of iron in China	
		3000	2000	1000	500

Legend:

- borders, 770–481
- Zhou state, 770–481
- Zhou royal domain, 770–481
- other state
- extent of Chinese cultural influence
- state capital
- city
- WU state with non-Chinese population
- (1–5) order of hegemons, late 8th to mid 6th century BC
- Mixu barbarian tribes
- barbarian attacks, late 9th to early 8th century BC
- barbarian attacks, 7th to early 6th century BC
- modern coastline and drainage where altered

SKILLED bronze casting was common to both the Shang and the Zhou dynasties. This ritual wine bucket is of early Zhou manufacture, c.1000.

0   400 km
0   300 mi

of Heaven". The ruler was the "Son of Heaven" and "All under Heaven" was his lawful domain so long as he was just and moral. Should a ruler become unjust, Heaven would send him a warning and if he failed to reform, the Mandate would be given to another. Di-xin had been a sadist so Heaven had transferred the right to rule to the Zhou. This theory, which could be used both to condemn disobedience to the ruler and to justify successful usurpation, remained central to Chinese imperial ideology.

The Zhou kingdom was a decentralized feudal state, divided into fiefs governed by dukes chosen from among the king's relatives and trusted supporters. Only the royal domain was directly ruled by the king. In 770 barbarian attacks on Hao forced the Zhou to move their capital to Luoyang. This event was a turning-point in the history of the dynasty and marks the beginning of the period of disorder and fragmentation known as the Springs and Autumns period (after the title of the annals of the state of Lu).

Luoyang was more centrally situated than Hao

but it removed the dynasty from its traditional heartland in the west; its authority began to decline. By this time the king controlled less land than most of his dukes who now became, in effect, the rulers of independent states, making almost constant war on one another. However, the dukes continued to recognize the sovereignty of the king and also recognized the duke of the leading state of the time as hegemon (with general primacy over all other states). The Springs and Autumns period turned into the Warring States period (480–221), which saw the decline of feudal relationships and the rise of a professional bureaucracy.

The Springs and Autumns period was a brutal age but it saw great creativity in literature and religious and philosophical thought. The end of the period saw Confucius found the ethical system, which remains fundamental to Chinese thought. Iron working was adopted around 600, probably in Wu, though iron tools and weapons did not replace bronze in everyday use until the 2nd century BC.

1 More than a hundred wet-rice farming villages (using flooded fields) were established in this region 6500–4000 BC.

2 Erlitou was the site of the first Chinese bronzes c.1900 BC; it was probably also the first Shang capital.

3 The city and ritual offering pits at Sanxingdui, discovered in the 1990s, are evidence of a bronze-using civilization contemporary with the Shang.

4 Hao, in the original Zhou heartland, was abandoned as the capital in 770 after barbarian attacks. The move initiated a decline in Zhou authority.

5 The Zhou royal domain was limited to a small area around Luoyang by the 7th century.

6 Wu, the dominant state in southern China in the late 6th century, was destroyed by Yue in 473 BC.

See also 1.03 (agriculture)

The domestication of maize around 2700 made possible the development of permanent farming villages in Mesoamerica by 2300. Most early farmers practiced slash-and-burn agriculture, which cannot support dense populations. However, on fertile river flood-plains in the tropical forests of southeastern Mexico, reliable rainfall and year-round warmth made it possible to raise four crops of maize a year, which provided the economic base for the Olmec civilization.

By 1250 BC the Olmec lived in chiefdoms or small states ruled by a powerful hereditary elite. The most important sites were ceremonial centers with earth pyramid mounds and monumental stone sculptures of gods and chiefs. Associated with the ceremonial centers were settlements of two to three thousand people. The ritual centers were periodically destroyed and sculptures defaced or buried. Though possibly due to warfare between chiefdoms or states, it is more likely that this served a ritual purpose, marking the end of calendrical cycles, the death of a ruler or the accession of a new dynasty. Trade and gift exchange played an important part in the Olmec way of life. The Olmec lands have few natural resources and the raw materials for everyday tools, stone sculpture and status enhancing display objects had to be imported over long distances. Gift exchange played an important part in the diffusion of Olmec culture as the emerging elites of neighboring communities took up Olmec beliefs and artifacts to enhance their prestige. Late in their history, the Olmec developed a rudimentary hieroglyphic script which was used mainly for astronomical inscriptions. They used – and may have originated – both the Mesoamerican 260-day sacred year and the 52-year "long-count" calendar.

The Maya originated about 1200 BC in the Guatemalan highlands, developing from earlier Archaic cultures, and began to spread out into the lowlands of the Yucatán peninsula around 1000. By draining and canalizing swamps the Maya were able to

CARVED in rare blue jade, this tiny bust of a woman has the distinctive monumental quality which characterizes all Olmec sculpture.

Olmec, c.1250–400
Maya, c.1000
Maya, c.800
Zapotec, c.1400–400
Olmec ceremonial center
site with Olmec or Olmec influenced art
Olmec trade route
source of basalt
source of hematite
source of jade
source of obsidian
source of serpentine
northern limit of farming cultures, c.500 BC

0   600 km
0   400 mi

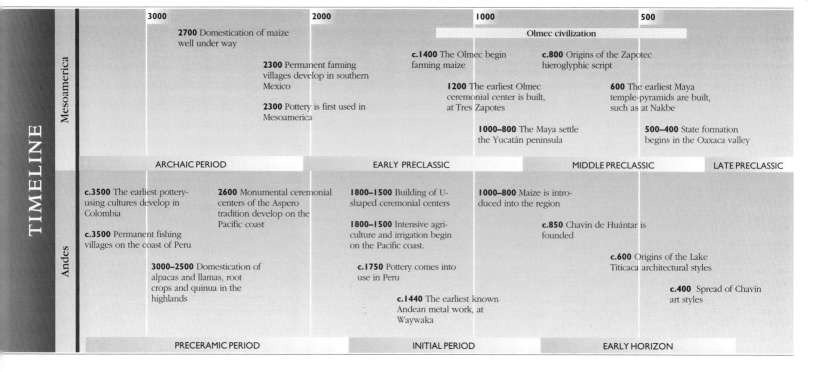

TIMELINE

Mesoamerica

	3000	2000	1000	500

2700 Domestication of maize well under way

2300 Permanent farming villages develop in southern Mexico

2300 Pottery is first used in Mesoamerica

Olmec civilization

c.1400 The Olmec begin farming maize

c.800 Origins of the Zapotec hieroglyphic script

1200 The earliest Olmec ceremonial center is built, at Tres Zapotes

600 The earliest Maya temple-pyramids are built, such as at Nakbe

1000–800 The Maya settle the Yucatán peninsula

500–400 State formation begins in the Oaxaca valley

ARCHAIC PERIOD — EARLY PRECLASSIC — MIDDLE PRECLASSIC — LATE PRECLASSIC

Andes

c.3500 The earliest pottery-using cultures develop in Colombia

c.3500 Permanent fishing villages on the coast of Peru

2600 Monumental ceremonial centers of the Aspero tradition develop on the Pacific coast

3000–2500 Domestication of alpacas and llamas, root crops and quinua in the highlands

1800–1500 Building of U-shaped ceremonial centers

1800–1500 Intensive agriculture and irrigation begin on the Pacific coast.

c.1750 Pottery comes into use in Peru

c.1440 The earliest known Andean metal work, at Waywaka

1000–800 Maize is introduced into the region

c.850 Chavín de Huántar is founded

c.600 Origins of the Lake Titicaca architectural styles

c.400 Spread of Chavín art styles

PRECERAMIC PERIOD — INITIAL PERIOD — EARLY HORIZON

produce sufficient food to support a complex society and by 600 towns, such as Nakbe and Komchen, with monumental temple pyramids, were developing. Complex societies also developed among the Zapotec people of the Oaxaca valley by the 1st millennium BC. Here food production was increased by simple irrigation techniques and terracing. By 400 BC there were at least seven small states in the valley, the most important of which was centered on Monte Albán, and a system of hieroglyphic writing had been developed. In the Valley of Mexico highly productive agriculture using *chinampas* – raised fields built on reclaimed swamps – led to the development of trading networks, a market economy, craft specialization and large villages by around 200 BC.

The earliest complex societies in South America developed on the desert coast of Peru in settled fishing communities during the Preceramic period (3750–1800 BC). The marine resources of this area are unusually rich and these communities were able to free labor for the construction of temples and ceremonial centers under the direction of village leaders. One of the earliest such centers was built at Aspero around 2600: it consisted of six mounds nine meters high, topped with masonry ceremonial structures. Cotton, squash and gourds (used as floats for fishing nets) were cultivated but farming did not make a significant contribution to the diet. In the highlands, herding alpacas or llamas and cultivation of root crops such as potatoes, ullucu and oca or quinua, a cereal, gradually replaced hunting and gathering during the Preceramic; permanent villages with small ceremonial buildings also developed.

During the Initial Period (1800–800 BC) the area of cultivable land in the coastal lowlands was greatly extended through irrigation works, diverting water from the rivers which flowed from the Andes through the desert to the coast. Pottery was adopted. Huge U-shaped ceremonial centers, requiring the control of considerable resources of labor, food supplies and raw materials, were constructed: one at Garagay is estimated to have required 3.2 million work-days to complete. These sites were probably focal points for local chiefdoms but burial practices show few distinctions of wealth or rank. Interaction between the fishing communities on the coast and the farming communities in the desert river valleys and the mountains was considerable, with salt, seaweed and dried fish from the coast being exchanged for carbohydrate foods such as root crops and grain from the highlands and river valleys.

The Early Horizon (about 800–200 BC) saw the development of sophisticated architecture and complex sculptural styles at the highland ceremonial center of Chavín de Huántar. The Chavín style was the culmination of styles which had originated as early as 1200 in other Andean and coastal sites and by 400 its influence had spread over a wide area of coastal and highland Peru. Chavín had a population of two to three thousand at its peak in the 4th century but thereafter it declined, without developing into a full urban civilization. Complex societies, united by common beliefs, also developed in the Lake Titicaca basin during the Early Horizon. Particularly important is the ceremonial center at Chiripa, built 600–400 BC, in which can be seen the origins of the architectural styles of the 5th-century AD Tiahuanaco state. Maize became an important crop in the Andes during this period.

Valdivia tradition, 3800–1700

Preceramic

Aspero tradition, 3000–1800

Kotosh tradition, 2300–1200

El Paraíso tradition, 2000–1800

Chinchoros tradition, 3000–500 (ceramic after 1200)

◆ site with monumental building

○ other important site

Initial Period and Early Horizon

El Paraíso, 1800–850

Chorrera culture, 1200–300

Chavín culture, 900–200

Paracas culture, 650–150

Yaya-Mama religious traditions, 600–400

◆ site with monumental building

• other important site

— possible trans-Andean route

coastal desert

tropical rainforest

0 — 600 km
0 — 400 mi

1 San Lorenzo was the first Olmec ceremonial center with earth pyramid mounds and monumental sculpture, flourishing c.1200–900.

2 The Zapotec script, the earliest in the Americas, was developed in the Oaxaca valley c.800–700.

3 The Maya originated in the Guatemalan highlands and settled the Yucatán peninsula by 800.

4 By the 7th century the Maya were constructing temple pyramids and other monumental buildings at sites such as Nakbe.

5 Valdivia has given its name to a culture, with early use of pottery (c.3000 BC), fishing, shellfish-gathering and maize-farming.

6 The earliest evidence of metal-working in the Andes is from Waywaka, where tools and beaten gold from c.1440 BC have been found.

7 Chavín de Huántar was a large ceremonial center occupied 850–200; its distinctive art style was adopted over a wide area of Peru c.400 BC.

8 More than four hundred mummies have been found at the necropolis of Paracas.

9 Chiripa was a mound-top ceremonial center of c.600 BC, with many features common to later civilizations in the region.

FANGED gods with human-animal attributes rendered in complex geometry, are found in the widespread Chavín style, seen here on a textile design.

See also 1.03 (agriculture)

Cross-referencing

References to other dictionary entries are identified in small capitals (e.g. ACROPOLIS*); references to map spreads are denoted by the use of an arrow (e.g. ▷ 1.21).*

Dating

For the purposes of this dictionary, the end of the Paleolithic period of early human prehistory, about 10,000 BC/12,000 years ago (i.e. the end of the Pleistocene Ice Age), is taken as the boundary between geological and historical time. Earlier dates are therefore given in years ago (ya), while dates after the end of the Paleolithic are given using the conventional BC/AD system.

Chinese spellings

Since 1979 the standard international system for the transliteration of Chinese names into Roman characters has been Pinyin, and this is the system used throughout this dictionary.

ABU SIMBEL

The site of two massive rock temples built by the Egyptian PHARAOH RAMESSES II (r.c.1290–1224 BC) on the Nile, 250 kilometers (155 miles) south of Aswan. The largest temple is fronted by four colossal statues of Ramesses. The smaller temple is dedicated to Ramesses' queen, Nefertari. In the 1960s, the temples were lifted and reconstructed above the waters of Lake Nasser. ▷ 1.18

ACHAEA, ACHAEANS

A region in the northwestern Peloponnese. The Achaeans were one of the peoples of Greece mentioned by HOMER as fighting at TROY. They were divided among a number of settlements, which shared common citizenship and COINAGE. Achaea formed a confederacy with other Peloponnesian cities in the Hellenistic period, but was overwhelmed by ROME in 146 BC. ▷ 1.23, 1.24

ACHEMENES

Founding ancestor of the ACHEMENID royal dynasty of Persia. He probably ruled the kingdom of Parsumash in western Iran in the early 7th century BC as a vassal of the MEDIAN EMPIRE. Achemenes may have led an army against King SENNACHERIB of ASSYRIA in 681 BC. ▷ 1.15

ACHEMENID EMPIRE

Persian empire ruled by the Achemenid dynasty (550–331 BC), named after its founding ancestor, ACHEMENES. The empire was established by CYRUS II (559–530 BC), who took over the MEDIAN throne (550 BC) and conquered LYDIA, BABYLONIA, Bactria and GANDHARA. By the reign of DARIUS I (522–530 BC), the empire extended from Greece to the Indus, and from the Persian Gulf to the Aral Sea, with an administrative capital at SUSA and royal center at PERSEPOLIS. This period is often regarded as a golden age

of Persian artistic and architectural achievement, and was important for the cultural contacts made possible between the Mediterranean civilizations and those of the Middle East and south Asia.

The empire was administered by 20 provincial governors (satraps), with a regular system of tribute and a large army of regular soldiers and levies controlled by the king. Imperial expansion came to an end after defeats by the Greeks in 490 and 480 BC. The empire gradually declined until it was conquered by Alexander the Great, who deposed the last of the Achemenids, Darius III, in 330 BC. ▷ 1.15, 1.26

ACHEULIAN

Cultural tradition of the LOWER PALEOLITHIC period that originated in Africa and spread to Europe with HOMO ERECTUS populations, about 1.5–0.2 million ya. The Acheulian is distinguished by the use of hand-axes, multi-purpose animal butchery and processing tools with a continuous, sharp working edge and a tapered or pointed end, that were designed for piercing, chopping, cutting and scraping. ▷ 1.01

ACROPOLIS

Literally the "high part" of any Greek city, often used as a center for defense. The most famous acropolis is in Athens; it became the ceremonial and religious center of the city and home of the Parthenon.

ADAD-NIRARI II

King of ASSYRIA (r.911–891 BC), who initiated renewed Assyrian expansion and the establishment of the Neo-Assyrian empire. He undertook campaigns against ARAMAEANS and Babylonians, securing Assyrian dominance in central MESOPOTAMIA. ▷ 1.13

ADENA

Complex HUNTER-GATHERER and farming culture of the middle Ohio river valley, in the eastern woodlands of North America (c.1000 BC–AD 100). Adena communities lived in permanent villages and had a rich material culture including pottery, smoking pipes, and COPPER, mica and seashell ornaments. Their mixed hunting, fishing, food-gathering and farming economy supported a large population, and their impressive burial and ceremonial monuments (such as Great Serpent Mound) suggest the development of social ranking and chiefly authority. This cultural tradition was elaborated by the succeeding Hopewell culture. ▷ 1.06

AEOLIA, AEOLIAN GREEKS

According to legend, the Aeolian Greeks fled from the Greek mainland after the collapse of the MYCENAEAN world in the 11th century BC. They came to settle on the west coast of Asia Minor, including the island of Lesbos, where they retained a distinctive dialect and developed their own style of architecture. Like

other Greeks, they developed city-states (POLIS) from the 8th century BC. ▷ 1.23, 1.24

AFANASEVO CULTURE

NEOLITHIC culture of southern Siberia from about 2300 to 1500 BC, in the steppe/taiga region to the north of the Altai mountains, along the upper reaches of the Yenisey and Ob rivers. It had a mixed hunting, farming and herding economy (domestic SHEEP, CATTLE and HORSES), a ROUND BARROW funerary tradition, and decorated pottery and COPPER metallurgy. Similar cultures occupied the steppes further to the west, from the Altai to southern Russia. ▷ 1.04

AGADE

See AKKAD

AGAMEMNON

Legendary king of MYCENAE and leader of the Greek forces to TROY. His quarrel with the hero Achilles is the main theme of HOMER's epic, the ILIAD. On his return to Mycenae he was murdered by his wife, Clytemnestra, and her lover, Aegisthus. ▷ 1.22

AHAB

King of ISRAEL (r.c.874–853 BC) and son of Omri. Often at war with JUDAH and ARAM-DAMASCUS, in 854 BC he led the alliance of Levantine states that were opposed to Assyrian expansion. ▷ 1.14

AHMOSE

Egyptian PHARAOH (r.1550–1525 BC) who successfully drove the HYKSOS from Egypt and led campaigns into Syria and southwards into NUBIA. Ahmose firmly established the foundations of the NEW KINGDOM (1532–1070 BC). ▷ 1.18

AKHENATEN

Egyptian PHARAOH (r.1353–1335 BC), also known as Amenophis IV, who reacted against the power of the priests at the sacred city of THEBES by establishing a monotheistic religion based on Aten, the sun disk, whose rays were shown in paintings as shining on Akhenaten ("glory of the sun disk") and his family. He set up his own capital at Akhetaten (now known as EL-AMARNA) in Middle Egypt. After his death Akhenaten was treated as a heretic, and the old gods were restored. ▷ 1.18

AKKAD

A region of south MESOPOTAMIA lying between the Euphrates and Tigris rivers to the northwest of SUMERIA. It was named after the unlocated city of Agade and was founded by SARGON OF AGADE in about 2300 BC, probably near BABYLON on the Euphrates. Akkad was the power base of Sargon's short-lived Akkadian dynasty, which established the first imperial STATE in world history (c.2330–2193 BC). At the height of its power, under Sargon's grandson, NARAM-SIN (c.2254–2218 BC), the Akkadian empire dominated all of Mesopotamia, the northern LEVANT and possibly southeast Anatolia and western Iran, before collapsing as a result of internal weakness and AMORITE and GUTIAN invasions. The Akkadians established their Semitic dialect as the official language and adopted Sumerian CUNEIFORM as a writing system. Akkadian formed the basis for later Babylonian and Assyrian writing. ▷ 1.04, 1.07, 1.10, 1.11

ALEUTS

Culture inhabiting the Aleutian Islands in the north Pacific, which extend from southwest Alaska towards the east coast of Siberia. The Aleuts had colonized the islands from the Alaskan mainland by about 2000 BC, living primarily by hunting marine and land mammals, and fishing. They had complex fishing technologies, sea-going boats and notable art traditions, particularly ceremonial masks, and bone and ivory carvings. ▷ 1.04, 1.05, 1.06

ALIGNMENT (MEGALITHIC)

Ceremonial monuments of the European NEOLITHIC that were probably used for processions and consist of large stones erected in lines. They are found mainly in Brittany (notably at CARNAC) and in western Britain (c.4000–2000 BC). Timber versions may also have existed. ▷ 1.20

ALTAMIRA

Cave site in northern Spain famous for its UPPER PALEOLITHIC paintings of bison and other animal and anthropomorphic figures. The cave was used by hunting communities over a long period, though the paintings are probably associated with SOLUTREAN and MAGDALENIAN occupation levels, (c.22,000–17,000 ya). ▷ 1.19

AMALEKITES

A group of nomadic tribes in southern JUDAH and Sinai in the early 1st millennium BC. The Amalekites were enemies of the HEBREWS, often raiding ISRAEL, but by the 8th century BC they were no longer a major threat. ▷ 1.14

AMENEMHET I

Egyptian PHARAOH of the MIDDLE KINGDOM (r.1991–1962 BC), who founded the 12th Dynasty and enforced strong Egyptian control over NUBIA. He initiated the practice of installing his son as co-ruler, so as to ensure a smoother succession from one pharaoh to the next. ▷ 1.18

AMENOPHIS IV

See AKHENATEN

AMORITES

Semitic people of Arabia, originally nomadic, who are mentioned in Mesopotamian records from about 2400 to 2000 BC, when their invasions contributed to the collapse of the

Akkadian empire (c.2193 BC) and later the Third Dynasty of UR (c.2000 BC). In the early 2nd millennium BC, Amorite kings established ruling dynasties in many Babylonian and Assyrian cities, assimilating Sumero-Akkadian culture. Amorites also settled in parts of Palestine in this period, and were sometimes associated with the CANAANITES. ▷ 1.11, 1.13

AMPHICTONIES

Leagues of cities associated with a particular Greek shrine (e.g. DELPHI). *Amphictonies* would oversee the arrangements for visitors and punish those who offended the dignity of the shrine. ▷ 1.24

ANDEAN CIVILIZATIONS

The cultures of the Andean region and adjacent coastal areas of western South America that developed CHIEFDOMS and later STATE systems, ceremonial centers, cities, and complex iconography and material culture. The history of Andean civilizations is divided into the following periods: PRECERAMIC (c.3750–2000 BC), INITIAL (2000–900 BC), EARLY HORIZON (900–200 BC), Early Intermediate (200 BC–AD 500), Middle Horizon (AD 500–1000), Late Intermediate (AD 1000–1475) and Late Horizon (AD 1475–1530). ▷ 1.04, 1.05, 1.06, 1.28

ANYANG

The last and most enduring of the SHANG capital cities ("Yin", c.1400–1100 BC), situated on a tributary of the Yellow river in Honan province, China. The urban settlement surrounded a palace and temple complex built on a massive, rammed earth platform. All the buildings were constructed of timber and clay, with thatch roofs, some elaborately painted. Stone and jade carvings, ORACLE BONES and evidence of bronze working and pottery manufacture have been found at the site. The royal cemetery nearby had at least 14 richly furnished tombs with grave goods that included magnificently decorated bronze vessels and other objects, and human and animal sacrifices. ▷ 1.27

ARAM, ARAMAEANS

Nomadic people who originally lived in Aram, a desert region in modern Syria, Jordan and western Iraq. The Aramaeans are first mentioned in Assyrian inscriptions in about 1100 BC, when they raided and settled in MESOPOTAMIA and the LEVANT. By 1000 BC Aramaean kingdoms were established from the Levant to BABYLONIA (where they were known as CHALDEANS). Western Aramaean kingdoms were eventually destroyed by the Assyrian king TIGLATH-PILESER III in 740–720 BC, while Aramaean dynasties in the east merged with the Babylonians. ▷ 1.12, 1.13, 1.14

ARAM-DAMASCUS

ARAMAEAN kingdom founded in about 1100 BC, with a capital at Damascus. It was a

major enemy of ISRAEL from the 10th to 8th centuries BC, until it was annexed by the Assyrians in 732 BC. ▷ 1.14

ARAMAIC LANGUAGE

Semitic language widely adopted in the Middle East following the ARAMAEAN migrations and the development of written Aramaic, using a phonetic script derived from the CANAANITE alphabet (by c.1100 BC). This became the main script used in the Middle East when it was adopted by the Assyrians from about 800 BC, replacing CUNEIFORM. ▷ 1.07, 1.12, 1.13, 1.15

ARCADIA

The central region of the Peloponnese. Although it is relatively unfertile, the Roman poet Virgil portrayed it as a haven of rural bliss, an image that has remained in the European imagination. ▷ 1.24

ARCHAIC PERIOD

A period of MESOAMERICAN CIVILIZATION from about 7000 to 2000 BC, in which HUNTER-GATHERER societies intensified food collection practices and modified plant habitats, domesticating several plant species, notably MAIZE (by c.2700 BC). Population growth, the development of permanent village settlements, intensive farming systems, the use of CERAMICS and long-distance OBSIDIAN exchange are all evident in Mexico by the late 3rd millennium BC.

ARCHAIC PERIOD (GREECE)

The period in Greek history before the Classical period, usually dated from about 750 to 480 BC. It saw the major expansion of the Greeks throughout the Mediterranean, the consolidation of the city-state (POLIS) and the appearance of important PAN-HELLENIC sites, such as OLYMPIA (the four-yearly OLYMPIC GAMES) and DELPHI (the ORACLE). The period also witnessed the birth of the Greek orders of architecture, the first marble sculptures and early lyric poetry. ▷ 1.24

ARDIPITHECUS RAMIDUS

The divergence of the evolutionary lineages of hominids and apes occurred about 6 million ya. Fossil remains of the earliest known hominid, *Ardipithecus ramidus* (found in Ethiopia), dating from about 4.4 million ya, show that it was a small animal about the size of a chimpanzee. It is not yet known whether it had developed the upright, bipedal gait characteristic of modern humans. This species probably evolved into the early australopithecines. ▷ 1.01

ARGOS

Greek city-state in the eastern Peloponnese and according to legend, the first to develop the HOPLITE phalanx as a means of defense. Argos was also a long-term rival of SPARTA, with whom it fought many wars between the 7th and 5th centuries BC. ▷ 1.24

ARVAD
City on the Levantine coast (modern Tripoli in Lebanon), probably founded by about 1000 BC. It was later the capital of a PHOENICIAN city-state, at times owing allegience to a succession of Assyrian, BABYLONIAN and ACHEMENID kings. ▷ 1.12, 1.13, 1.14

ARYANS
Pastoralist people from central Asia with an INDO-EUROPEAN LANGUAGE, who invaded Iran and India in about 1500 BC. They may have been related to the KASSITES, who invaded the Middle East in about 1600 BC. The Aryans are described in Indian epic poems, the Rigvedas, which were first composed orally in archaic Sanskrit (c.1500–800 BC) and only later recorded in writing. They absorbed aspects of local culture and, by 900 BC, ruled most of northern India, establishing small kingdoms, which coalesced into larger states in the following centuries. The relevance of the Aryans to the question of Indo-European language origins is much disputed, and the identification of an Aryan "race" has no foundation in biological anthropology. ▷ 1.05, 1.06, 1.26

ARZAWA
Kingdom in western Anatolia that was conquered on several occasions by the HITTITES, and a vassal of the Hittite empire for a period in the 17th century BC. Arzawa was at its most powerful from the 15th to 14th centuries BC, but was reconquered by the Hittites in about 1300 BC and later became embroiled in power struggles within the Hittite empire. The collapse of the Hittites in about 1200 BC left Arzawa fragmented and it lost its separate political identity. ▷ 1.12

ASHUR
City in north MESOPOTAMIA situated on the river Tigris, at a strategic point on trade routes from SUMERIA to Anatolia and the LEVANT. It was founded in the 3rd millennium BC and had become a major trade center by about 1800 BC, when it was siezed by the Amorite king, SHAMSHI-ADAD. An Akkadian dynasty ruled Ashur from about 1600 BC, overthrowing Mittanian domination in about 1330 BC, and renaming their kingdom ASSYRIA (after Ashur). It remained the Assyrian capital until about 878 BC, and continued to be the religious capital when the political center moved elsewhere. The city was destroyed by the BABYLONIANS in 614 BC. ▷ 1.11, 1.12, 1.13

ASHURBANIPAL
The last great king of ASSYRIA (r.668–627 BC). He completed the conquest of Egypt, installing Necho I as vassal ruler. Assyrian garrisons were later expelled, but Egypt was no longer a threat to Assyrian dominance. He suppressed rebellions in the LEVANT, expelled the CIMMERIANS, reconquered BABYLONIA and conquered ELAM by 639 BC. Ashurbanipal greatly overstretched the resources of the empire, while his tyrannical rule created wide discontent. After his death the empire rapidly declined, due to MEDIAN invasions and the resurgence of BABYLON. ▷ 1.13, 1.15

ASHURNASIRPAL II
King of ASSYRIA (r.883–859 BC). Ashurnasirpal III conquered north MESOPOTAMIA and the Levantine coast, using cavalry on a large scale, and enforced Assyrian dominance by means of terror tactics and the resettlement of conquered populations. He moved the royal capital to KALHU. ▷ 1.13

ASPERO TRADITION
Cultural tradition of the Andean PRECERAMIC PERIOD that produced the first ceremonial monument complexes in South America (c.3000–1800 BC), with sedentary settlement and an increasing reliance on agriculture. It is named after the site of Aspero, one of the earliest ceremonial sites in lowland Peru, consisting of six large earthen mounds with masonry temples (c.2600 BC). ▷ 1.04, 1.28

ASSYRIA
Region of north MESOPOTAMIA centered on the Upper Tigris in modern Iraq. The name derives from ASHUR, an early city-state that was siezed by SHAMSHI-ADAD (c.1800 BC), who established a short-lived empire (the Old Assyrian period). The Akkadian dynasty, which ruled Assyria from about 1600 BC, were vassals of MITTANI or BABYLON until Ashuruballit I overthrew Mittanian domination in about 1330 BC. This initiated the Middle Assyrian empire (c.1330–1076 BC), which at its greatest extent under Tukulti-Ninurta I (r.1243–1207 BC) controlled Mesopotamia and dominated most of the LEVANT, Anatolia and ELAM. The empire collapsed in the face of ARAMAEAN invasions.

The Neo-Assyrian empire (c.911–612 BC), the period of Assyria's greatest expansion and cultural achievement, was initiated by ADAD-NIRARI II (r.911–891 BC) and maintained by a series of powerful and warlike kings. The empire reached its greatest extent under ASHURBANIPAL (668–627 BC), but disintegrated after his death and was destroyed by the MEDES and Babylonians in 612 BC. Assyrian imperialism is notable for its military innovations (the mass production of iron weaponry, huge professional armies and mass cavalry tactics), and its extreme ruthlessness (the use of terror and resettlement of conquered populations). The Assyrians are also noted for their architectural and sculptural achievements, especially monumental temples, fortifications, narrative friezes depicting campaigns and hunts, and huge gateway statues of winged bulls. ▷ 1.11, 1,12, 1.13

ATTICA
The territory of Athens, extending for 2,500 square kilometers (965 square miles) around the city. Originally controlled by aristocratic clans, by the 5th century BC its inhabitants were well integrated into the city's democratic system through their membership of *demes*, local "village" communities. ▷ 1.24

AURIGNACIAN CULTURE
The earliest UPPER PALEOLITHIC stone tool industry in Europe (c.40,000–29,000 ya), associated with the colonization of the region by anatomically modern humans. It was characterized by a diverse new range of specialized stone and bone tools, such as burins, scrapers and projectile points, and by the appearance of complex works of art, including engraved pebbles, bone and ivory carvings, clay figurines and cave paintings (by 30,000 ya). ▷ 1.19

AUSTRALOPITHECUS AFARENSIS
The earliest australopithecine hominid, living about 4 million to 3 million ya. Fossil remains have been found at HADAR in Ethiopia and at LAETOLI in Tanzania. Lightly built and fully bipedal (though not a tool user), this species evolved into two later types of hominid – gracile AUSTRALOPITHECUS AFRICANUS and the larger AUSTRALOPITHECUS ROBUSTUS – and was possibly ancestral to the genus *Homo*. ▷ 1.01

AUSTRALOPITHECUS AFRICANUS
Hominid that lived in Africa about 3 million to 2 million ya and was contemporary with the related, but more heavily built, AUSTALOPITHECUS ROBUSTUS. Fossils from Taung and Makapansgat in South Africa and KOOBI FORA in Tanzania suggest that this was a small, gracile hominid with teeth similar to those of humans. It is possibly the ancestor of HOMO HABILIS, though the human genus may have evolved from AUSTRALOPITHECUS AFARENSIS at an earlier date. ▷ 1.01

AUSTRALOPITHECUS ROBUSTUS
A heavily-built hominid that lived in Africa about 3 to 1 million ya, alongside the gracile AUSTRALOPITHECUS AFRICANUS and the earliest humans. It was characterized by massive jaws and teeth that were adapted to the consumption of tough vegetable foods rather than meat. Fossil remains have been found in eastern and southern Africa (notably at KOOBI FORA, OMO, OLDUVAI, SWARTKRANS and Sterkfontein). This species probably became extinct when HOMO ERECTUS, a sophisticated tool user, began to colonize new habitats, becoming more numerous and marginalizing australopithecine populations. ▷ 1.01

AVEBURY HENGE
Late NEOLITHIC enclosure in southern Britain, built in about 2800–2500 BC. It consists of a massive circular embankment, about 425 meters (1,394 feet) in diameter with an interior quarry ditch, enclosing the three largest STONE CIRCLES in Europe. The site was approached by an avenue of standing stones,

1.6 kilometers (1 mile) long, which lead from another stone circle (the Sanctuary). SILBURY HILL is located to the south. ▷ 1.20

BA

Early state with a non-Chinese population near the confluence of the Yangtze and Jialing rivers in Sichuan province, China. Ba became a feudal state, with Chinese over-lords, that owed allegiance to the Western ZHOU in the 11th century BC. It was incorpo-rated into the QIN empire from the late 4th century BC. ▷ 1.27

BABYLON

City on the Euphrates and the most important religious and cultural center of ancient MESOPOTAMIA. Probably founded in the mid-3rd millennium BC, it was the capital of an AMORITE dynasty from about 1895 BC, the best-known ruler being HAMMURABI, until it was destroyed by the HITTITES in 1595 BC. It was the capital of a KASSITE dynasty from 1570 until 1158 BC, when it was sacked by the Elamites.

Babylon was subsequently ruled by a series of short-lived ARAMAEAN and CHALDEAN dynasties under Assyrian dominance, until the restoration of Babylonian independence in 626 BC. It was reconstructed by NEBUCHADNEZZAR (c.600 BC) to become the largest city in the world, covering 1,000 hectares (2,500 acres) with a population of over 100,000, and was defended by a massive double wall on both sides of the Euphrates. The most famous buildings in Babylon date from this period, including the ZIGGURAT of Marduk (the Tower of Babel) and the Ishtar Gate. The Greek historian Herodotus also mentions the Hanging Gardens, possibly part of one of the two palace complexes. Babylon was captured by the Persians in 539 BC and a revolt in 482 BC led to the widespread destruction of its ancient temples and fortifi-cations. ▷ 1.11, 1.12, 1.13, 1.14, 1.15, 1.23

BABYLONIA

A region of south MESOPOTAMIA named after the city of BABYLON. It became a province of the Third Dynasty of UR in the late 3rd millennium BC and was established as an independent kingdom during the Old Babylonian period (c.1895–1595 BC), under the AMORITE dynasty founded by king Sumuabum (c.1895). Expansion into northern Mesopotamia by King HAMMURABI in about 1790–1755 BC briefly established Babylonia as the leading imperial power in the Middle East. After Hammurabi's death, Babylonia declined and after Babylon was sacked by the HITTITES in 1595 BC, it was so weakened that it was unable to resist a KASSITE invasion (c.1570 BC). Under the Kassites, Babylonia became a powerful state once again, and was frequently at war with its ASSYRIAN, Elamite and ARAMAEAN neighbors. This dynasty was swept away when the Elamites sacked Babylon in 1157 BC, opening the way to a

series of Aramaean and CHALDEAN dynasties. Babylonia became a mere vassal of the Assyrian empire from the mid-9th century BC, until its revival in the 7th century BC.

During the Neo-Babylonian empire (c.626–539 BC), Babylonian independence was reasserted by King NABOPOLASSAR, who attacked Assyria and destroyed NINEVEH in 612 BC, ending Assyrian power and taking over their domains. His son, NEBUCHADNEZZAR, defeated the Egyptians in 605 BC, ensuring supremacy in the Middle East. The empire lasted until 539 BC, when Babylonia was taken over by CYRUS the Great, becoming the wealthiest satrapy of the ACHEMENID EMPIRE. The rich cultural heritage of SUMER and AKKAD was adopted by later Babylonian rulers, who maintained their religious, artistic, architectural and literary traditions until conquest by the Persians in the 6th century BC. ▷ 1.12, 1.13, 1.15

BANAS CULTURE

Culture of the Banas valley, Rajasthan, influenced by the late INDUS CIVILIZATION, with stone and clay houses, Black-and-Red ware pottery and bronze tools. The principal settlement at Ahar is dated from about 2200 to 1500 BC. The Banas culture survived the collapse of the Indus civilization and Black-and-Red ware pottery became widespread across southern India after 1800 BC. ▷ 1.26

BANDKERAMIK CULTURE

The earliest farming culture of the central European NEOLITHIC, from 5400 to 4500 BC, characterized by distinctive round-based dec-orated pottery, large timber LONGHOUSES, and slash-and-burn horticulture. It spread through a gradual colonization process from the Balkans across the loess lands of central Europe, as far as Poland, the Netherlands and France, exploiting domestic plant and animal species that were derived from the Near East. ▷ 1.20

BANTU

An African language group that originated in the equatorial region of Cameroon. Bantu-speaking herders and farmers, with their iron-working technology, spread eastwards and southwards from about 500 BC, replacing or influencing indigenous populations. Bantu speakers were dominant throughout central and southern Africa by AD 400. ▷ 1.06

BARLEY

Cereal plant native to the temperate regions of the Old World, from China to southern Europe and Egypt. Two varieties of barley were domesticated in the Middle East by 8000 BC. It was one of the staple crops of NEOLITHIC farming communities. ▷ 1.03, 1.08, 1.09, 1.16

BARROW, LONG

A type of early NEOLITHIC burial monument found in Europe in about 5000–2500 BC,

consisting of an elongated rectangular, trapezoidal or oval mound built of earth or rock. The mounds cover one or more burials, often collective deposits of disarticulated skeletons, sometimes housed in timber or MEGALITHIC mortuary houses. ▷ 1.20

BARROW, ROUND

Multi-period burial monument found in many parts of the Old World, especially associated with NEOLITHIC and BRONZE AGE cultures of temperate Europe from about 3000 to 1000 BC, and steppe cultures (such as the SCYTHIANS) from about 3000 to 200 BC. Built of turf, earth and/or rock, sometimes with timber structures and mortuary houses, they usually cover single articulated burials, some with lavish grave goods. ▷ 1.21

BASILEUS

Literally Greek for "king", the word is normally used to describe Greek nobles of the 10th to 8th centuries BC, a class portrayed by HOMER. A CATTLE-owning aristocracy, they idealized feasting and the heroism of war. In the medieval Byzantine empire the word was used to describe the emperor.

BELL BEAKER CULTURES

Late NEOLITHIC and early BRONZE AGE cultures of Europe associated with distinctive decorated drinking vessels (beakers) and other objects, including COPPER and bronze items, often found as grave goods with single burials under ROUND BARROWS in about 2800–1800 BC. This tradition emerged in the Rhineland and the Netherlands and spread to Britain, central Europe, Atlantic France and Spain, probably adopted by local populations as a cult package. ▷ 1.04, 1.20, 1.21

BERINGIA

Continental shelf between Siberia and Alaska that was exposed as dry land several times during the last glaciation (c.45,000–40,000 ya; 33,000–28,000 ya; 22,000–12,000 ya), forming the Bering land-bridge across which humans migrated from Asia to America. The date of this is disputed, but PALEOINDIAN populations were present in North America by about 15,000–12,000 ya. ▷ 1.02

BIBLE LANDS

A region of the Middle East comprising most of modern Israel, Jordan, Lebanon and Syria. It is referred to in detail in the Old Testament, during the period of HEBREW colonization from the 12th century BC until the destruction of the last of the Hebrew kingdoms in about 587 BC. ▷ 1.14

BIMBISARA

King of Magadha (c.520–491 BC), one of the major Indian states of the Gangetic civiliza-tion. He expanded his territory by annexing neighboring kingdoms, forming the core area of the later Mauryan Empire. He was a friend and patron of the BUDDHA. ▷ 1.26

BOEOTIA
Region of central Greece, neighboring ATTICA, that was a fertile area of many settlements, the most prominent of which was Thebes. Its central position made it the focus of many wars between surrounding city-states. ▷ 1.24

BOOK OF THE DEAD
A book of spells that was designed to help Egyptians make the transition into the next world safely. Usually written on papyrus, it was placed beside the mummified body of the deceased.

BOW AND ARROW
A hunting and fighting weapon used for precision killing at a distance from the target. The earliest preserved examples are MESOLITHIC in date, but stone and bone arrow points found in Europe and Africa suggest that they were first used by modern humans about 20,000 ya. The bow was introduced into the Americas from Asia in about 2000 BC. ▷ 1.18

BOWL CULTURES
First farming cultures of northwest Europe (c.4500–3300 BC), with regional traditions of round-based CERAMICS, tomb building (PASSAGE GRAVES and LONG BARROWS), and ceremonial enclosures. These cultures developed from MESOLITHIC communities who adopted ceramics and agriculture, at first perhaps more for ritual than subsistence purposes. ▷ 1.20

BOXGROVE
LOWER PALEOLITHIC fossil beach in southern Britain with the earliest human remains yet found in Europe (HOMO ERECTUS), about 500,000 years old. ACHEULIAN hand-axes and animal remains found *in situ* on the ancient beach surface provide important information about tool manufacture and butchery practices, with implications for early human cognition. ▷ 1.01

BRONZE AGE
A subdivision of the THREE AGE SYSTEM. It is now recognized that the idea of a Bronze Age is of limited value, being applicable only to Eurasia and north Africa, beginning at different times in different regions (e.g. c.4000 BC in MESOPOTAMIA and c.2000 BC in China), and being too general to describe the great variety of bronze-using cultures. ▷ 1.04, 1.05, 1.06, 1.09, 1.10, 1.11, 1.12, 1.16, 1.20, 1.21, 1.26, 1.27

BUDDHA (SIDDHARTHA GAUTAMA)
Founder of the Buddhist religion who was born at LUMBINI in north India in about 563 BC, son of the king of the Sakyas. He renounced his royal status and embarked on a period of learning, formulating a doctrine of personal spiritual enlightenment that attracted a growing number of disciples. He

was highly regarded by King BIMBISARA of Magadha. His teachings inspired a religious movement that spread rapidly, though it did not become a major organized religion until the 3rd century BC. The Buddha died at Kusinagara in about 483 BC. ▷ 1.06, 1.26

BYBLOS
NEOLITHIC settlement on the Levantine coast that became a major trading center, especially for the export of cedar wood to Egypt, by 2500 BC. It was the main city of PHOENICIA in the 11th century BC, but later declined as its rivals SIDON and TYRE grew more powerful. ▷ 1.09, 1.10, 1.11, 1.12, 1.13, 1.14

CALENDAR
Once it was realized that there was a regular year of 365 days, calendars came into operation to mark the passing of the year. They could be based on the cycles of the moon (hence the 12 months of the Egyptian, Greek and Roman calendars), or the sun. Any calendar based on full (e.g. 365) days is bound to become inaccurate with time (the true length of a year is approximately 365 ¼ days), so additional days or even months have to be entered to maintain accuracy. The Roman emperor Julius Caesar adapted an Egyptian solar calendar to solve inaccuracies in the Roman calendar, and it is this Julian calender, with some modifications (Pope Gregory, 1582), that is used today. The practice of dividing a day or night into 12 hours is Egyptian, and that of dividing hours into 60 minutes, Babylonian.

CAMBYSES II
ACHEMENID king of Persia (r.529–522 BC) and the son of CYRUS II. He annexed Egypt after the Battle of Pelusium and the capture of MEMPHIS in 525 BC, but failed to conquer the Nubian state of MEROË. He was possibly murdered in Syria in 522 BC by his brother, SMERDIS, who was deposed by DARIUS. ▷ 1.15

CANAANITES
Semitic people who had settled in the LEVANT, from Sinai to the Orontes river, by about 2000 BC, and established small city-states with a shared religion and alphabet. The Canaanites were culturally heterogenous with elements of pre-Semitic, Semitic and Mesopotamian culture, and Egyptian, Anatolian and Aegean influences. In southern Palestine they were conquered by the Israelites and PHILISTINES (c.1200 BC), the last enclaves being annexed by king DAVID in the early 10th century BC. Further north, the PHOENICIANS were partly descended from the Canaanites and maintained some Canaanite cultural traditions. ▷ 1.05, 1.07, 1.11, 1.12, 1.14, 1.23

CANAANITE ALPHABET
The Canaanite language appears to have been an early form of HEBREW. The CANAANITES developed the first known

phonetic alphabet, which was widely adapted in the LEVANT and Middle East from the late 2nd millennium BC. The PHOENICIAN version of this alphabet was the basis for the Old HEBREW, GREEK and LATIN (via Etruscan) alphabets. ▷ 1.07, 1.12, 1.14, 1.23

CARCHEMISH
City situated on the upper Euphrates, that was strategically placed to command the main trade routes from MESOPOTAMIA to the LEVANT and Anatolia. It was important in the 2nd millennium BC as a trading city and the administrative center of MITTANI (c.1500–1350 BC), a vassal state dominated by the HITTITES (c.1350–1200 BC), and the most powerful of the Neo-Hittite city-states (c.1200–880 BC). Carchemish later became a vassal of the Neo-Assyrian empire and was annexed by SARGON II in 716 BC. In 605 BC it was the site of a battle between the Egyptians and Babylonians, which ended Egyptian attempts to regain their power in the Near East. ▷ 1.12, 1.13, 1.14

CARNAC
NEOLITHIC ceremonial center to the north of the Gulf of Morbihan in Brittany, with a dense concentration of MEGALITHIC tombs and alignments (c.4500–2000 BC). The alignments consist of parallel lines of menhirs (standing stones) in several segments on a line about 4 kilometers (2.5 miles) in length, some with enclosures at the ends, that were probably used for processions and other rituals. ▷ 1.20

CATACOMB GRAVE CULTURES
Early BRONZE AGE pastoral nomad cultures of the south Russian steppes (c.2300–1800 BC), characterized by ROUND BARROWS covering burial chambers, some of which contain wheeled vehicles. This was one phase of the longer Kurgan tradition (*kurgan* means "mound"), preceded by the Pit Grave culture, (c.3500–2300 BC) and followed by the Timber Grave phase. SCYTHIAN round-barrow burials are a later version of this tradition. ▷ 1.21

CATTLE
Animals derived from the wild aurochs (*Bos primigenius*), that were domesticated in Anatolia and the Balkans by about 6500 BC, giving rise to *Bos taurus* breeds in Europe and the Middle East, and *Bos indicus* (or humped zebu) breeds in India and east Asia. Central to early farming economies for meat and leather, cattle were increasingly exploited for dairy products and traction from about 4500 BC. The water buffalo (*Bubalus bubalis*) is derived from a different ruminant species domesticated in Asia by about 5000 BC. ▷ 1.03, 1.05, 1.08, 1.16, 1.20

CAUSEWAYED CAMP
A type of NEOLITHIC enclosure found in Britain (e.g. WINDMILL HILL) and Denmark, built in about 3800–3000 BC, that consists of one or more ditch and bank circuits

interrupted by causeways. Most had settlement or ceremonial functions (including possible exposure of the dead). ▷ 1.20

CAVE AND ROCK ART

The earliest examples of art, consisting of paintings and engravings on the walls of caves and rock shelters, produced by the UPPER PALEOLITHIC hunters of Europe, Africa and Australia. In Africa and Australia these traditions continued into modern times. In the case of Upper Paleolithic Europe, the cave art is associated with modern humans, dating mostly from about 25,000 to 10,000 ya, and is dominated by representations of animals, some of them extraordinarily naturalistic, human figures, hand prints and abstract symbols. Especially impressive friezes survive at LASCAUX (France) and ALTAMIRA (Spain). These paintings are believed to have had considerable religious and social significance. ▷ 1.02, 1.16, 1.19

CERAMICS

Materials and objects made of fired clay, including pottery (containers and other vessels) and terracotta (fine building materials, clay tablets and statuary). The earliest known fired-clay objects are the "Venus" figurines and animal models of the UPPER PALEOLITHIC GRAVETTIAN CULTURE of Europe. The use of pottery is sometimes equated with early farming cultures, though the first NEOLITHIC societies of the LEVANT (9th millennium BC) were aceramic, while the HUNTER-GATHERER JOMON CULTURE of Japan made pottery from about 12,500 ya. ▷ 1.04, 1.06, 1.08, 1.10, 1.12, 1.17, 1.27

CHALDEANS

ARAMAEAN people of northern Arabia who settled in MESOPOTAMIA in the early 1st millennium BC, establishing ruling dynasties in several cities. The famous Chaldean 11th dynasty of BABYLON destroyed the Assyrians and re-established the Babylonian empire. ▷ 1.12, 1.13

CHAMBERED TOMB

A type of collective burial monument found in many parts of the world, that consists of a stone mortuary chamber covered by an earth or stone mound. The earliest examples are the early NEOLITHIC MEGALITHIC tombs of Europe, such as PASSAGE GRAVES and chambered LONG BARROWS, built by the earliest farming societies in France and Britain in about 4500–3400 BC, with later types found throughout western Europe. ▷ 1.20

CHATAL HUYUK

An exceptionally large early agricultural settlement, sometimes described as a town, that is situated on the edge of the Konya plateau in southern Anatolia and dates from about 6500 BC. The densely-clustered clay-built houses were entered through rooftop openings, some with shrine rooms which

contained clay-modeled bull's heads and frescoes. The settlement had a mixed farming economy that supported a population of about 6,000 people, importing materials such as OBSIDIAN for tools. There is evidence in late occupation levels of early COPPER WORKING. ▷ 1.03, 1.09

CHÂTELPERRONIAN CULTURE

Initial stage of the European UPPER PALEOLITHIC, defined by a distinctive set of stone tools, including backed knives. Dating from about 40,000 to 30,000 ya, it was once thought to be the earliest cultural evidence of modern humans in Europe, though it is now believed to be a product of late Neanderthal populations, copying the AURIGNACIAN blade-tool technologies of the modern human communities. ▷ 1.19

CHAVÍN DE HUÁNTAR

Ceremonial center in the Andes, occupied from about 850 to 200 BC, with several large temple platforms and sunken courts linked by pavements and stairs. The stone buildings, especially gates, are decorated with relief carvings of humans and animals. The site gives its name to the Chavín style of art and architecture (c.900–200 BC), and is probably related to a religious cult that had spread throughout the Andes and coastal Peru by 400 BC. ▷ 1.06, 1.28

CHAYONU

A rare transitional HUNTER-GATHERER and early agricultural settlement in north MESOPOTAMIA, occupied from about 8500 to 6500 BC. It is also notable for the very early evidence (c.7300 BC) of COPPER metallurgy (cold hammering of "native" copper in its free metallic state) to make tools and ornaments. ▷ 1.08

CHESOWANJA

LOWER PALEOLITHIC site in ancient lake sediments and tuffs at Lake Baringo, Kenya, dating from about 2.4 to 1.3 million ya, with remains of AUSTRALOPITHECUS ROBUSTUS, layers containing OLDOWAN chopper tools, and a later ACHEULIAN hand-ax industry. There is also possible evidence of the earliest controlled use of FIRE (c.1.6 million ya). ▷ 1.01

CHIEFDOM

A type of social system characterized by centralized chiefly and religious authority, tribute-giving, the exhange and redistribution of prestige goods, the building of ceremonial centers, alliance networks, and competition between polities. Chiefdoms are usually regarded as an evolutionary stage following tribal or simple ranked societies, and preceding the development of STATES and urbanism, and are recognized in many parts of the world at different times. ▷ 1.04, 1.05, 1.06

CHINCHOROS TRADITION

Long-lived HUNTER-GATHERER culture of the coastal region of South America, in modern

north Chile, spanning both the PRECERAMIC and INITIAL periods (3000–500 BC). As well as fishing and hunting equipment, the Chinchorros had knowledge of basketry and textiles, and made pottery from about 1200 BC. ▷ 1.04, 1.06, 1.15

CHINESE LANGUAGE AND SCRIPT

Chinese is a language group of the Sino-Tibetan language family and consists of a number of separate languages, though all use a common writing system. The earliest Chinese scripts were pictographic, of the SHANG period (from c.1600 BC), when they were used for recording divinations. Refinements to this writing system gave rise to a LOGOGRAPHIC SCRIPT from about 900 BC (standardized in the 3rd century BC), in which each sign represented a unit of meaning rather than sound. This script is the world's oldest continually used writing system. ▷ 1.07, 1.27

CHIRIPA CULTURE

Culture of the Andean EARLY HORIZON PERIOD named after the ceremonial center at Chiripa (600–400 BC), at the south end of Lake Titicaca, Bolivia. Little is known about its origins or development, but the communities of the Titicaca Basin probably shared a religious tradition (YAYA-MAMA), and the architectural styles seen at Chiripa are similar to those of the later Tiahuanaco state in the same area in about AD 500. ▷ 1.05, 1.28

CHOGA MAMI

Early agricultural settlement of the 7th to 6th millennia BC, to the east of the Tigris river on the edge of the Mesopotamian plains. It is the site of the earliest recorded canal IRRIGATION system, built by about 5500 BC. ▷ 1.09

CHORRERA CULTURE

Early farming culture in southern Ecuador with a sophisticated CERAMIC tradition spanning the INITIAL and EARLY HORIZON periods (1200–300 BC), which expanded from the long-settled VALDIVIA coastal region into the Andean highlands to grow MAIZE and manioc. ▷ 1.05, 1.06, 1.28

CHU

Major feudal state of the ZHOU kingdom in southern China in about 1100–250 BC, with a capital at Ying. It was constantly at war with its powerful northern enemy, JIN, during the later SPRINGS AND AUTUMNS PERIOD and briefly became the leading state (hegemon) in about 710–690 BC, under King Zhuang. It lost its position as the pre-eminent southern Zhou state as its rivals, WU and Yue, grew more powerful in the late 6th century BC. ▷ 1.27

CIMMERIANS

Nomadic people of the steppes to the north of the Caucasus who migrated southwards in the 8th century BC. They were repulsed by the Assyrians and driven into Anatolia, where they conquered PHRYGIA (705–696 BC) and LYDIA (652 BC). Their power was broken by the Lydians and Babylonians in the late 7th century BC. ▷ 1.13

CLOVIS CULTURE

Earliest distinct PALEOINDIAN culture of North America (c.9500–9000 BC), characterized by stone tools, including projectile points with concave bases (Clovis points) used for big-game hunting of mammoths and bison. The origins of the Clovis culture are unclear but must lie in the preceding little-known Lower Lithic Paleoindian traditions. ▷ 1.02

COINAGE

Stamped pieces of metal were first given to the Greek mercenaries of the king of LYDIA in about 600 BC and spread quickly into the Greek world. (Coinage was invented independently in China at about the same time.) At first they were used for state transactions and for the receipt of taxes. By the end of the 6th century BC, many Greek cities were minting their own smaller coins in silver, and these were used for everyday transactions. The use of coin faces for propaganda and for the glorification of a city, ruler or successful victory was soon widespread. Coinage quickly spread from Greece to Italy, and then the rest of Europe. ▷ 1.24

COLCHIS

An area enclosed by the Caucasus mountains, stretching from the east coast of the Black Sea. The coastline was colonized by the Greek city of MILETOS in the 6th century BC, and the area was later absorbed into the Roman province of Cappadocia. ▷ 1.15, 1.23

CONFUCIUS

Chinese philosopher and teacher born in 551 BC in the state of LU, who was a member of the minor aristocracy, or bureaucratic class. Confucius advocated moral rectitude, education for all, service to the state and responsible government. His writings established an influential ethical code for the exercise of power and citizenship. He died in 479 BC. ▷ 1.06, 1.27

COPPER WORKING

Copper was one of the first metals used for making tools and ornaments. It is easily worked and may exist in a pure form, though it usually requires extraction from ores by smelting. Copper working began independently in different parts of the world: in MESOPOTAMIA by about 7000 BC, China by about 3000 BC and the Americas by about 1000 BC. In the western Old World, a Copper Age is sometimes identified as a separate period. ▷ 1.08, 1.27, 1.28

CORD IMPRESSED WARE CULTURE

Late NEOLITHIC culture of central Europe that influenced the farming societies of northern

Europe from the Meuse to the Volga in 3000–2400 BC. It is distinguished by its pottery beakers with cord-impressed decoration, stone battle-axes, and burials under ROUND BARROWS. The Cord Impressed Ware culture marked a new emphasis on PASTORAL-ISM and social hierarchy, and was a precursor of the BELL BEAKER cultures of western Europe. ▷ 1.04, 1.20

CORINTH

The leading Greek city-state of the 7th century BC, heavily involved in Mediterranean trading and shipbuilding, and the pioneer of Doric architecture. Corinth's central position meant that it was drawn into the wars of the 5th and 4th centuries BC, at first in support of SPARTA (Peloponnesian War) and then against it. The Romans sacked Corinth in 146 BC, but later founded a new colony there, which regained the original city's prosperity. It was the home of an early Christian community made famous by the letters it received from St Paul. ▷ 1.22, 1.23, 1.24

CORTAILLOD

Early farming and fishing village beside Lake Neuchâtel in Switzerland, that gave its name to the early NEOLITHIC of the north Alpine region in about 3800–3000 BC. Cortaillod settlements are famous for the preservation of wooden houses and artifacts in the lake sediments. ▷ 1.20

COTTON

Seed-hair fiber from plants of the genus *Gossypium*, found in sub-tropical regions and cultivated for making textiles and thread. The earliest use of cotton was in the Indian sub-continent, where it was domesticated by 5000 BC, and in South America, where cotton textiles of the 3rd millennium BC have been recorded (ASPERO culture). ▷ 1.03, 1.26, 1.28

CROESUS

King of LYDIA (r.c.560–546 BC) who lives on in legend for his immense wealth. Croesus had many links with the Greek world, but found himself isolated when he attacked CYRUS of Persia, who defeated him and annexed his kingdom to the ACHEMENID EMPIRE (546–545 BC). ▷ 1.15

CUMAE

See KYMAI

CUNEIFORM

Writing system invented in MESOPOTAMIA in the 3rd millennium BC, derived from Sumerian pictographs that were refined to include phonetic and syllabic values. Early inscriptions were written in Sumerian, but cuneiform was widely adopted in the Middle East for writing other languages, notably AKKADIAN. It fell out of use as ARAMAIC LANGUAGES and versions of CANAANITE phonetic alphabets became widespread in the 1st millennium BC. ▷ 1.07, 1.10, 1.15

CYRUS II (THE GREAT)

King of Persia (r.559–30 BC) who founded the ACHEMENID EMPIRE by overthrowing his MEDIAN overlord, King Astyages, and appropriating his extensive empire. He confirmed his position by destroying his main rival to the west, CROESUS of LYDIA, in Asia Minor (547–546 BC) and annexing BABYLONIA (539 BC). Cyrus was known for his diplomacy as well as his use of force. His eastern campaigns and fortress-building (546–530 BC) consolidated the empire, but Cyrus was killed in battle on the frontier in 530 BC. ▷ 1.13, 1.14, 1.15

DARIUS I (THE GREAT)

Achemenid king of Persia (r.521–486 BC) who ruled the ACHEMENID EMPIRE when it was at the height of its power. He seized the throne after the death of CAMBYSES and secured the northern frontiers by defeating the SCYTHIANS. He conquered the Indus valley by 518 BC and Thrace by 513 BC, but failed to conquer Greece (490 BC). He reorganized the empire by establishing a federal system of satrapies, efficient taxation and postal systems, and a new military organization. He marked his reign by building a new royal capital at PERSEPOLIS. ▷ 1.15

DAVID

King of ISRAEL (r.c.1006–965 BC), proclaimed ruler of JUDAH and later of Israel after the death of King SAUL. David conquered JERUSALEM and made it the capital of a united kingdom in about 1000 BC. He defeated the PHILISTINES and consolidated the kingdom of Israel by dominating vassal states such as EDOM, MOAB and ARAM-DAMASCUS. ▷ 1.14

DELPHI

Important shrine of Apollo, situated on the slopes of Mount Parnassus, central Greece. Its famous ORACLE attracted visitors from all parts of the Greek world, and the Pythian Games held at the shrine were second only to those held at OLYMPIA. The site was crowded with treasuries, temples and statues donated by cities and supplicants. Delphi played an important role during the period of Greek colonization, advising migrants where they should settle. ▷ 1.24

DI-XIN

Last king of the SHANG dynasty of China, who was overthrown by his vassal, King WU of the ZHOU family, at the Battle of Chaoge in 1122 BC. He was later seen as a sadistic despot who was morally unfit to rule, and was therefore justly removed according to the doctrine known as the "Mandate of Heaven", under which political power was subject to divine judgement. ▷ 1.27

DIASPORA

Greek word meaning "dispersion" that is used to describe the scattering of Jewish populations and their exile from Palestine.

The first Diaspora took place in 587 BC, when NEBUCHADNEZZAR, king of BABYLON, suppressed a revolt in JUDAH and forcibly resettled HEBREW communities in BABYLONIA. When CYRUS the Great of Persia permitted a return to their homeland in 539 BC, many Jews stayed behind. Later Diaspora scattered the Jews still further. ▷ 1.14

DILMUN
Early state and trading center in the Persian Gulf that is mentioned in Sumerian records and was probably on the island of Bahrain, where a large fortified city existed in about 2800–1800 BC. Dilmun was at the center of a thriving trade system, largely based on commerce between MESOPOTAMIA and the Indus valley in the 3rd millennium BC. It may have been conquered by SARGON of AGADE, becoming part of the Akkadian empire in the 23rd century BC. ▷ 1.11

DJOSER
Founder of the 3rd Dynasty of Egyptian PHARAOHS, Djoser ruled from 2677 until 2648 BC. He is chiefly remembered for his burial place, the STEP PYRAMID at SAQQARA, designed by the architect Imhotep. ▷ 1.17

DOG
The first animal to be tamed by humans, the wolf probably being its main ancestral species. There is evidence of early domestic dogs in several parts of the world, with the earliest in the Middle East (c.3000 ya), though earlier hunters may have initiated the domestication process. Dogs were used for protection, herding and food (in the Americas), and as pets. ▷ 1.08

DOLMEN
Term used by early European archeologists to describe MEGALITHIC tomb chambers of the NEOLITHIC period, especially those consisting of upright orthostats with a large capstone on top. The term is now rarely used, except to describe the "portal-dolmen", a specific type of tomb. ▷ 1.20

DORIANS
One of the tribes of Greeks whose foundation myths told of their arrival in the Peloponnese after the fall of TROY. Some archeologists and historians have dated this to about 1100 BC, but others point to a later foundation (c.900 BC) of the main Dorian city, SPARTA. By the 5th century BC the Dorians were deadly rivals of the IONIANS, whose mother city was Athens. ▷ 1.12, 1.22, 1.23, 1.24

DRAVIDIANS
People of southern India, sometimes regarded as the original pre-ARYAN HUNTER-GATHERER population, which adopted farming from the 4th millennium BC. The ethnic and racial distinctiveness of the Dravidians is open to question, and the term is now used mainly to describe speakers of the Dravidian languages, widely spoken in southern India. ▷ 1.04, 1.05, 1.06, 1.26

DUR-KURIGALZU
City in south MESOPOTAMIA near to the confluence of the Tigris and Diyala rivers, founded in the 14th century BC by a KASSITE king of BABYLON, Kurigalzu I or Kurigalzu II. The city contained a ZIGGURAT and temples dedicated to Sumerian gods, as well as a royal palace. ▷ 1.12, 1.13

DYUKHTAI TRADITION
UPPER PALEOLITHIC stone-tool industry (c.20,000–12,000 ya) that represents the first human colonization of far northeast Asia (eastern Siberia). It is characterized by bifacial spear points for big-game hunting. Communities from this region migrated eastwards in this period and eventually crossed BERINGIA to colonize the Americas. ▷ 1.02

EARLY HORIZON PERIOD
Period of ANDEAN CIVILIZATION from about 900 to 200 BC. It is marked by the spread of the Chavín artistic and temple-building tradition across the formerly diverse regional cultures of the central Andes, after which coastal areas adopted highland architectural styles. This process of cultural integration may have been due to the adoption of a single religious cult. The decline of Chavín influence after 200 BC resulted in the renewed regionalization of cultures such as the Mochica, Nazca and Lima. ▷ 1.28

EARLY DYNASTIC PERIOD
Period of MESOPOTAMIAN CIVILIZATION (c.2900–2334 BC) that saw the emergence of the first documented royal dynasties in the region. A definitive chronology for the period has not been established, due to the fragmentary nature of the sources. The end of the period is marked by the accession of SARGON OF AGADE in 2334 BC, which is the first reliable established date in the history of the Middle East. ▷ 1.10

EARLY PRECLASSIC PERIOD
Period of MESOAMERICAN CIVILIZATION from about 2000 to 800 BC, marked by the adoption of farming, the growth of village settlements and the use of pottery throughout Mesoamerica. Most significant was the development of complex hierarchical societies with large settlements and ceremonial centers, such as the Maya, OLMECS and ZAPOTECS, and the emergence of the Olmec civilization in the lowland region to the south of the Gulf of Mexico from about 1200 BC. Extensive trade networks, religious architecture and monumental stone sculpture all appeared in this period. ▷ 1.05, 1.28

EDOM
Region of Palestine between the Dead Sea and the Gulf of Aqaba, occupied by the Edomites from the 14th to the 6th centuries BC. Although well-placed to exploit the Red Sea trade route, Edom was often dominated by ISRAEL or JUDAH (c.1000–843 BC). The region lost its political and cultural identity following its conquest by the Babylonians in about 600 BC. ▷ 1.13, 1.14

EGYPTIAN CIVILIZATION
Ancient Egypt was blessed with annual floods of the Nile, which brought fertile silt and water, making the lower Nile valley the most favorable agricultural area in the ancient world. After 2,500 years of settled cultivation, a unified Egyptian kingdom was created by NARMER (r.c.3000 BC). The Egyptian hieroglyphic writing system and styles of art and architecture emerged with unification. Ancient Egypt was a highly centralized state focused on the semi-divine king (or PHARAOH, as he was later called). The kings showed their authority through grand building projects, such as PYRAMID complexes and temples. Egypt enjoyed long periods of stability (under the OLD KINGDOM, MIDDLE KINGDOM and NEW KINGDOM), broken by periods of fragmentation (Intermediate periods).

Egyptian society was highly ritualized; every activity was related to the gods, who were appeased through elaborate rituals in temples or by means of magic and spells in the home. Those who behaved correctly were promised an afterlife, though this depended on their body being preserved through MUMMIFICATION after death. The Egyptians were expert craftsmen in fields such as sculpture, architecture, painting and jewelry-making. They also had a reputation for wisdom in science, astronomy, mathematics and medicine, though there is little evidence of creative thinking in these areas.

By 1070 BC Egypt was in decline and after the 8th century BC it was usually under foreign rule, but its civilization survived until it was undermined by Christianity in the fourth century AD. ▷ 1.05, 1.07, 1.10, 1.13, 1.14, 1.15, 1.16, 1.17, 1.18, 1.23

EL PARAISO TRADITION
Cultural tradition of coastal Peru in about 1800–850 BC, that was contemporary with the Andean KOTOSH TRADITION. The largest PRECERAMIC monument complex in South America is named after El Paraiso; it consists of massive mounds forming U-shaped platforms, with a temple at the end and central sunken courts. This style of architecture was widely adopted along the coast, together with IRRIGATION farming and pottery, from about 1800 BC. ▷ 1.28

ELAM
Plains region to the east of MESOPOTAMIA, between the Zagros mountains and the Persian Gulf. Cultural developments in Mesopotamia were closely paralleled in Elam, where cities, states and writing (proto-Elamite pictographs) existed by about 3500 BC. The

KINGS OF EGYPT

LATE PREDYNASTIC PERIOD
c.3000 BC
Zekhen
Narmer

EARLY DYNASTIC PERIOD
2920–2575

1st Dynasty	2920–2770
Menes	
Djer	
Djet	
Wadj	
Den	
Adjib	
Semerkhet	
Qa'a	

2nd Dynasty	2770–2649
Hotepsekhemwy	
Reneb	
Ninetjer	
Peribsen	
Khasekhemwy	

3rd Dynasty	2649–2575
Zanakht	2649–2630
Djoser	2630–2611
Sekhemkhet	2611–2603
Khaba	2603–2599
Huni	2599–2575

OLD KINGDOM
2575–2134

4th Dynasty	2575–2465
Snefru	2575–2551
Khufu (Cheops)	2551–2528
Radjedef	2528–2520
Khephren	2520–2494
Menkaure (Mycerinus)	2490–2472
Shepseskaf	2472–2467

5th Dynasty	2465–2323
Userkaf	2465–2458
Sahure	2458–2446
Kakai	2446–2426
Ini	2426–2419
Raneferef	2419–2416
Izi	2416–2392
Menkauhor	2396–2388
Izezi	2388–2356
Unas	2356–2323

6th Dynasty	2323–2150
Teti	2323–2291
Pepi I	2289–2255
Nemtyemzaf	2255–2246
Pepi II	2246–2152

7th/8th Dynasty	2150–2134
Numerous kings, including Neferkare	

1st INTERMEDIATE PERIOD
2134–2040

9th/10th Dynasty	2134–2040
Several kings called	
Khety	
Merykare	
Ity	

11th Dynasty	2134–2040
Inyotef I (Sehertawy)	2134–2118
Inyotef II (Wahankh)	2118–2069
Inyotef III	2069–2061
(Nakhtnebtepnufer)	
Mentuhotpe II	2061–2010

MIDDLE KINGDOM
2040–1640

11th Dynasty	2040–1991
Mentuhotpe II	2061–2010
(ruler of all Egypt from 2040)	
Mentuhotpe III	2010–1998
Mentuhotpe IV	1998–1991

12th Dynasty	1991–1783
Amenemhet I	1991–1962
Senwosret I	1971–1926
Amenemhet II	1929–1982
Senwosret II	1987–1878
Senwosret III	1878–1841?
Amenemhet III	1844–1797
Amenemhet IV	1799–1787
Nefrusobk	1787–1783

13th Dynasty	1783–after 1640
About 70 kings, including	
Wegaf 1	1783–1779
Amenemhet V	
Harnedjheriotef	
Amenyqemau	
Sebekhotpe 1	c.1750
Hor	
Amenemhet VII	
Sebekhotpe II	
Khendjer	
Sebekhotpe III	c.1745
Neferhotep I	c.1741–1730
Sebekhotpe IV	c.1730–1720
Sebekhotpe V	c.1720–1715
Aya	c.1704–1690
Mentuemzaf	
Dedumose II	
Neferhotep III	

14th Dynasty	
A group of kings probably contemporary with the 13th or 15th Dynasty	

2nd INTERMEDIATE PERIOD
1640–1532

15th Dynasty (Hyksos)	
Salitis	
Sheshi	
Khian	
Apophis	c.1585–1542
Khamudi	c.1542–1532

16th Dynasty	
Minor Hyksos rulers, contemporary with the 15th Dynasty	

17th Dynasty	1640–1550
Numerous kings, including	
Inyotef V	c.1640–1635
Sebekemzaf I	
Nebireyeraw	
Sebekemzaf II	
Ta'o (or Djehuti'o) I	
Ta'o (or Djehuti'o) II	
Kamose	c.1555–1550

NEW KINGDOM
1532–1070

18th Dynasty	1550–1307
Ahmose	1550–1525
(ruler of all Egypt from 1532)	
Amenophis I	1525–1504
Tuthmosis I	1504–1492
Tuthmosis II	1492–1479
Tuthmosis III	1479–1425
Hatshepsut	1473–1458
Amenophis II	1427–1401
Tuthmosis IV	1401–1391
Amenophis III	1391–1353
Amenophis IV (Akhenaten)	1353–1335
Smenkhkare	1335–1333
Tutankhamun	1333–1323
Aya	1323–1319
Haremhab	1319–1307

19th Dynasty	1307–1196
Ramesses I	1307–1306
Sethos I	1306–1290
Ramesses II	1290–1224
Merneptah	1224–1214
Sethos II	1214–1204
Siptah	1204–1198
Twosre	1198–1196

20th Dynasty	1196–1070
Sethnakhte	1196–1194
Ramesses III	1194–1163
Ramesses IV	1163–1156
Ramesses V	1156–1151
Ramesses VI	1151–1143
Ramesses VII	1143–1136
Ramesses VIII	1136–1131
Ramesses IX	1131–1112
Ramesses X	1112–1100
Ramesses XI	1100–1070

Elamites briefly conquered SUMERIA and sacked UR in 2004 BC, and were a major threat to Mesopotamian states in the 2nd millennium BC. In the 13th century BC Elam emerged as a powerful unified kingdom, under a series of warrior kings who conquered much of south Mesopotamia, but it declined rapidly from about 1110 BC, when the capital at SUSA was captured by the Babylonians, later becoming a vassal of Assyrian and Babylonian empires, and one of the richest satrapies of the ACHEMENID EMPIRE. Little is known about Elamite society or religion; its artistic and architectural achievements were predominantly BABYLONIAN in style. ▷ 1.10, 1.11, 1.12, 1.13, 1.15

EL-AMARNA
Modern name for the site of Akhetaten, the capital of the "heretic" PHARAOH AKHENATEN, in Middle Egypt from 1350 to 1325 BC. The city was abandoned at Akhenaten's death and the site remained well-preserved. The ceremonial procession way and great royal hall for public audiences have been recognized as well as residential suburbs. The site also contained the famous El-Amarna letters, detailing the relationship between Egypt and the cities and states of the Near East. ▷ 1.18

ELEUSIS
Important sanctuary west of Athens, known throughout the Greek world for its Mysteries into which suppliants could be initiated. The presiding goddesses were Demeter and her daughter Persephone, themselves at the center of complex cults of fertility and rebirth. ▷ 1.24

ELIJAH
Biblical prophet of the 9th century BC who, with the prophet ELISHA, asserted a monotheistic religious doctrine and successfully encouraged the Israelites to reject CANAANITE beliefs and the worship of Baal (c.860–853 BC). ▷ 1.14

ELISHA
Biblical prophet who, with his mentor ELIJAH, persuaded the Israelites to reject the god Baal. He directed the civil war that led to the death of King AHAB (853 BC) and Jehu's seizure of the throne. Elisha succeeded Elijah as the most influential religious figure in ISRAEL. ▷ 1.14

ENLIL
Sumerian deity (Bel in Akkadian) of the air, winds and farming. One of a triad of gods (with An and Enki), Enlil was especially important because of his role in ensuring fertility and agricultural productivity. Control of the cult center at NIPPUR was essential for Sumerian and Akkadian kings. ▷ 1.11

ENSETE
Plant of the banana family that produces an edible root, domesticated in Ethiopia at a very early date (by c.4000 BC). It is one of several indigenous farming innovations based on local plants (including teff and finger MILLET) that were independent of Middle Eastern agriculture. ▷ 1.16

EPIPALEOLITHIC
Period in the post-glacial period prior to the adoption of agriculture, in which HUNTER-GATHERER societies – including cultures in the LEVANT (such as the NATUFIANS) and north Africa – continued to use UPPER PALEOLITHIC stone-tool and hunting technologies. ▷ 1.08, 1.16

EPIRUS
An area of northwestern Greece known from early times for its ORACLE to Apollo at Dodona. Gradually Hellenized by Greek colonies on the coast, the area was united into a single kingdom under a chieftain from the central Molossian tribe in the 4th century BC. Epirus' greatest period of prosperity then followed. Its most famous king was Pyrrhus. The kingdom collapsed in the 3rd century BC and, in 167 BC, Epirus was conquered by the Romans, who reputedly enslaved 150,000 of its inhabitants. ▷ 1.24, 1.25

ERIDU
Sumerian city to the south of UR, referred to in ancient king lists as the first city of SUMER. Founded in the mid-6th millennium BC, Eridu was one of the leading cities of MESOPOTAMIA by the EARLY DYNASTIC period (c.2500 BC), and was continuously occupied until about 600 BC. Its political importance declined after the rise of the Third Dynasty of Ur. ▷ 1.09, 1.10, 1.11

ERLITOU CULTURE
The first bronze-using culture of China (c.1900–1650 BC), named after the city of Erlitou situated on the Yellow river in the heartland of the later Shang state. The Erlitou culture is probably equivalent to the first phase of the SHANG CIVILIZATION and is notable for its sophisticated cast-bronze work. ▷ 1.27

ERTEBOLLE CULTURE
Late MESOLITHIC HUNTER-GATHERER-fisher culture of Denmark (c.6000–3500 BC). It is characterized by its distinctive stone tools, massive shell middens at coastal sites, cemeteries with grave goods, and the adoption of pottery, polished stone axes and agricultural methods from neighboring farmers. Several canoes and examples of wood-carved art have been found in water-logged sediments. ▷ 1.19

ESARHADDON
King of ASSYRIA (r.680–669 BC), who re-established peaceful dominion over BABYLONIA but lost contol of the northern provinces due to SCYTHIAN and CIMMERIAN invasions. Esarhaddon suppressed revolts in the LEVANT and conquered Egypt, but failed to consolidate Assyrian rule. Esarhaddon's successor, ASHURBANIPAL, was forced to reconquer the country. ▷ 1.13

ESHNUNNA
City on the Diyali river in central MESOPOTAMIA and an important city-state of the EARLY DYNASTIC PERIOD. It was conquered by the Akkadians (c.2250 BC) and later ruled by the Third Dynasty of UR, before regaining its independence in about 2000 BC. It was the last major Mesopotamian state to be conquered by HAMMURABI of BABYLON (1755 BC). ▷ 1.10, 1.11

ETRUSCANS
The leading pre-Roman people of Italy, located between the Tiber and Arno rivers, with offshoots in the Po valley and Campania. Recognizable in the early IRON AGE Villanovan cultural group of the 9th and 8th centuries BC, the Etruscans soon developed prosperous city-states supported by agriculture, COPPER and iron deposits, and extensive trading contacts throughout the Mediterranean. The leading cities were loosely organized in the league of Twelve Cities (the Etruscan league), which met periodically at the sanctuary of Voltumna in central Etruria. From 396 BC, with the fall of Veii, the Etruscans gradually came under Roman control and their assimilation was complete by the end of the republic. They were famed for their artistic skills, and many Etruscan wall-paintings, terracottas and bronzes have been discovered in tombs and sanctuaries dating from the 7th to the 1st centuries BC. ▷ 1.06, 1.07, 1.23, 1.25

FERTILE CRESCENT
Region of the ancient Middle East in which the earliest agricultural economies and sedentary village societies developed (c.9000–7000 BC), with domesticated cereals (einkorn and emmer WHEAT, and BARLEY) and animal species (SHEEP and GOAT). These species co-existed in the wild in the crescent-shaped region extending from the southern LEVANT, through northwest Syria to the Zagros mountains in Iran. ▷ 1.08, 1.09

FIRE, EARLIEST USE
The earliest evidence of the controlled use of fire by hominids (probably HOMO ERECTUS) is dated to about 1.6 million ya, at CHESOWANJA, Kenya and at SWARTKRANS, South Africa. Consistent fire making, however, was probably a later development associated with the human colonization of temperate regions after about 600,000 ya. The earliest evidence of the use of fire in Europe comes from near Bury St Edmunds in eastern England and dates from about 400,000 ya. ▷ 1.01

FLOOD, THE
Biblical story with earlier origins in Middle Eastern culture. CUNEIFORM tablets dating

from about 2000 BC, found at NINEVEH and other sites in MESOPOTAMIA, record parts of the "Epic of Gilgamesh" (the earliest surviving literary tale). It includes an account of a great flood that left only one family alive. ▷ 1.10

FOLSOM CULTURE
Early PALEOINDIAN culture (c.9000–8000 BC) of the North American plains and adjacent regions, characterized by stone projectile points with concave bases (Folsom points) used in big-game hunting, especially of bison (mammoths were extinct by this period). The Folsom culture developed as a regional specialization of the preceding CLOVIS tradition. ▷ 1.02

FUNNEL-NECKED BEAKER CULTURE
The earliest NEOLITHIC culture of northern Europe (c.4200–2800 BC), with distinctive necked pottery styles, MEGALITHIC CHAMBERED TOMBS and long mounds, settlements of small timber buildings or LONGHOUSES, and enclosures. It is associated with the first use of PLOWS, animal traction and wheeled transport in north-central Europe. ▷ 1.20

GADES
City on the Atlantic coast of Spain (modern Cadiz), founded as a seasonal trading post (possibly before 1000 BC) by PHOENICIANS from the LEVANT. It had become a major trading center by the 8th century BC and probably part of the powerful native kingdom of TARTESSOS by about 600 BC. It was controlled by the Carthaginians from about 500 BC. ▷ 1.23, 1.25

GANDHARA
Satrapy of the ACHEMENID EMPIRE in the mountainous region of east Afghanistan and northwest Pakistan. Gandhara was strategically important as a focus for trade routes from Iran and central Asia to India through the Khyber Pass, and sent silver, bulls and weapons as tribute to the Persian king. After the conquest of the Achemenid empire by Alexander the Great, Gandhara came under Greek rule (the last Greek principalities in the area were extinguished at about the time of Jesus Christ). The Gandhara style of art, a fusion of Greek and Indian influences that developed in the last centuries BC, became the most important style of Buddhist art in southeast Asia. ▷ 1.15

GAVRINIS
Island in the Gulf of Morbihan in Brittany, France, on which a large, early NEOLITHIC PASSAGE GRAVE was built in the 4th millennium BC. It is notable for its elaborate carved stone decoration, bearing abstract curvilinear designs and depictions of stone axes. ▷ 1.20

GERMANS, PROTO-
Peoples of north and north-central Europe who spoke proto-Germanic languages and shared cultural features during the IRON AGE.

Their origins are uncertain but proto-Germanic languages probably developed in the late BRONZE AGE (by c.800 BC). ▷ 1.06

GEZER
A major CANAANITE city of the 2nd millennium BC, sometimes held by the Egyptians. It was refortified by King SOLOMON of ISRAEL in about 950 BC, before abandonment in about 900 BC. Early examples of the Canaanite alphabet (c.1800 BC) and of HEBREW writing (the GEZER calendar, c.1000 BC) have been discovered at the site. ▷ 1.14

GIRSU
See LAGASH

GOAT
Animal first domesticated in the highland regions of the Middle East, with early evidence (c.7500 BC) from sites such as Jarmo in the foothills of the Zagros mountains. Goats were used as a source of milk and cheese, WOOL, meat and leather. ▷ 1.03, 1.08, 1.16, 1.20

GORDION
City in Anatolia, the capital of the Phrygian kingdom from about 800 BC. It was destroyed by the CIMMERIANS in 695 BC, when the last king of the PHRYGIANS, MITAS, was killed. The city was re-established as a provincial center by the ACHEMENID empire in the 6th century BC. ▷ 1.13

GRAVETTIAN CULTURE
A phase (c.28,000–23,000 ya) of the European UPPER PALEOLITHIC that is characterized by a stone-tool industry with small pointed blades used for big-game hunting (bison, horse, reindeer and mammoth). It is divided into two regional groups: the western Gravettian, mostly known from cave sites in France, and the eastern Gravettian, with open sites of specialized mammoth hunters on the plains of central Europe and Russia. Some early examples of CAVE ART, and the famous "Venus" figurines were made by Gravettian artists. ▷ 1.19

GREEK ALPHABET
The Greeks adopted an alphabet from the PHOENICIANS in about 750 BC, but adapted it for their own use by adding vowels. There were 23 standard letters, but some city-states used variations. The alphabet was passed on to Italy in the 8th century BC and, as adapted by the Romans, forms the basis of the Western alphabet. ▷ 1.07

GUTIANS
Tribal people of the hill region between the Mesopotamian plains and the Zagros mountains. The Gutians raided SUMERIA and AKKAD, and briefly dominated the lowlands in the 22nd century BC. Mesopotamian kings often attempted to conquer them and they finally lost their cultural identity when

the Assyrian empire expanded during the 9th century BC. ▷ 1.10, 1.11, 1.12

HADAR
Site of hominid fossil finds in Ethiopia, where the remains, dating about 3 million ya, of 30 individuals of the species AUSTRALOPITHECUS AFARENSIS – including the most complete skeleton of an early hominid (LUCY) – have been discovered in ancient lake silts. ▷ 1.01

HALAFIAN CULTURE
Late NEOLITHIC culture (c.6000–5400 BC) of central and north MESOPOTAMIA, named after the site of Tell Halaf. It is characterized by burnished and painted pottery, small villages of clay-built houses, a mixed dry-farming economy and evidence of weaving. The Halafians used stone tools, imported OBSIDIAN, and made increasing use of COPPER and bronze. Storehouses and prestige goods suggest the development of chiefly authority and social ranking. ▷ 1.09

HALLSTATT CULTURE
The general term for the late BRONZE AGE URNFIELD CULTURES (Hallstatt phases A and B, c.1150–750 BC) and the early IRON AGE cultures (Hallstatt C and D, c.750–450 BC) of central and western Europe, named after the cemetery and salt-mining center at Hallstatt in Austria. Each phase of the culture is characterized by distinctive metalwork and burial practices, with the appearance of iron and large HILLFORTS at the beginning of Hallstatt C. From about 600 BC, there is evidence of increasing trade in luxury goods, and of other contacts with Greek and Etruscan cities in the Mediterranean. ▷ 1.06, 1.25

HAMMURABI
AMORITE king of BABYLON (r.1792–1750 BC). Hammurabi inherited a strong state from his father, SIN-MUBALLIT, and later conquered most of MESOPOTAMIA (c.1764–1750 BC), capturing the Assyrian capital at SHUBAT-ENLIL, and defeating his last major rival, ESHNUNNA, in 1755 BC. His empire stretched from SUMERIA to north Syria, but he failed to establish an effective bureaucracy and the empire declined after his death. Hammurabi is most famous for his law code, one of the earliest to have survived. Though not a complete legal system, it provides a valuable source for the structure of early Babylonian society. The code is heavily reliant on retaliatory punishments involving the death or mutilation of offenders, or members of their family. ▷ 1.11

HAO
The first capital city of the ZHOU DYNASTY from about 1122 to 770 BC, situated on the WEI river in the Zhou heartland (the state of QIN) in northwest China. It was attacked by an alliance of barbarian tribes and rebellious noblemen in 771 BC, prompting the Zhou to move their capital to LUOYANG. ▷ 1.27

HARAPPA
Second largest city of the INDUS CIVILIZATION, with an estimated population of 30,000, situated beside the river Ravi in modern northeast Pakistan. Founded in the mid-3rd millennium BC on the site of a pre-Indus settlement, the city consisted of a heavily fortified citadel, a cereal-processing and storage complex and a planned workers' quarter, with uniform housing units on a grid layout. It was probably abandoned after 1800 BC. ▷ 1.26

HASSUNA CULTURE
NEOLITHIC cultural phase (c.6500–6000 BC) marking the first agricultural settlement of the central Mesopotamian plains, with small villages of clay-built houses, a mixed dry-farming economy, the first permanent kilns for pottery manufacture, distinctive painted CERAMICS, the use of COPPER, and stamp seals to denote ownership. It developed directly into the succeeding SAMARRAN and HALAFIAN cultural traditions. ▷ 1.09

HATSHEPSUT
Appointed regent to her stepson, TUTHMOSIS III, on her husband's death, Hatshepsut seized power in Egypt in 1473 BC to become the only female PHARAOH. She shrewdly used "male" images of herself when appropriate to maintain loyalties. The reliefs on her impressive burial complex at Deir el-Bahri detail a famous voyage to the exotic kingdom of Punt. After her death in 1458 BC her memory was erased by later pharaohs. ▷ 1.18

HATTI
Assyrian name for the people of central Anatolia who spoke a non-INDO-EUROPEAN LANGUAGE (Hattian) in the late 3rd millennium BC. This region was occupied from about 2000 BC by the Indo-European HITTITES, who are sometimes confusingly identified with the Hatti, though the latter were one of several distinct populations ruled by Hittite kings. ▷ 1.12

HATTUSAS
(Modern Boghazkoy) Settlement in central Anatolia first occupied in the 3rd millennium BC. It was a major HITTITE city by 1800 BC and the capital from about 1650 until its destruction by the PHRYGIANS (c.1200 BC). By the New Kingdom period (c.1450–1190 BC) the city extended across several hills and deep valleys, with a fortified royal residence, an upper town with temples and official buildings, and a lower town with a Great Temple and merchants' houses. ▷ 1.12

HEBREW LANGUAGE AND ALPHABET
Semitic language closely related to CANAANITE. "Old Hebrew" was spoken in Palestine until the 3rd century BC. The earliest examples of written Hebrew date to the 10th century BC, using a version of the phonetic PHOENICIAN alphabet (notably the GEZER calendar), which was later supplanted by an ARAMAIC script. ▷ 1.07

HEBREWS
People with a shared language and religious identity whose ancestors may once have lived in northwest MESOPOTAMIA before settling in Palestine (Canaan) in the mid-2nd millennium BC. Some Hebrews probably migrated to Egypt, where they lived as serfs before returning to the LEVANT in the late 13th century BC (the biblical stories of Moses and JOSHUA), colonizing areas previously dominated by CANAANITE and PHILISTINE cities. The monotheistic religious doctrine of Judaism was firmly established in the 9th century BC. ▷ 1.12, 1.14, 1.18, 1.23

HELLENES
The name the Greeks called themselves. It originally referred only to the inhabitants of a small area of central Greece, but gradually came to refer to all Greeks. ▷ 1.24

HELOT
The helots were the enslaved population of MESSENIA (southwest Peloponnese), brought into subjection when SPARTA conquered the area in the 8th century BC. They were tied to the land and forced to produce food for their Spartan overlords, who could then train full-time to maintain their supremacy.

HENGE
Circular ceremonial enclosure of the late NEOLITHIC period in Britain (c.3000–2000 BC). Henges are usually symmetrical in plan and typically have a ditch on the inside of the bank, varying from about 50 to 450 meters (165 to 150 feet) in diameter. Some enclose either STONE CIRCLES (e.g. AVEBURY) or timber circles (e.g. DURRINGTON WALLS). The larger sites suggest a complex social organization, perhaps indicative of CHIEFDOMS. The STONEHENGE enclosure, from which they take their name, is not a classic henge. ▷ 1.20

HEUNEBURG
HILLFORT of the HALLSTATT period situated on the Upper Danube in south Germany that was refortified in the 6th century BC using Greek-style building methods, with mud-brick walls on stone foundations with projecting bastions. Imports of Greek wine amphorae and tableware indicate Mediterranean trade contacts. A royal burial mound, with grave goods that may have included silk fabrics, is located nearby. ▷ 1.25

HIEROGLYPHS
A distinctive script that emerged in Egypt in about 3200 BC. It consisted of more than 1,000 signs and took many years for scribes to master. Traditionally used for carved inscriptions on religious or royal monuments, it fell into disuse in early Christian times and remained undeciphered until the early 19th century.

HILLFORTS
Fortified hilltop enclosures of the European late BRONZE AGE and IRON AGE (c.1100–50 BC), with stone, earth, and/or timber ramparts. Hillforts had diverse functions: as settlement centers and refuges, royal residences and defended storage complexes. The largest and most elaborately fortified sites date mainly from the middle Iron Age (c.600–200 BC). ▷ 1.05

HINDUISM
Religion of the Indian subcontinent with a complex set of beliefs and practices, which refer to a pantheon of deities, numerous sacred texts and a sacred geography of temples and shrines. Hinduism is difficult to characterize, however, as it has no single founder, doctrine, or authoritative scripture, and no ecclesiastical organization. Some features may be traced back to the INDUS CIVILIZATION and DRAVIDIAN traditions of the late 3rd millennium BC, but the earliest Hindu scriptures are the Vedas, hymns composed from about 1500 BC by ARYAN settlers in India. By 500 BC the principal features of historical Hinduism were codified in the Vedic texts, the caste system, and religious law books that defined moral lifestyles. ▷ 1.26

HIPPIAS
TYRANT of Athens (r.527–510 BC) who succeeded his father, PEISISTRATUS. He was responsible for extensive building programs in Athens. Increasingly tyrannical, he was overthrown by the Athenians, who were helped by the Spartans, in 510 BC. The Persians attempted to restore him as a manageable ruler of Athens in 490 BC. ▷ 1.24

HIRAM
PHOENICIAN king of TYRE (r.c.969–936 BC) and an ally of ISRAEL. He contributed craftsmen and materials for the building of SOLOMON's Temple at JERUSALEM, and received tribute and territory on the Levantine coast in return. ▷ 1.23

HIT
Settlement on the middle Euphrates where the river runs into the lowland floodplains of southern MESOPOTAMIA. Important nearby sources of bitumen were intensively exploited by the Mesopotamians for bonding courses of mud brick in building work. ▷ 1.10

HITTITES
People with an INDO-EUROPEAN LANGUAGE who settled in Anatolia (c.2000 BC), possibly from the Ukraine or Caucasus. They founded several kingdoms that dominated native populations, including the non-Indo-European HATTI; by about 1750 BC a unified Hittite state had emerged. The Hittite state was organized on a devolved feudal basis, which could be unstable when succession to the throne was disputed. The high king had supreme power, partly theocratic in nature

(after death he gained the status of a god). Little is known about Hittite religion or art.

The later history of the Hittites can be divided into three main periods: the Old Kingdom period, New Kingdom (Empire) period and Neo-Hittite period. During the Old Kingdom period (1750–1450 BC), the Hittites established a capital at Kussara, and then at Hattusas (c.1650 BC), extending their rule into north MESOPOTAMIA. Under King MURSILIS they briefly annexed ASSYRIA and sacked BABYLON (1595 BC), but could not sustain their conquests. Hittite power declined in the 16th century BC in the face of Egyptian and Mittanian expansion and internal instability, and reached a low point in the 15th century BC, when little is known about Hittite affairs.

Under the New Kingdom (Empire) period (c.1450–1190 BC) the revival of the Hittite empire took place, as MITTANI power waned and the Egyptians were distracted by internal affairs. The empire reached its greatest extent in about 1325 BC under King SUPPILULIUMAS, who consolidated Hittite rule in Anatolia and conquered the northern parts of Syria and the LEVANT. Confrontations with the Egyptians in the early 13th century BC over control of the Levant ended in stalemate. The collapse of the empire (c.1205–1190 BC) is attributed to PHRYGIAN invasions (which destroyed the capital at Hattusas), attacks by the SEA PEOPLES and political fragmentation.

After the Phrygian conquests, during the Neo-Hittite period (1190–700 BC), Hittite cultural identity was maintained only in small city-states and kingdoms in south Anatolia and north Syria, the most powerful being CARCHEMISH. Their independence, and the last remnants of Hittite culture, were finally destroyed by the Assyrians in the 8th century BC. ▷ 1.11, 1.12, 1.13, 1.14, 1.18, 1.21, 1.22

HOMER

Greek poet who is associated with the final composition of the two great Greek epics, the ILIAD and the ODYSSEY, in the late 8th century BC. The Ionic dialect of the poems suggests that he may have come from Asia Minor, the eastern Aegean or Euboea. Homer probably brought together earlier oral poems and consolidated them into coherent stories. ▷ 1.22, 1.24

HOMINOID APES

Large primates belonging to three main groups (*Sivapithecus*, *Dryopithecus* and *Proconsul*) that evolved in the MIOCENE EPOCH and spread throughout the Old World. The evolutionary lineage of hominids, including humans, probably diverged from other apes only 6 million ya. ▷ 1.01

HOMO ERECTUS

Human species that had evolved in Africa from HOMO HABILIS by about 1.5 million ya. Though probably slightly taller, *Homo erectus* was physically similar to modern humans. Its brain size ranged from two-thirds that of a modern human in early examples of the species, to three-quarters in later examples. *Homo erectus* developed more effective technology than *Homo habilis*, notably the use of hand axes, wooden spears and FIRE. *Homo erectus* was so successful adaptively that populations grew to colonize a wide range of new habitats, spreading from Africa to Eurasia, reaching Britain (BOXGROVE), China (ZHOUKOUDIEN) and Indonesia (Sangiran). Between 500,000 and 100,000 ya *Homo erectus* evolved into anatomically modern HOMO SAPIENS SAPIENS in Africa. In Europe it evolved into HOMO SAPIENS NEANDERTHALENSIS, while in southeast Asia it may have survived until about 60,000 ya, becoming extinct only with the arrival of anatomically modern humans in the region. ▷ 1.01, 1.02

HOMO HABILIS

The earliest human species, probably evolved from AUSTRALOPITHECUS AFARENSIS or AUSTRALOPITHECUS AFRICANUS, that lived in eastern and southern Africa, about 2.5–1.5 million ya. Fossils from OLDUVAI GORGE, KOOBI FORA and SWARTKRANS show that this gracile hominid had hands that were capable of the precise manipulation of objects, and discoveries of contemporary stone tools suggest that *Homo habilis* was the first tool-using hominid. Its brain size was about half that of a modern human. ▷ 1.01

HOMO SAPIENS

Although the origins of *Homo sapiens* ("Wise Man") are debated, this species probably evolved from HOMO ERECTUS populations in Africa and Eurasia, with some distinct regional traits, such as the cold-adapted groups in Europe (which later developed into the NEANDERTHALS). As a sophisticated tool user, *Homo sapiens* developed effective hunting equipment for the first time (projectiles for close-impact spearing of animals), had a wider range of specialized tool industries, may have built shelters, and were adept at using FIRE. ▷ 1.01, 1.02

HOMO SAPIENS NEANDERTHALENSIS

(NEANDERTHAL man) Specialized cold-adapted human species that evolved in west Eurasia and the Middle East from late HOMO ERECTUS, about 230,000–150,000 ya. The recent recovery of Neanderthal DNA has shown that they were not ancestral to modern humans. The Neanderthals had short, thick skeletal frames to reduce surface body area exposed to the cold, and heavy facial structures to protect the sinuses and lungs from cold air. They used MIDDLE PALEOLITHIC tools, hunted a range of animals, lived in open settlements and cave sites, and were the first humans to express aesthetic qualities and religious beliefs (formal burials). They became extinct about 28,000 ya, as more numerous and versatile HOMO SAPIENS SAPIENS populations colonized their territories. ▷ 1.01, 1.02, 1.19

HOMO SAPIENS SAPIENS

Anatomically modern man, a regional human adaptation that evolved in Africa about 150,000–100,000 ya, with enhanced cognitive and linguistic capabilities, increasingly complex technologies and social institutions, and new forms of cultural expression in art and ritual. The adaptational success of modern humans, with developed UPPER PALEOLITHIC tool-kits, led to population growth and rapid global colonization, spreading from Africa to east Asia by about 75,000 ya, to Europe by about 40,000 ya, and to the Americas by about 15,000 ya, replacing existing human groups (HOMO SAPIENS variants). All humans today are descendents of the *Homo sapiens sapiens* population that evolved in Africa. ▷ 1.01, 1.02

HOPLITE

Greek infantry soldier of the 7th to 4th centuries BC, notable for his large shield (hoplon), which – joined alongside those of others – enabled him to fight in a heavily protected line. Hoplite battles consisted of tightly packed bodies of troops (phalanxes), about 12 ranks deep, pushing and jabbing their opponents until one side gave way.

HORSE, DOMESTICATION

Probably first domesticated as a food source in the steppe region of southeast Europe and central Asia in the 4th millennium BC, the use of horses as draft animals for pulling wagons and chariots developed in this region from about 2500 BC and spread to the Middle East by about 1700 BC. Horse-riding equipment was invented by the pastoralist cultures of the Eurasian steppes (c.1500–1000 BC), enabling them to adopt a fully nomadic way of life. ▷ 1.03, 1.06, 1.11, 1.19, 1.20, 1.21, 1.22, 1.23

HUANG DI

Mythical third emperor of China and founder of Chinese civilization, traditionally dated to 2698 BC, who "invented" wooden houses, wheeled transport, the bow, writing and moral government. His reign was regarded as a golden age of order and prosperity. ▷ 1.27

HUELVA

See TARTESSOS

HUNTER-GATHERERS

People that depend on wild resources for their subsistence by hunting wild animals, fishing, and gathering plant foods and other materials. All humans were hunter-gatherers until the development of farming about 10,000 ya, each group adapting to local ecological conditions, with highly specialized social and economic systems. By 500 BC agriculture was the dominant mode of livelihood in most parts of the world, and hunter-gatherers were restricted to Arctic regions, North America, parts of South America, southern Africa and Australia. ▷ 1.01, 1.02, 1.03, 1.04, 1.05, 1.06, 1.08, 1.16, 1.19, 1.20

HURRIANS
People closely related to the Urartians, from the area to the southwest of the Caspian Sea, who moved into MESOPOTAMIA and Anatolia in the late 3rd millennium BC. They settled in northern Mesopotamia and Syria, overran ASSYRIA in about 1680 BC, and had established the powerful kingdom of MITTANI by about 500 BC. ▷ 1.11, 1.12

HYKSOS
Literally "chiefs of foreign lands", Semitic peoples who migrated from Asia to the Nile Delta in the 17th century BC, and whose influence spread throughout Lower Egypt at a time when central Egyptian government was weak (the 2nd Intermediate period). They were expelled from Egypt by AHMOSE I in about 1550 BC. ▷ 1.18

ICE AGES
The cold phases of the PLEISTOCENE EPOCH, a period of extreme oscillation in global temperatures with extensions and contractions of the polar ice sheets. The long-accepted sequence of four glacial/inter-glacial phases from 750,000 ya, recognized in the northern hemisphere, is now known to be too simplistic. Recent studies of polar ice cores and ocean sediments have identified at least 22 major warm and cold phases in the same period. ▷ 1.01, 1.02, 1.08, 1.16, 1.18, 1.19

ICE MAN
The frozen body of a man, dating from about 3350–3120 BC, discovered in an Alpine glacier on the Italian–Austrian border. Preserved equipment lying nearby included leather clothing, a fur hat, BOWS AND ARROWS, COPPER and stone tools, and a backpack made of wood and animal skins. The man had several small linear tatoos on his arms, legs and back. The discovery revealed that metal tools had come into use in west-central Europe far earlier than previously supposed. ▷ 1.20

ILIAD
One of Europe's great epics, traditionally ascribed to HOMER, which tells the story of the hero Achilles during the Greek siege of TROY. A poem about war and the pity of war, it explores the nature of heroism and leadership. It was probably brought to its final form in about 750 BC, but contains material that may be dated to MYCENAEAN times. ▷ 1.24

IMPRESSED POTTERY CULTURES
The earliest farming societies (c.6000–4000 BC) of the west Mediterranean region, characterized by pottery with impressed decoration, such as the Cardial Wares of southern France, and village settlements. Their farming economy, based on cereals, legumes and domestic animals, probably spread along the coast from the Balkans. ▷ 1.20, 1.21

INDO-EUROPEAN LANGUAGES
Group of related languages spoken in Europe, the Middle East and India, the origins of which are disputed. The prevailing view is that they derive from dialects spoken in the west Eurasian steppe region in the 4th to 3rd millennia BC, which spread as a result of population migrations. An alternative argument sees Indo-European origins in the adoption of Middle Eastern farming and associated economic and social practices, which spread throughout the Indo-European area in the NEOLITHIC period, from about 7000 to 5000 BC. ▷ 1.11, 1.12, 1.26

INDO-IRANIAN PEOPLES
Peoples who spoke Indo-Iranian languages, the easternmost branch of the INDO-EUROPEAN LANGUAGE group, who were probably originally pastoral nomads of the central Eurasian steppes. These included the ARYANS, who migrated into northern India in the mid-2nd millennium BC, and the CIMMERIANS, SCYTHIANS, MEDES and Persians who migrated into different parts of the Middle East, Anatolia and Ukraine in the 9th–7th centuries BC. ▷ 1.13, 1.26

INDUS CIVILIZATION
A civilization that had emerged in the Indus valley by 2500 BC, with consistent features across a vast area from the Hindu Kush to the Arabian Sea, and from Baluchistan to Gujarat. STATE formation and URBANIZATION in the early 3rd millennium BC may have been partly stimulated by trade with MESOPOTAMIA. Planned towns, built of mud brick, included walled citadels with monumental buildings, civic granaries and housing areas. The two largest centers, at HARAPPA and MOHENJO-DARO, were probably capital cities, though their relative status is unknown.

The Indus economy was based on IRRIGATION farming of cereals, RICE, legumes and COTTON, with CATTLE for dairy products and traction. Domesticated elephants and camels were also exploited. Evidence exists of long-distance trade in silver, COPPER and lapis lazuli, with distant trading colonies such as SHORTHUGAI in the Hindu Kush, and maritime trade with SUMERIA. Little is known about Indus political organization or religion, but features such as the ritual bath at Mohenjo-Daro are found in later Hindu contexts. Monumental art works are rare, but terracotta figurines, painted pottery, stone seals and an undeciphered pictographic script give the impression of a complex cultural life.

The decline and collapse of the Indus civilization in about 2000–1700 BC has not been fully explained, though flooding, soil degradation, over-population and political fragmentation have been suggested, with the final collapse of an already impoverished society at the time of the ARYAN invasions. Urban state cultures did not develop again in the Indian subcontinent for several centuries. ▷ 1.07, 1.26

INITIAL PERIOD
Period of ANDEAN CIVILIZATION from about 2000 to 900 BC, marked by full dependence on agriculture, farming villages, impressive ceremonial and temple complexes, IRRIGATION systems in the coastal lowlands, and the widespread introduction of pottery and COTTON-weaving. Marked regional cultures in this period gave way after 900 BC to the spread of the Chavín tradition. ▷ 1.28

IONIA, IONIAN GREEKS
A division of the Greek peoples, traditionally descendants of settlers from the Ionian "mother city" of Athens, found in communities on the central-western coast and islands of Asia Minor. Ionians pioneered the Ionic style of architecture and fostered early Greek philosophy. ▷ 1.23

IRON AGE
A subdivision of the THREE AGE SYSTEM that commences and ends at different times in different regions (it could be argued that it continued until the modern industrial era, c.AD 1750). It is misleading as a means of characterizing very complex and varied iron-using cultures. Iron metallurgy was practiced in Anatolia by about 1500 BC and spread rapidly throughout the Old World, except southern Africa, from 1100 to 500 BC. ▷ 1.05, 1.06, 1.12, 1.16, 1.21, 1.24, 1.26, 1.27

IRRIGATION
A means of controlling plant growth by ensuring and regulating water supply to produce consistent harvests and intensify production. Irrigation agriculture was a key factor in the development of complex civilizations in many parts of the world, particularly in MESOPOTAMIA and the Indus valley from the 6th to 3rd millennia BC, north China by 4000 BC, and in Mesoamerica and South America from the 2nd to 1st millennia BC. ▷ 1.03, 1.09, 1.17, 1.26, 1.27, 1.28

ISAIAH
HEBREW prophet of the mid-8th century BC who warned the Israelites about the impending threat of Assyrian conquest (c.735 BC), which he saw in a vision and interpreted as a sign of divine condemnation of Israelite godlessness. ▷ 1.14

ISIN
City in south MESOPOTAMIA, ruled by an AMORITE dynasty by about 2000 BC. It briefly dominated SUMERIA in the 20th century BC, but lost its political independence to Larsa and then BABYLON from about 1800 BC. It reasserted its independence in the 12th and 11th centuries BC, when several kings of Isin dominated BABYLONIA. ▷ 1.11, 1.12

ISRAEL, ANCIENT
HEBREW kingdom founded in the late 11th century BC by King SAUL and consolidated by DAVID (c.1006–965 BC). It reached its greatest

extent under SOLOMON (c.965–928 BC), who dominated the region from Sinai to the Euphrates, but split into the two separate kingdoms of JUDAH and Israel in about 920 BC. Thereafter, as Egyptian and Assyrian power revived and internal disunity and hostilities with Judah continued, Israel declined and by the mid-8th century BC it had become a vassal of the Assyrian empire. A rebellion by Hoshea in 727–724 BC was crushed, resulting in the annexation of Israel and the deportation of much of the population. ▷ 1.13, 1.14

ITALICS
Indigenous peoples of Italy from the early IRON AGE, excluding the ETRUSCANS, Greeks and PHOENICIANS. The main groups are the Veneti, UMBRIANS, SABINES, LATINS, SAMNITES, LIGURIANS and OSCANS. They were generally organized into tribes in the earlier 1st millennium BC, and spoke INDO-EUROPEAN Italic languages. ▷ 1.23, 1.25

JANAPADAS
Collective name for the small Hindu kingdoms that developed on the Gangetic plains from about 1000 BC, based on intensive WHEAT and RICE cultivation. These coalesced into 16 larger states (*mahajanapadas*) by about 700 BC. ▷ 1.26

JEBUSITES
People of mixed cultural origins, predominantly CANAANITE, whose city-state, centered on JERUSALEM, was conquered by King DAVID of ISRAEL in about 1000 BC. ▷ 1.14

JEMDET NASR
Transitional phase of Sumerian history, from about 3200 to 2900 BC, at the end of the URUK PERIOD. It was marked by distinctive painted pottery, rich metalwork, the wider use of writing, urban growth and the appearance of monumental sculpture. It precedes the EARLY DYNASTIC period. ▷ 1.10

JERICHO
Important early farming settlement situated in the Jordan valley at the north end of the Dead Sea. The first settlement dates to the late 9th millennium BC, when a NATUFIAN HUNTER-GATHERER village was replaced by the earliest-known town, with a stone defensive wall and mud-brick houses, inhabited by an aceramic farming community. Occupation of the site saw several phases of abandonment and renewal, with a major urban settlement in the 3rd millennium BC, and an urban revival by the CANAANITES in the early 2nd millennium BC. Jericho was occupied by the Israelites in the 12th century BC. ▷ 1.08, 1.09

JERUSALEM
City in Palestine that was founded in the 3rd millennium BC and was a major CANAANITE center by about 2000 BC. Occupied by the JEBUSITES in the late 2nd millennium BC, the city was captured by King DAVID in about 1000 BC and made the capital of ISRAEL. Jerusalem was massively rebuilt by SOLOMON (c.965–928 BC), with elaborate fortifications and the Great Temple. It was the capital of JUDAH from 922 BC to 586 BC, when the city was destroyed and the population deported by King NEBUCHADNEZZAR of BABYLON. The city was rebuilt when the HEBREWS were allowed to return to Palestine by CYRUS the Great in 538 BC. There was a further major phase of building during the reign of Herod the Great (37–4 BC), but the city suffered serious destruction during the Jewish revolts against Roman rule in the 1st and 2nd centuries AD. ▷ 1.12, 1.13, 1.14, 1.15, 1.23

JIN
Major feudal state of the ZHOU kingdom in northern China in about 1100–250 BC, with a capital at Jiang. It twice became the leading state (hegemon) during the SPRINGS AND AUTUMNS PERIOD: in the late 7th century BC under Duke Wen, and in the early 6th century under Duke Diao. It was constantly at war with its powerful southern neighbor, CHU. Both states declined in the late 6th century as other southern states, WU and Yue, grew more powerful. ▷ 1.27

JOMON CULTURE
Complex HUNTER-GATHERER and early farming culture of Japan, dating from 14,000–2300 ya (300 BC). It is notable for making the earliest pottery in the world (c.13,000 ya). Early Jomon communities were already semi-sedentary, with a rich fishing, food-collecting and hunting economy, living much of the year in permanent settlements of round houses. This tradition continued in the Middle and Late Jomon periods, with a gradual transition to agriculture from about 4000 BC (MILLET, buckwheat and CATTLE), and RICE farming from about 300 BC. ▷ 1.03, 1.04, 1.05, 1.06

JOSHUA
HEBREW warrior who succeeded Moses as leader of the Israelites. According to the Bible he led the invasion of Canaan, though other evidence indicates a more episodic process of conquest and peaceful colonization during the 12th–11th centuries BC. ▷ 1.14

JOSIAH
King of JUDAH (r.c.640–609 BC) who restored its independence and undertook religious reforms, destroying idols and establishing the Great Temple at JERUSALEM as the only official place of worship. His territorial ambitions ended in defeat by the Egyptians at MEGIDDO. ▷ 1.14

JUDAH
Region of Palestine named after one of the tribes of ISRAEL. It became an independent HEBREW kingdom in 922 BC, when civil war led to the division of Israel, and remained loyal to King REHOBOAM and the Davidic dynasty. Judah remained a separate state, often at war with Israel and other neighbors, until it was conquered by the Assyrians in about 730 BC. King JOSIAH briefly restored independence in about 630 BC, but died fighting the Egyptians. Judah became a vassal state of the neo-Babylonian empire in 605 BC, but rebellions in 597 and 587 BC led to the annexation of the kingdom and the deportion of its population to BABYLONIA. ▷ 1.13, 1.14, 1.18

KALHU
City in ASSYRIA situated on the upper Euphrates, also known as Nimrud, founded by King Shalmaneser I in about 1260 BC. The city was refounded on a larger scale by ASHURNASIRPAL II (c.878 BC) to replace ASHUR as the Assyrian capital (until 707 BC), with massive defences 8 kilometers (5 miles) in circumference, a citadel, a huge ZIGGURAT and palaces richly adorned with sculpted friezes. The city was destroyed by the Babylonians and MEDES in 612 BC. ▷ 1.13

KANESH
City in Anatolia founded in the 3rd millennium BC (the Kultepe TELL site), outside which an Assyrian merchant colony was established in the 19th century BC. Important clay tablets from the Assyrian quarter have revealed details of the Mesopotamian–Anatolian trade in textiles and metals, and of political relations before the rise of the HITTITES. ▷ 1.11, 1.12

KARASUK CULTURE
BRONZE AGE pastoral nomad culture of the Siberian steppes (c.1200–700 BC) that succeeded the AFANASEVO-Andronovo tradition. They were skilled bronze workers, with distant cultural contacts, particularly with late-SHANG China to the east. ▷ 1.05

KARNAK
A vast complex of Egyptian temples on the outskirts of THEBES in Upper Egypt. The most vigorous period of building was the NEW KINGDOM, and the greatest temple that of the god Amun. ▷ 1.18

KASKAS
Tribal people of the mountain areas of northern Anatolia in about 1600–1200 BC. They are mentioned by the HITTITES, who saw them as a major threat because of raiding. Campaigns to control the Kaskas were largely unsuccessful, and in the 14th century BC the Hittites had to build forts to protect their northern frontier. ▷ 1.12

KASSITES
People from the Zagros mountains (Iran–Iraq border) who spoke an INDO-EUROPEAN LANGUAGE and settled in MESOPOTAMIA in the 16th century BC. They established royal dynasties in several cities, notably BABYLON,

imposing a system of feudal rule. They were rapidly assimilated by Babylonian aristocracies and native populations. The dynasty that ruled Babylon was destroyed by the Elamites in the mid-12th century BC. ▷ 1.11, 1.12, 1.13

KAUSAMBI
Pre-Mauryan city in the Ganges valley, India, founded by about 800 BC, when it was probably the capital of Kuru (one of the 16 Gangetic *mahajanapadas* or "great realms"). In the 6th century BC the city was enclosed by brick ramparts more than 5 kilometers (3 miles) in circumference. ▷ 1.26

KERMA
Town on the Nile in Upper NUBIA, the capital of the KUSH peoples during the 2nd Intermediate period (during which Egypt was unable to exercise control over Nubia). It gives its name to the Kerma culture (c.2500–1500 BC). ▷ 1.18

KHEPHREN
Fourth PHARAOH (r.2558–2532 BC) of the 4th Dynasty of Egypt, whose monument is the second of the three great PYRAMIDS at Giza. The GREAT SPHINX is part of his burial complex. ▷ 1.17

KHILAKKU
Neo-Hittite kingdom of Cilicia, south Anatolia (c.1200–750 BC), formerly a province of the HITTITE empire. Although elements of Hittite culture survived, from about 900 BC the region was increasingly influenced by Greek colonies on the coast. Khilakku was conquered by the Assyrians in the mid-8th century BC. ▷ 1.13

KHOISAN
Holocene HUNTER-GATHERERS of southern Africa, with related languages (the Khoisan language group) and similar stone-tool technologies and economies evident in the archeological record from about 8000 BC. Although some Khoisan peoples adopted animal-herding from 500 BC, they were increasingly marginalized by BANTU colonists in the 1st millennium AD; a few groups survived into the modern era (e.g. San Bushmen and Hottentots). ▷ 1.04, 1.05, 1.06

KHUFU
Second PHARAOH (r.2589–2566 BC) of the 4th Dynasty of Egypt, responsible for the Great PYRAMID at Giza, the construction of which earned him a reputation for tyranny. Virtually nothing else is known about him. ▷ 1.17

KISH
City in south MESOPOTAMIA that, according to Sumerian tradition, was the first to be founded after the FLOOD. Established by about 3000 BC, the city was a major rival of URUK and UR in the EARLY DYNASTIC PERIOD and King Mesilim of Kish appears to have been pre-eminent in SUMERIA in the early 25th

century BC. The city lost its independence after 2400 BC but remained a prestigious religious center. ▷ 1.10, 1.11

KIZZUWATNA
Kingdom in Cilicia, south Anatolia, mentioned in HITTITE texts in the 2nd millennium BC. Although powerful in the 15th century BC, its status depended on Hittite imperial fortunes, as Kizzuwatna was usually a vassal state. After the collapse of the Hittites in about 1200 BC, the region fragmented into several Neo-Hittite kingdoms. ▷ 1.12

KLEISTHENES
Athenian statesman who was responsible for an important program of constitutional reform in 508–507 BC. It saw the encouragement of local democracy throughout ATTICA and the reorganization of citizens into new tribes, breaking down traditional regional alliances and allowing all to focus their political energies on the city-state (POLIS) itself. The reforms paved the way for full democracy in 461 BC. ▷ 1.15, 1.24

KLEOMENES
King of SPARTA (r.520–490 BC), remembered for his aggressive foreign policy. He crushed Sparta's old enemy, ARGOS, organized the remaining Peloponnesian cities into the so-called Spartan (Peloponnesian) league (an alliance of states under the leadership of Sparta), and ousted the TYRANT HIPPIAS from Athens (510 BC). ▷ 1.24

KNOSSOS
One of the oldest inhabited sites in CRETE and, from 2000 BC, the site of the most impressive and sophisticated palace complex of the MINOAN CIVILIZATION. It was even designed to withstand earthquakes. At its height in about 1600 BC, the palace and its rulers probably controlled most of the island. It was also a center for sophisticated religious rituals, including bull-leaping. The palace appears to have been taken over by the MYCENAEANS (c.1450 BC) and probably collapsed with their civilization in about 1200 BC. ▷ 1.22

KOOBI FORA
Site of early hominid fossil finds on the east side of Lake Turkana in Kenya, east Africa. The deep deposits of ancient lake sediments contain remains of AUSTRALOPITHECUS ROBUSTUS, HOMO HABILIS and HOMO ERECTUS, as well as evidence of stone-tool working (chopper and flake tools) and animal butchery sites dating from about 2.5 to 1.3 million ya. ▷ 1.01

KOSALA
One of the *mahajanapadas* ("great realms"), an ancient kingdom of northern India, which rose to prominence in the 6th century BC. It was the setting for several stories in Sanskrit literature, including the *Ramayana*. Its capital

was Ayodhya (later moved to Sravasti). In about 500 BC it controlled most of the trade routes in the Ganges basin, but in the following decades it was conquered by Magadha.

KOTOSH TRADITION
Cultural tradition of the PRECERAMIC and INITIAL periods in the Andean highlands of South America from about 2300 to 1200 BC. It is characterized by the development of permanent villages, root crops and cereal farming, camelid herding, monumental architecture, and the earliest pottery in the Andes region (from c.1750 BC). It is named after the site of a temple complex. ▷ 1.28

KOW SWAMP
Early cemetery in south Australia, with formal burials of about 50 individuals dating from about 14,000 to 8000 ya (6000 BC). It is the largest burial population of the late PLEISTOCENE period. Although all anatomically modern humans (HOMO SAPIENS SAPIENS), the skulls have robust archaic features. Grave goods found in some of the burials included shells and stone tools. ▷ 1.02

KULLI
Early BRONZE AGE urban culture of the highland area to the west of the Indus in Baluchistan, with distinctive painted pottery and carved stone vessels. Towns such as Nindowari and Kulli, founded in the early 4th millennium BC, traded in metals with the Indus valley and were possibly influenced by Mesopotamian trade contacts along the coast. The Kulli region fell within the territory of the INDUS CIVILIZATION in the mid-3rd millennium BC. ▷ 1.26

KULTEPE
See KANESH

KUSH
The land of Kush lay to the south of Egypt in NUBIA and was controlled by the strong Egyptian dynasties. In the so-called Kushite period (747–656 BC), kings from Kush controlled Egypt in their turn. They later moved their capital further up the Nile to MEROË (fl.c.300 BC–AD 350). ▷ 1.16, 1.18

KYMAI (CUMAE)
Located at modern Cuma in Campania, this was a Euboean colony founded in about 740 BC. It dominated coastal Campania from 700 to 474 BC, but fell to the OSCANS in 421 BC. Kymai was an ally of ROME in the Punic wars and flourished under the empire. The Cumaean sibyl and the cult of Apollo was important in Augustan ideology, and the area was a popular location for elite Roman villas. The site declined in the 3rd and 4th centuries AD. ▷ 1.23, 1.25

LA VENTA
Largest OLMEC ceremonial center, situated on an island surrounded by swamps, near the

Gulf of Mexico. The main monument complex had a linear arrangement of platforms, pavements, shrines and enclosures oriented on the Great Pyramid, a 30-meter (100-foot) high clay mound. These were adorned with fine stone sculptures and offerings of jade figurines. The principal monuments were built from about 1000 BC, and the site was violently destroyed in about 400 BC.

LACHISH
City in Palestine founded in the mid-3rd millennium BC and a CANAANITE town and religious center from about 1500 BC. It was occupied by the Israelites in the 10th century BC and fortified by REHOBOAM. Lachish was sacked in 701 BC by the Assyrian king SENNACHERIB, who had the event recorded in reliefs at his palace at NINEVEH. The city was again sacked, by the Babylonians, in 588–587 BC and was finally abandoned in the 2nd century BC. ▷ 1.14

LACONIA
Mountainous region in the central-southern Peloponnese and the home territory of SPARTA, which drew on the fertility of the Eurotas valley between the main mountain ranges. The word "laconic" reflects the tradition that the Spartans – unlike most Greeks – were uncommunicative by nature. ▷ 1.24

LAETOLI
Site of hominid fossil finds close to OLDUVAI GORGE in Tanzania, east Africa. Remains of AUSTRALOPITHECUS AFARAENSIS were found in wind-blown sediments, together with remarkable footprints, about 3.6 million years old, of fully bipedal hominids preserved in ancient muds. Later discoveries included the early remains of HOMO SAPIENS dating from about 120,000 ya. ▷ 1.01

LAGASH
Sumerian city that became a major city-state in the EARLY DYNASTIC PERIOD and briefly dominated south MESOPOTAMIA after King Eannatum conquered the city of KISH (c.2400 BC). Control of Lagash later fell to UMMA and to SARGON of AGADE, but its power revived in the 22nd century BC when it was rebuilt by Gudea, a vassal king of GUTIAN overlords. The city declined after its capture by Larsa in about 2100 BC. ▷ 1.09, 1.10, 1.11

LASCAUX
Cave site in southwest France, famous for its magnificent UPPER PALEOLITHIC paintings and engravings of animals, especially aurochs, red deer and horses. The cave was probably used for ritual purposes in the MAGDALENIAN period (c.17,000–14,000 ya). ▷ 1.19

LATINS, LATIUM
The Latins were an ITALIC group occupying the area between the Tiber and Campania, known in antiquity as Latium Vetus. By the 6th century BC the main settlements had become city-states. ROME, also a Latin city, had conquered the whole area by 300 BC, and the Latial cities declined as Rome developed and as the area was disturbed by warfare during the late republic. ▷ 1.25

LEPENSKI VIR
Late MESOLITHIC settlement of the 7th millennium BC, beside the river Danube in Serbia. The community was semi-sedentary, living in permanent trapezoidal houses, with a complex fishing and hunting economy. Several houses had human burials in the floors, and notable carved stone statuettes of human heads, some with fish-like features. ▷ 1.19

LEVANT
East Mediterranean region between Anatolia and Sinai, extending inland to the Arabian desert. Sometimes described as the "Near East", it comprises the modern countries of Israel, Palestine, Lebanon, west Jordan and west Syria. The earliest farming societies developed in this region in the 9th millennium BC. It was a key area of URBANIZATION and STATE formation from the 4th millennium BC, and the main stage for imperial struggles between Egypt, ASSYRIA, MITTANI, the HITTITES and the Israelites in the 2nd–1st millennia BC. ▷ 1.07, 1.08, 1.09, 1.10, 1.11, 1.12, 1.13, 1.14, 1.18, 1.23

LIGURIANS
Indigenous group of southern France and northeast Italy that became Celticized from the 3rd century BC, through amicable relations with neighboring Gauls. Greek settlements developed on the Mediterranean coast from about 600 BC, and the area was conquered by the Romans between 238 and 117 BC. No archeological culture can be equated with the Ligurians. ▷ 1.23, 1.25

LINEAR A SCRIPT
Script that evolved in CRETE in about 1800 BC and was used by the Minoans to record quantities of goods, the ownership of produce and – in some cases – religious texts. Linear A signs stand for syllables. The script has not been deciphered, and disappeared in about 1450 BC. ▷ 1.22

LINEAR B SCRIPT
Script similar to LINEAR A but in a different language, that first appeared on CRETE in about 1450 BC and spread to the Greek mainland. Linear B script was used to record quantities of goods and administrative matters. Decipherment by Michael Ventris in 1952 revealed the language to be an early form of GREEK and showed that the Mycenaeans had adopted the script from Linear A. ▷ 1.22

LINEAR POTTERY CULTURE
See BANDKERAMIK CULTURE

LINEN (FLAX)
Woven fabric made from cultivated plant fiber (flax), first produced in the Middle East in the 7th millennium BC. This plant and associated weaving technologies spread across the Middle East to Anatolia and Europe: there is evidence of linen clothing in Egypt and at NEOLITHIC lake villages in Switzerland by the 4th millennium BC. ▷ 1.03, 1.08, 1.09, 1.16

LLAMA
Camelid domesticated in the Andes of South America, possibly as early as the 5th millennium BC, closely related to the alpaca, wild guanaco and vicuna. Llamas were mainly used as pack animals and as sources of WOOL, food and leather. ▷ 1.03, 1.28

LOGOGRAPHIC SCRIPTS
Writing systems in which signs represent units of meaning (morphemes) rather than units of sound, as in phonographic scripts. The most widely used logographic script is CHINESE, which developed in the 1st millennium BC and has thousands of signs, each with a different meaning or set of meanings depending on the context of use. ▷ 1.07

LONGHOUSES, NEOLITHIC
Elongated rectangular or trapezoidal buildings of the early Neolithic BANDKERAMIK CULTURE of central Europe (c.5500–4500 BC). Longhouses were massive constructions, up to 50 meters (160 feet) in length, some with rows of entire tree trunks set in pits to support the superstructure. They probably housed extended families of between 20 and 40 people, similar to more recent examples in southeast Asia and North America. ▷ 1.20

LONGSHAN CULTURE
Late NEOLITHIC culture (c.3200–1800 BC) of the Yellow river region in northern China, with distinctive wheel-thrown pottery, polished stone tools, ORACLE BONES for divination, and intensive RICE cultivation. Their large settlements, rammed earth fortifications and evidence of warfare and prestige goods indicate a CHIEFDOM society that was more complex and hierarchical than the preceding YANGSHAO farming culture. ▷ 1.04, 1.05, 1.27

LOS MILLARES
Important Copper Age settlement in southern Spain, consisting of a heavily fortified village protected by several outlying citadels, with a large cemetery of collective tombs nearby. The scale and prosperity of the site in the 3rd millennium BC was based on a rich agricultural economy, control of local COPPER sources and trade in prestige goods. ▷ 1.20, 1.21

LOTHAL
Southern port of the INDUS CIVILIZATION, situated at the head of the Gulf of Khambat, Gujarat. The rectangular town was enclosed by a brick wall, with a citadel, granaries, and

a housing and craft-working quarter. Outside the town was a large brick-built basin, possibly a dock or reservoir. Artifacts from the site indicate trade contacts with the Persian Gulf. ▷ 1.26

LU
Large feudal state of the ZHOU kingdom, with a capital city at Qufu, in about 1100–250 BC. It was the home of the philosopher CONFUCIUS (c.551–479 BC), who served as a bureaucrat. Lu played only a minor role in the power struggles of the SPRINGS AND AUTUMNS PERIOD as the authority of the Zhou dynasty declined (from c.770 BC). ▷ 1.27

LUCY (AUSTRALOPITHECUS AFARENSIS)
The most complete fossil remains (about 40 percent) of an individual AUSTRALOPITHECUS AFARENSIS hominid, about 3.5 million years old, found at HADAR in Ethiopia. Nicknamed "Lucy" by the excavators, the female australopithecine was bipedal and stood only about 1.2 meters (4 feet) tall. ▷ 1.01

LUGALZAGESI
King of the city of UMMA (c.2375–2350 BC) in south MESOPOTAMIA. He established a short-lived empire by conquering the pre-eminent city of LAGASH, along with KISH, UR and URUK, but was in turn conquered by SARGON of AGADE, who took over his dominions. ▷ 1.10, 1.11

LULLUBIANS
Tribal people of the Zagros mountains who are mentioned in Akkadian inscriptions of the late 3rd millennium BC, when they raided or traded with lowland communites. The Lullubians were later absorbed by the Elamite kingdom. ▷ 1.11

LUMBINI
Mythical grove in the foothills of the Himalayas where Queen Maha Maya gave birth to Siddhartha Gautama, the future BUDDHA, in about 563 BC. ▷ 1.26

LUOYANG
City to the south of the Yellow river in Honan province, northern China, founded in the 12th century BC. It became the capital of the ZHOU state in about 770 BC, after their ancient capital at HAO was exposed to barbarian attacks. The city was captured by QIN in about 256 BC. ▷ 1.27

LUVIANS
People of southwest Anatolia in the 2nd millennium BC, who spoke an INDO-EUROPEAN LANGUAGE that was related to HITTITE and Lydian. The Luvians may have contributed to the collapse of the Hittite empire. The latest hieroglyphic Luvian inscriptions date from the 7th century BC, and Lycian (written from about 600 to 200 BC) is believed to derive from a Luvian dialect. ▷ 1.05, 1.12

LUXOR
The site of an important NEW KINGDOM temple to the Egyptian god Amun. Each year, at the Festival of Opet, when the Nile began reflooding, a cult statue of the god was carried from his temple at KARNAK to a ceremony at Luxor symbolizing the sexual relationship between the god and the mother of the reigning PHARAOH. ▷ 1.18

LYDIA, LYDIANS
An area of central Asia Minor consolidated as a kingdom under the Mermnad dynasty (c.700–545 BC). Lydia exploited its central position on trade routes to become conspicuously wealthy, and is credited with the invention of COINAGE in about 600 BC. It was absorbed into the ACHEMENID EMPIRE in 545 BC, after the defeat of its last king, CROESUS. ▷ 1.15, 1.23, 1.24

MAES HOWE
Famous early NEOLITHIC PASSAGE GRAVE in ORKNEY, dating from the early 3rd millennium BC, with a finely built MEGALITHIC tomb structure covered by an enormous mound and surrounded by a rock-cut ditch. The passage is oriented towards sunset at the midwinter solstice. ▷ 1.20

MAGDALENIAN
The last cultural phase (c.17,000–11,000 ya) of the UPPER PALEOLITHIC period in western and central Europe. The Magdalenian communities were specialized reindeer hunters, and later turned to sea-mammal hunting using distinctive bone harpoons. They are also renowned for their works of art and the most accomplished and impressive cave paintings are Magdalenian in date, including those at LASCAUX and ALTAMIRA. ▷ 1.19

MAGNA GRAECIA
"Greater Greece", the name given to southern Italy (sometimes including Sicily) after its extensive colonization by the Greeks from the 8th century BC. ▷ 1.25

MAHAJANAPADAS
See JANAPADAS

MAIZE
Cereal plant that was domesticated in Mesoamerica in the early 3rd millennium BC. By about 2300 BC, maize formed the staple crop of farming communities in Mesoamerica, spreading to South America in about 1000–800 BC and to the southwestern deserts of North America by about AD 300. With the development of cold-resistant strains, maize also became a staple food crop in the eastern woodlands of North America by about AD 800. Maize cultivation facilitated surplus production and reliable food storage, which led to the development of permanent villages and population growth. ▷ 1.03, 1.28

MANNEANS
People to the east of Lake Urmia who are mentioned in Assyrian and Urartuan texts of the 9th–7th centuries BC. Little is known of their history or culture, though they may have spoken a language related to Hurrian. They were overrun by the SCYTHIANS and MEDES in the 7th century BC. ▷ 1.13

MARI
City in central MESOPOTAMIA beside the Euphrates in modern Syria, strategically situated to control the trade route between SUMERIA and the LEVANT. It was one of the most powerful Mesopotamian city-states in the 3rd millennium BC. Thousands of clay tablets have been found in the palace of the last king, Zimri-lim (c.1790–1757 BC), including diplomatic correspondence, historical and legal archives, and treasury records. The city was destroyed by HAMMURABI of BABYLON in 1757 BC and never regained its former power. ▷ 1.10, 1.11

MASSILIA
The modern Marseilles, founded as a Greek colony by the Phocaeans (from the coast of Asia Minor) in about 600 BC. It exploited the trade routes up the Rhône to the Celtic heartlands of Gaul, and is credited with the introduction of the vine and the olive to France. ▷ 1.23, 1.25

MASTABAS
Egyptian tombs in which the underground chamber is surmounted by a rectangular structure whose walls slope inwards. *Mastabas* were used for royal and noble burials during the early dynasties. The name comes from the similarly shaped benches found outside modern Egyptian homes. ▷ 1.17

MEDES, MEDIAN EMPIRE
INDO-IRANIAN PEOPLE, originally pastoral nomads from central Asia, who settled in northwest Iran in the 9th century BC. The Medes established a unified kingdom in the 8th century BC, with a capital at Hamadan. Little is known about Median culture, as written records have not survived, and most of their works of art appear to be Assyrian-inspired.
Under King Cyaxares (r.c.625–585 BC), the Medes became a major power in the Middle East by destroying the Assyrian empire, sacking ASHUR in 614 BC, and (with the Babylonians) capturing NINEVEH in 612. Cyaxares and his son, Astyages (r.585–550 BC), established a short-lived empire which extended from central Iran to the Persian Gulf and Anatolia. The empire disintegrated in 550 BC when CYRUS the Great of Persia rebelled against Median rule, defeating Astyages at PASARGADAE. The Median aristocracy submitted and were given senior roles in the new administration; Media became a satrapy of the ACHEMENID EMPIRE. ▷ 1.13, 1.15

MEDITERRANEAN TRIAD

The so-called Mediterranean triad consisted of three staple crops: cereals, olives and vines. They could be farmed together on the same land and even in the most disastrous of years, at least one would crop. They formed the backbone of the Greek agricultural economy from the 8th century BC, with olives and vines spreading overseas with Greek settlements.

MEGALITHIC MONUMENT

Ceremonial or mortuary structure built of "large stones" (from the Greek words *megas* and *lithikos*). The term is mainly applied to the NEOLITHIC and BRONZE AGE stone architecture of Europe, including CHAMBERED TOMBS, STONE CIRCLES and avenues, but is also applicable to building traditions such as the IRON AGE MEGALITHIC TOMB culture of India. ▷ 1.04, 1.20, 1.21, 1.26

MEGALITHIC TOMB CULTURE (INDIA)

Small-scale IRON AGE agricultural societies of southern India in the 1st millennium BC that built distinctive MEGALITHIC tombs and other ceremonial monuments. This cultural tradition had indigenous NEOLITHIC origins and developed largely independently of the urban, state-organized societies of northern India. One of the culture's most important sites, Brahmagiri, contains more than 300 tombs and STONE CIRCLES. ▷ 1.26

MEGIDDO

Strategic town in Palestine, founded in the 4th millennium BC. It was often sacked and rebuilt, and owed allegiance to a succession of Egyptian, CANAANITE and Israelite rulers. It was refortified by SOLOMON of ISRAEL in about 1000 BC, and was a major fortress of the kingdom of JUDAH. ▷ 1.14

MEHRGARH

NEOLITHIC village in Baluchistan that was occupied from the 7th to 4th millennia BC. The adoption of Middle Eastern domesticates and similarities with aceramic farming settlements in the FERTILE CRESCENT suggest that agriculture spread rapidly across Iran. The long occupation sequence, with numerous layers of mud-brick houses, also provides important evidence of cultural change from the first village to the proto-urban center of the 4th millennium BC. ▷ 1.26

MEMPHIS

Strategically situated where the narrow Nile valley begins to broaden out into the Delta, Memphis was the natural choice for an Egyptian capital after the first unification of the country in about 3100 BC. The city remained an important administrative center throughout Egyptian history, and only fell into decline when Alexandria was built in the late 4th century BC. ▷ 1.13, 1.15, 1.17, 1.18

MENTUHOTPE II

Egyptian PHARAOH (r.2061–2010 BC) who is remembered for restoring order to the borders of Egypt following the breakdown of authority in the 1st Intermediate period. His impressive burial complex near THEBES, his capital, drew heavily on OLD KINGDOM models, doubtless as a means of asserting his legitimacy. ▷ 1.18

MEROË

Town situated on the Nile in NUBIA. It was the capital city of the Kushite kingdom in the 5th century BC, after the Kushites had retreated southwards from Egypt. An important center for IRON WORKING, the town later gave its name to the Meroitic kingdom, which was at its height from 300 BC to AD 350. Meroitic culture was heavily Egyptianized; its rulers were buried in small PYRAMIDS and worshipped Egyptian gods. ▷ 1.06, 1.15

MESILIM OF KISH

See KISH

MESOAMERICAN CIVILIZATIONS

A series of related Mesoamerican cultures that developed complex societies with STATE systems, ceremonial centers, cities and rich iconography and material culture, as well as the only fully literate culture of the ancient Americas (the Maya civilization of the Classic period). The history of Mesoamerican civilizations is divided into the following periods: ARCHAIC (c.7000–2000 BC), EARLY PRECLASSIC (c.2000–800 BC), MIDDLE PRECLASSIC (c.800–300 BC), Late Preclassic (c.300 BC–AD 300), Classic (c.AD 300–800), and Postclassic (c.AD 800–1520). ▷ 1.04, 1.05, 1.06, 1.07, 1.28

MESOLITHIC

The period of cultural transition in Europe (c.8000–4000 BC), following the end of the last glaciation, when UPPER PALEOLITHIC HUNTER-GATHERERS developed specialized cultural systems adapted to changing climatic conditions and new habitats. Mesolithic communities used sophisticated tool-kits with MICROLITHIC technology and a new emphasis on fishing equipment. In resource-rich coastal areas, such as Brittany and Denmark, the appearance in the late Mesolithic of semi-permanent settlements, ritual sites and formal burials suggests population growth and more complex social systems (e.g. ERTEBOLLE culture). These were the last groups in western Europe to adopt agricultural practices, and the first to build MEGALITHIC tombs. ▷ 1.19, 1.20

MESOPOTAMIAN CIVILIZATION

The distinctive STATE-organized urban cultures of the Tigris and Euphrates river system that formed a core area of civilization from the 4th millennium BC. Its key features include the first cities and large-scale IRRIGATION (by 3500 BC), the earliest writing system (Sumerian pictographs and CUNEIFORM), and

first imperial state (SARGON OF AGADE's Akkadian empire, c.2330 BC). Mesopotamian civilization was highly varied because of its diverse origins in independent city-states and its distinct ethnic communities, but it developed a shared religious and literate tradition with a considerable degree of continuity and integration, as each new dominant state tolerated local customs and adopted cultural and political features of their predecessors.

The complex history of the region can be divided into the following periods (with intermediate periods of political and cultural instability): URUK (c.4300–3100 BC), JEMDET NASR (c.3200–2900 BC), EARLY DYNASTIC (c.2900–2334 BC), Akkadian empire (c.2350–2200 BC), Third Dynasty of UR (c.2100–2000 BC), Old Babylonian and Old Assyrian (c.1900–1600 BC), Middle Assyrian empire (c.1360–1075 BC), Neo-Assyrian empire (c.930–612 BC) and Neo-Babylonian empire (612–539 BC). ▷ 1.04, 1.05, 1.10, 1.11, 1.12, 1.13, 1.14, 1.15

MESSENIA

Plain in the southwest Peloponnese annexed by SPARTA in the 8th century BC. Its native Greek peoples, the HELOTS as they became known, were treated as slaves by the Spartans and forced to work the land for their overlords. The area was liberated from Spartan control by the Thebans in the mid-4th century BC. ▷ 1.24

MEZHIRICH

UPPER PALEOLITHIC settlement in the Ukraine with a hut built partly of mammoth bones, dating from about 20,000 ya. The bones were probably used to weigh down tent awnings, but may also have had some social or religious significance. ▷ 1.19

MICHELSBERG

Late NEOLITHIC post-BANDKERAMIK CULTURE of the Rhineland and northern France, between about 4000 and 2800 BC. It is named after a ceremonial enclosure site in the middle Rhine valley, with distinctive material culture and settlement sites. ▷ 1.20

MICROLITHIC TOOLS

Composite tools made of tiny, stone blade fragments, or "microliths", set in hafts singly (such as arrowheads) or edge-to-edge in groups (such as projectile barbs and sickle blades). Microliths are often geometric in shape and were made by snapping long blades into pieces for more versatile use. Microlithic tools are characteristic of the MESOLITHIC period in Europe but were used by many other cultures. ▷ 1.19

MIDAS

See MITAS

MIDDLE KINGDOM

Period in Egyptian history (c.2055–1650 BC) characterized by stability and prosperity. The

PHARAOH MENTUHOTPE II (12th Dynasty) successfully stabilized the kingdom over a long reign and order was maintained until a succession of weaker pharaohs of the 13th Dynasty lost control of the Delta and allowed the infiltration of the HYKSOS people. At its height the Middle Kingdom saw effective Egyptian control over NUBIA. It was also an age that produced the most famous of the so-called "Wisdom Texts', which extolled the virtues of good administration. ▷ 1.18

MIDDLE PRECLASSIC PERIOD
Period of MESOAMERICAN CIVILIZATION from about 800 to 300 BC, in which OLMEC CIVILIZATION reached the height of its cultural achievement, particularly in stone sculpture, jade carving and temple building, before it collapsed in the 5th to 4th centuries BC. Mayan civilization, which emerged in highland Guatemala and the Yucatán peninsula, has many features in common with the Olmecs, but also developed large-scale IRRIGATION farming systems that facilitated settlement growth and STATE formation (c.600–300 BC). Another complex society emerged in this period in the OAXACA VALLEY, Mexico, where the earliest writing system in the New World (ZAPOTEC hieroglyphic) was invented in the 8th century BC. ▷ 1.06, 1.07, 1.28

MILETOS
Important Greek city-state on the west coast of Asia Minor whose wealth came from its rich territory and trade. In the 6th century BC Miletos was an effective colonizer of the Black Sea coast, and the same period saw the work of its famous philosophers, Thales, Anaximander and Anaximenes. A leader of the unsuccessful IONIAN revolt against the Persians (499 BC), it never fully recovered its prosperity. ▷ 1.22, 1.23, 1.24

MILLET
Several species of grasses that produce small edible seeds, domesticated in different parts of the world at different times, notably in China, sub-Saharan Africa and Ethiopia by the 6th millennium BC, and in the Middle East by the 4th millennium BC. ▷ 1.03, 1.16, 1.27

MINOAN PALACE CIVILIZATION
Important civilization that flourished on CRETE between 2000 and 1450 BC. It was centered on large palaces (KHANIA, KNOSSOS, MALLIA and PHAISTOS), which were also religious and administrative centers. Originally relying on an agricultural economy, the Minoans also traded extensively in the Aegean and were fine craftsmen and fresco painters. Their civilization collapsed, probably as the result of a MYCENAEAN invasion. ▷ 1.07, 1.20, 1.22

MIOCENE EPOCH
Period of the Tertiary era (c.25–5 million ya), marked by cooling climatic conditions in which mammal species increasingly dominated terrestrial fauna, with hominid evolution in eastern Africa. ▷ 1.01

MITAS (MIDAS)
King of PHRYGIA, whose dates are traditionally given as 738–695 BC. A figure of fun for the Greeks, his greed is remembered in the story that he wished for everything he touched to be turned to gold, and then found he could not eat or drink anything. ▷ 1.13

MITTANI
A kingdom of north MESOPOTAMIA and Syria founded by HURRIAN invaders by about 1550 BC, after the decline of the Assyrian and Babylonian states which had ruled the region in the 19–17th centuries BC. Mittani controlled the strategic routes linking Hittite Anatolia, Mesopotamia, the Levantine ports, the Aegean states and Egypt, and was a major regional power from about 1500 to 1350 BC. It collapsed in the early 13th century BC after the HITTITES sacked the capital, WASHUKANNI, and conquered the western part of the kingdom (c.1340 BC), leaving the remainder to be conquered by the Assyrians (by c.1270 BC). Little is known about the political organization or culture of the Mittani state, which left few written records. ▷ 1.12, 1.18

MOAB
Highland region of Palestine to the east of the Dead Sea occupied in biblical times by the Moabites, a Semitic people closely related to the Israelites, who may have settled in Palestine in the 14th century BC. The Moabite kingdom was often at war with ISRAEL and JUDAH, and was destroyed by the Babylonians in about 582 BC. ▷ 1.13, 1.14

MOHENJO-DARO
The largest of the two great cities of the INDUS CIVILIZATION (the other being HARAPPA), situated beside the Indus river in Sind (south Pakistan). The city was probably founded in the early 3rd millennium BC, laid out in a series of residential blocks with a grid street plan and drainage system. On one side of the city was a monumental brick-built citadel which may have served as the royal and religious center of the Indus state, with a huge granary, residential buildings, aisled ceremonial halls and a ritual bath. Massive flooding and local environmental deterioration probably led to its decline and eventual abandonment by about 1700 BC. ▷ 1.26

MOUSTERIAN CULTURE
MIDDLE PALEOLITHIC tool industry of west Eurasia and north Africa, about 150,000 to 40,000 ya, that is often associated with HOMO SAPIENS NEANDERTHALENSIS. The Mousterian culture is characterized by its distinctive flaking techniques and range of tools, including small hand axes, flake tools, and the first hafted projectiles (spears for close-impact hunting of large game). Differences in tool assemblages from site to site may indicate cultural variation or seasonal specializations. ▷ 1.01, 1.19

MUMMIFICATION
The process, used by the ancient Egyptians, of preserving a corpse in preparation for burial, in the belief that only a preserved body ("mummy") could enjoy an afterlife. Carried out in accordance with strict rules over a period of some 70 days, it involved preserving some organs separately, while soaking the rest of the body in natron, a natural drying agent. The body was then bound in cloth and placed in a coffin.

MURSILIS I
King of the HITTITES (r.c.1620–1590 BC). The most successful king of the Old Kingdom period, he extended Hittite rule in Anatolia and northern Syria, and undertook a campaign down the Euphrates, sacking BABYLON in 1595 BC. He was killed in a palace coup. ▷ 1.11

MUSHKI (MYSIANS)
People who were related to the PHRYGIANS and who settled in northeast Anatolia in the 12th century BC, after the collapse of the HITTITE empire. Allied with native HURRIANS and KASKAS, they invaded MESOPOTAMIA but were defeated by TIGLATH-PILESER I of ASSYRIA in 1115 BC. ▷ 1.12

MUWATALLIS II
King of the HITTITES (r.1295–1271 BC). He opposed the Egyptian attempt under PHAROAH RAMESSES II to regain control of Syria and inflicted a strategic defeat on the Egyptian PHARAOH at the Battle of QADESH (c.1285 BC), successfully extending Hittite control as far south as Damascus. ▷ 1.12

MYCENAE
An impressively fortified hilltop city with a palace and lavishly furnished royal tombs in the Peloponnese, occupied from the 16th to 12th centuries BC. Its most famous features are the famous Lion Gate and the so-called "Treasury of Atreus", actually a magnificent THOLOS tomb. Mycenae was excavated in the 19th century by the pioneering German archeologist, Heinrich Schliemann, and many spectacular artifacts, including gold death masks, were discovered. ▷ 1.21, 1.22, 1.23

MYCENAEAN CIVILIZATION
First GREEK-speaking civilization (c.1600–1200 BC), named after MYCENAE, its most important site. The Mycenaean civilization centered on a number of independent rulers, each with their own stronghold. Mycenaeans traded extensively overseas and conquered CRETE in about 1450 BC, where they adapted the LINEAR A script to write their own language (LINEAR B). Excavations at many Mycenaean sites, including Mycenae, indicate that the civilization came to a violent end, though its attackers are unknown. ▷ 1.21, 1.22, 1.23

NABATEAN ALPHABET
Variant of the CANAANITE phonetic alphabet developed by the Nabataeans in Arabia for writing their ARAMAIC LANGUAGE (c.1000 BC). It was most widely used in the Nabataean kingdom of Petra from about 150 BC to AD 150, and gave rise to the Arabic scripts of the Middle Ages. ▷ 1.07

NABONIDUS
The last king of BABYLON (r.555–539 BC). An imperial official crowned by the ruling aristocracy, Nabonidus was defeated by CYRUS the Great of Persia in 539 BC, after which BABYLONIA submitted peacefully to ACHEMENID rule. ▷ 1.13, 1.15

NABOPOLASSAR
King of BABYLON (r.626–605 BC) and the king of the CHALDEAN 11th dynasty, who reasserted Babylonian independence. Nabopolassar drove the Assyrians out of BABYLONIA before attacking ASSYRIA. He destroyed the Assyrian capital at NINEVEH in 612 BC and took over Assyrian domains. ▷ 1.13

NAPATA
District of NUBIA that served as the center of the Kushite kingdom between 1000 BC and 300 BC, before the kingdom moved southwards to MEROË.

NARAM-SIN
King of AKKAD (r.2254–2218 BC), who was the grandson of SARGON OF AGADE and ruled the Akkadian empire at the height of its power. He consolidated Akkadian domains, protected key trade routes, founded numerous temples and may have assumed theocratic powers. ▷ 1.11

NARMER
Early Egyptian ruler who was possibly responsible for the first unification of Egypt (c.3000 BC) and the foundation of the capital at MEMPHIS. The famous Narmer palette found at HIERAKONPOLIS shows for the first time a king wearing the Crowns of both Lower and Upper Egypt. ▷ 1.17

NATUFIAN CULTURE
Late glacial and early Holocene EPIPALEOLITHIC culture, dating from about 12,500 to 10,500 ya (8500 BC), of the LEVANT and Syriax, with an intensive cereal-collecting and gazelle-hunting economy. They became increasingly settled, living in small villages of permanent houses at sites such as JERICHO, with shrines and formal burials, and selectively modified plant-growing conditions that led to incipient farming. ▷ 1.08

NEANDERTHALS
See HOMO SAPIENS NEANDERTHALENSIS

NEBUCHADNEZZAR
King of BABYLON (r.604–562 BC), the son of NABOPOLASSAR. While he was still crown-prince he defeated the Egyptians at CARCHEMISH in Syria in 605 BC, and undertook campaigns in Syria, ELAM and the LEVANT, ensuring Babylonian supremacy in the Middle East by about 590 BC. He crushed revolts in JUDAH in 597 and 587 BC, and deported the population to BABYLONIA. He rebuilt his capital at Babylon on a vast and magnificent scale. His dynasty was overthrown soon after his death. ▷ 1.13, 1.15

NECHO II
Egyptian PHARAOH (r.610–595 BC), the third of the Saite dynasty, who founded Egypt's first navy and reconquered the LEVANT as the ASSYRIAN EMPIRE disintegrated. He was finally checked by the Babylonians in 605 BC. ▷ 1.13

NEOLITHIC
The final phase of the STONE AGE, in which farming was the main form of subsistence production, leading to population growth, village settlements and ranking, while stone remained the principal material used in tool manufacture. The term is still used to refer to early agricultural societies in the Old World. ▷ 1.03, 1.04, 1.06, 1.08, 1.09, 1.10, 1.16, 1.19, 1.20, 1.27

NEW KINGDOM
The third and final of the three great kingdoms of ancient Egypt (1550–1070 BC). The period saw the extension of Egyptian power into Syria and Palestine and the intense exploitation of NUBIA. Among its great PHARAOHS was the conqueror TUTHMOSIS III, the heretic king AKHENATEN and the great builder RAMESSES II; among its most spectacular legacies are the contents of the tomb of TUTANKHAMUN. In the late New Kingdom the power of the temple priesthoods was greatly increased through excessive grants of land by the pharaohs, leading to the decline of royal authority and the loss of Egypt's empire in Nubia and the Near East. ▷ 1.18

NEWGRANGE
Enormous early NEOLITHIC PASSAGE GRAVE located in the Boyne valley ceremonial center in Ireland, built in about 3000 BC. The passage is oriented on sunrise at the midwinter solstice, when the sun's rays illuminate the central chamber. The stone kerb around the mound is elaborately decorated with carvings. Two similar monuments (Knowth and Dowth) are located nearby, as well as numerous satellite tombs. ▷ 1.20

NINEVEH
Assyrian city situated beside the Tigris in central MESOPOTAMIA. Although an important commercial and religious center by 3000 BC, it did not play a major role in Assyrian history until the 9th to 7th centuries BC, when successive rulers built large temples and palaces. It became the Assyrian capital in 705 BC, provided with magnificent buildings and replanned on a grandiose scale, with wide streets, a water-supply system, monumental gates, arsenal and palaces (including ASHURBANIPAL's palace and library, from which thousands of clay tablets have been recovered). The city was destroyed in 612 BC when the Babylonians and MEDES overthrew the Assyrian empire. Nineveh was rediscovered by the pioneering Victorian archeologist, Austen Henry Layard, in 1849. ▷ 1.09, 1.10, 1.11, 1.12, 1.13, 1.15

NIPPUR
Major city and the most important religious center in SUMERIA, founded by 4000 BC. Nippur was the site of the temple of ENLIL, the storm god responsible for sanctifying secular power, making control of the city essential for any ambitious MESOPOTAMIAN king. The final temple sanctuary was built by UR-NAMMU, king of UR, in about 2100 BC. ▷ 1.09, 1.10, 1.12, 1.13

NUBIA
Region along the Nile, south of Egypt, that acted as a corridor between Egypt and the rest of Africa. The more powerful Egyptian kingdoms, especially the NEW KINGDOM, exploited its resources mercilessly, but at times of Egyptian weakness it maintained its own cultures (the KERMA culture) and kingdoms (the Kushite). The Kushite dynasty (747–656 BC) from NAPATA was powerful enough to rule Egypt itself. ▷ 1.14, 1.15, 1.16, 1.17, 1.18

OAXACA VALLEY
Highland area of south Mexico where complex societies developed in the 2nd millennium BC, influenced from about 1200 BC by the OLMECS. It was the core area of ZAPOTEC civilization, which developed in the 1st millennium BC, with an early ceremonial center at Monté Albán and hillside agricultural terraces and settlements. ▷ 1.28

OBSIDIAN
Volcanic glass with flaking properties similar (but superior) to flint, widely used and highly valued for toolmaking in many parts of the world, notably in MESOPOTAMIA, where long-distance trade in obsidian was important by 7500 BC, and in Mesoamerica, where control of obsidian resources was essential for the lowland civilizations of the OLMEC and Maya. ▷ 1.08, 1.09, 1.28

ODYSSEY
Greek epic poem attributed to HOMER (c.700 BC), that tells the story of the hero Odysseus' return from the TROJAN WAR. His adventures include encounters with gods, monsters (the Cyclops) and the hazards of the sea. He eventually arrives at his homeland, Ithaca, to be reunited with his wife, Penelope. The *Odyssey* is the archetypal story of a hero battling against great odds to reach ultimate happiness. ▷ 1.24

OLD KINGDOM
The first of the great kingdoms of ancient Egypt (2686–2181 BC). It was characterized by powerful rulers who diverted enormous resources towards the building of the PYRAMIDS as their burial places. The strain on the economy, possibly intensified by climatic changes, led to the slow disintegration of the kingdom and a period of disorder (the 1st Intermediate period). ▷ 1.17

OLDOWAN CULTURE
The earliest tool industry (c.2.4–1.4 million ya) that is associated with the first humans (HOMO HABILIS) at sites in east Africa, such as OLDUVAI GORGE (after which it is named), KOOBI FORA and OMO. Flaked pebble tools, choppers and flakes were used for crushing, cutting and scraping. The more consistent Developed Oldowan industry (c.1.5–0.7 million ya), contemporary with early ACHEULIAN industries, was probably employed by hand-ax users for specific tasks. ▷ 1.01

OLDUVAI GORGE
A complex of ravines in the African Rift Valley, Tanzania, cutting through volcanic deposits and ancient lake and river sediments. They contain important early hominid remains (HOMO HABILIS, AUSTRALOPITHECUS ROBUSTUS, HOMO ERECTUS and HOMO SAPIENS), and the longest sequence of PALEOLITHIC tool industries (c.2.1 million–15,000 ya), with a succession of OLDOWAN, ACHEULIAN, MIDDLE PALEOLITHIC and UPPER PALEOLITHIC assemblages. ▷ 1.01

OLMEC CIVILIZATION
The earliest MESOAMERICAN CIVILIZATION, which developed in the humid lowland region along the Gulf coast of southern Mexico from 1250 BC. The Olmecs established a set of political, religious and aesthetic traditions which influenced later Mesoamerican cultures, with large ceremonial centers (notably TRES ZAPOTES, LA VENTA and SAN LORENZO), platform mounds and step pyramids, monumental stone carving, expansive and warlike states, and distinctive religious iconography.

Most stone resources used for the building of monuments (basalt and serpentine) and for portable material culture (OBSIDIAN and jade) had to be imported from highland regions, extending the Olmec sphere of influence. Hieroglyphic writing and a complex calendar had been invented for ritual purposes by about 700 BC, though there is no evidence that the Olmecs developed a literary culture. The decline of Olmec civilization and the destruction of its ceremonial centers took place between about 600 and 400 BC, probably as a result of political fragmentation and economic stresses. The Maya, who were deeply influenced by the Olmecs, became the dominant cultural force in Mesoamerica from about 400 BC. ▷ 1.28

OLYMPIA
Site of the OLYMPIC GAMES, Olympia is situated in the fertile Alpheus valley, in the north west Peloponnese. The site was an important PAN-HELLENIC sanctuary to the god Zeus, whose festivals came to be dominated by the famous games. The temple to Zeus, dating from the mid-5th century BC, contains fine classical sculptures. ▷ 1.24

OLYMPIC GAMES
Games held at OLYMPIA every four years between 776 BC and AD 393, at which aristocratic athletes from throughout the Greek world would compete in a range of events, including athletics, wrestling and chariot racing. The prizes were modest, but the honor of winning was great. ▷ 1.24

OMO
Region at the north end of Lake Turkana in Ethiopia, with ancient lake and river sediments dating from about 4 million ya, rich in early hominid fossil remains (australopithecines and HOMO ERECTUS) and tool industries (early pebble tools). Perhaps most significant is the discovery made there of the earliest fossils – about 135,000 years old – of HOMO SAPIENS SAPIENS. ▷ 1.01, 1.02

OPIS, BATTLE OF
Defeat of the last king of BABYLONIA, NABONIDUS, by CYRUS the Great in 539 BC, removing the last serious threat to the early ACHEMENID EMPIRE. ▷ 1.15

ORACLE BONES
Animal bones, especially ox scapulae and turtle shells, with engraved or painted inscriptions (pictographs), that were used for divination in China during the LONGSHAN and SHANG periods (from c.2500 BC). Cracks in the bone caused by applying heat were interpreted according to their patterns and relation to inscriptions (China's first written script). ▷ 1.27

ORACLE, GREEK
Both city-states and individuals used oracles as a means of divining the future or receiving advice on matters as diverse as marriage, overseas settlement or whether to go to war. The most celebrated oracle was at DELPHI, where answers were given by a priestess who entered a trance to consult the god Apollo. ▷ 1.24

ORKNEY, NEOLITHIC
Group of islands off the north coast of Britain with important NEOLITHIC remains dating from about 3500 to 2000 BC. These include the well-preserved SKARA BRAE settlement, the MAES HOWE PASSAGE GRAVE, and many other MEGALITHIC sites (e.g. the Ring of Brodgar and Stenness STONE CIRCLES). This concentration of monuments offers an unusually detailed view of Neolithic settlement, social organization and ritual practices. ▷ 1.20

OSCANS
Proto-historic inhabitants of southern Italy who are difficult to identify with historically documented groups. The language of the same name – Oscan – was spoken by various Italian groups (notably the SAMNITES, Frentani, Lucani, Bruttii and Apuli). Oscan is an INDO-EUROPEAN Italic language that was widely used until the 1st century BC; it then survived in some local dialects into the imperial period. Many Oscan inscriptions survive, most dating from 300 to 90 BC. ▷ 1.25

PAINTED WARE CULTURES
Earliest farming cultures of Anatolia and the Balkans (c.7000–6000 BC), where native populations adopted Near Eastern domesticates, ceramic technologies and similar social institutions, with village communities, mud-brick houses and long-lived TELL settlement sites. These cultures produced distinctive styles of painted pottery. ▷ 1.20

PALEOINDIANS
Earliest human populations in the Americas, the descendents of HUNTER-GATHERER bands who colonized the New World from at least 15,000 ya, crossing the Bering Straits land-bridge from Siberia. The first "Lower Lithic" cultures remain elusive. The best-known Paleoindian cultures are the CLOVIS-FOLSOM big-game hunters of North America. ▷ 1.02

PALEOLITHIC
The first phase of the STONE AGE of the THREE AGE SYSTEM and the earliest period of human toolmaking. The Paleolithic is itself divided into three stages – the LOWER PALEOLITHIC, MIDDLE PALEOLITHIC and UPPER PALEOLITHIC, each with distinctive stone technologies and tool-kits, and each associated with different human species and different forms of human subsistence and social organization. ▷ 1.01, 1.02, 1.19

PALEOLITHIC, LOWER
Tool industries of the early human species HOMO HABILIS and HOMO ERECTUS, dating from about 2.4 million to 230,000 ya. The earliest pebble tool industries, such as the OLDOWAN, were largely replaced by hand-ax industries, such as the ACHEULIAN. These tools were used mainly for scavenging and food processing, rather than hunting. ▷ 1.01

PALEOLITHIC, MIDDLE
Tool industries of the archaic HOMO SAPIENS and regional variants, such as the NEANDERTHALS in west Eurasia (associated with the MOUSTERIAN industry), characterized by an emphasis on the use of flake tools for a more flexible adaptation to local resources and specialized tasks, including the use of spears for hunting. ▷ 1.01, 1.02, 1.19

PALEOLITHIC, UPPER
Tool industries of HOMO SAPIENS SAPIENS that were based on blade technologies and

composite tools developed in Africa from about 70,000 ya and used by humans throughout the world by 12,000 ya. These technologies produced lightweight task-specific tools, and allowed for creative innovation, enabling modern humans to be highly adaptable in exploiting new regions in the course of global colonization. ▷ 1.19

PAN-HELLENIC FESTIVALS
Festivals that drew Greeks from their settlements throughout the Mediterranean and helped to maintain a sense of common Greek identity. Most centered on competitive games (OLYMPIA, DELPHI, Nemea) and were independent of any city-state (POLIS). Others, such as the Panathenaea in Athens, were unashamedly propagandist events for a particular city. ▷ 1.24

PARTHIA
Satrapy of the ACHEMENID EMPIRE located to the southeast of the Caspian Sea, that sent camels and vessels as tribute to the Persian emperor. After the fall of the Achemenid empire, Parthia was settled by the nomadic Parni from the east Caspian steppe region. Their ruling Arsacid dynasty became vassals of the Seleucid kingdom until Arsaces I established Parthia as an independent kingdom in 238 BC. Mithridates I (r.170–138 BC) turned Parthia into a major power by conquering Persia and MESOPOTAMIA. In the 1st century BC, Parthia came under attack by the Roman empire. Despite a crushing victory over the Romans at Carrhae (53 BC), a long series of debilitating wars followed, leading ultimately to the fall of the Arsacid dynasty and the takeover of the Parthian empire by the Persian Sasanian dynasty in AD 224–26. Under the Arsacids Parthia developed as a decentralized feudalistic state. ▷ 1.15

PASARGADAE
The first capital of the ACHEMENID EMPIRE, founded by CYRUS the Great in about 540 BC, near the site of his victory over the MEDES. The extensive un-walled city had splendid palaces, a royal park, monumental buildings and a great citadel, and was the site of Cyrus' tomb. PERSEPOLIS, linked to Pasargadae by a rock-cut avenue, replaced it as the capital in 522 BC. ▷ 1.15

PASSAGE GRAVE
Type of MEGALITHIC MONUMENT of the European NEOLITHIC, constructed in about 4500–2500 BC, that consists of a passage leading to a chamber beneath an earthen or stone mound, usually circular. These were tombs for the collective burial of the dead of a descent group or community. Many have stone carvings, and in some cases the passages were oriented on celestial events. Notable examples of passage graves include GAVRINIS, NEWGRANGE and MAES HOWE. ▷ 1.20

PASTORALISM
A specialized form of farming based on the intensive exploitation of domestic animal herds for meat, leather, fur and secondary products, such as milk and WOOL. Fully nomadic pastoralism developed in the steppe regions of Eurasia from about 2000 BC, when HORSE DOMESTICATION allowed for the increased mobility of herding communities. ▷ 1.03, 1.04, 1.05, 1.06, 1.16

PEISISTRATUS
TYRANT who seized power briefly in Athens in the 560s BC, and then permanently from 546 to 527 BC. He was a relatively benign ruler who presided over Athens at a time of increasing prosperity. He appears to have built temples and may have instituted the great Panathenaic festival. ▷ 1.24

PERSEPOLIS
The royal capital of the ACHEMENID EMPIRE, founded by DARIUS I in 522 BC in a remote mountain region of central Persia, with magnificent palaces and the tombs of the Achemenid kings. It had no significant admininstrative role, as the empire was ruled mainly from SUSA and BABYLON. Persepolis was sacked by Alexander the Great in 330 BC. ▷ 1.15

PHAISTOS
MINOAN palace site on the south coast of CRETE, important from 2000 BC until it was destroyed with the other Minoan palaces in about 1450 BC. It is famous for the Phaistos disk, whose circular inscription – though Minoan in form – is unique and as yet undecipherable. ▷ 1.22

PHARAOHS
The word comes from *per-aa* ("the great house") and was first used in about 1400 BC, but has come to be used generally for the kings of ancient Egypt. ▷ 1.18

PHILISTINES
One of the SEA PEOPLES who settled on the Levantine coast, expelling the CANAANITES. By 1150 BC they had established a confederacy of city-states (Ashkelon, Gaza, Ashdod, Gath and Ekron). The Philistines were conquered by ISRAEL in about 1000 BC but soon regained their independence. From about 650 BC they were vassals of the Assyrians, Egyptians and Babylonians. ▷ 1.12, 1.13, 1.14

PHOENICIA, PHOENICIANS
A general name for the territory and inhabitants of the ancient city-states of the Levantine coast, including ARVAD, Berytus, SIDON and TYRE. The name is probably derived from the purple dye they produced. The Phoenicians were a Semitic-speaking peoples related to the CANAANITES. They were expert sailors and enterprising traders who, from the 10th to the 5th centuries BC, were heavily involved in Mediterranean trade and colonization. They had a considerable cultural influence on the Greeks, to whom they gave the alphabet, and on the native peoples of southern Spain, including the Tartessians. Conquered by Persia in the 530s BC, the Phoenicians provided the bulk of the Persian fleet in their wars with the Greeks. After the Persian conquest, the Phoenician settlements in the western Mediterranean became independent under the leadership of Carthage. ▷ 1.13, 1.14, 1.15, 1.23, 1.24, 1.25

PHOENICIAN ALPHABET
The earliest alphabet, based on single signs for the 20 or so consonants, was developed by the CANAANITES in the ancient Near East in about 1600 BC. The PHOENICIANS adapted this between 1300 and 1000 BC, and passed it on to the Greeks in the 8th century BC. ▷ 1.07

PHRYGIA, PHRYGIANS
Central area of western Asia Minor whose native rulers included MITAS. Absorbed into LYDIA, it became part of the ACHEMENID EMPIRE in 545 BC, then fell under Greek and finally Roman influence. The area was divided between the provinces of Asia and Galatia. ▷ 1.12, 1.13, 1.22, 1.23

PIG
Animal that was domesticated independently in the Middle East (by c.6500 BC), Europe (from the wild boar) and East Asia (by c.5000 BC). They were exploited mainly for meat and fat. Modern pig breeds derive from a native southeast Asian species. ▷ 1.03, 1.08, 1.09, 1.20, 1.27

PLEISTOCENE EPOCH
Geo-climatic period following the PLIOCENE. Dating from about 1.6 million ya, it is marked by global temperature oscillations, general cooling and a series of cold glacial phases (ICE AGES). It is arguable whether the present post-Glacial era (from 12,000 ya), termed the Holocene, is a new climatic epoch or simply a warm phase of the Pleistocene. ▷ 1.01, 1.02

PLIOCENE EPOCH
Geo-climatic period following the MIOCENE, dating from about 5 to 1.6 million ya. It is marked by global cooling, numerous extinctions, and the evolution of large mammals (e.g. mastodons) and advanced hominids, such as the australopithecines and earliest humans. ▷ 1.01

PLOW
Agricultural tool used for breaking the soil surface to allow for planting, dragged by oxen, horses or men. The earliest plows, with simple chisel-like blades, were known as ards and were invented in the Middle East by 4500 BC, replacing hoes. Ards usually needed cross-plowing to be effective and were most suited to light soils. Heavy plows for clay soils were invented in Europe in the 1st millennium BC. ▷ 1.03, 1.09, 1.20, 1.21

POLIS

Greek city-state typically centered on a city, complete with temples and other public buildings, that was supported by its surrounding territory. There were many hundreds of city-states scattered throughout the Mediterranean. A high degree of political and social involvement was normally demanded of the citizens of a *polis*. ▷ 1.24

POTATO

Plant with edible tubers that was domesticated in the central Andes of South America by about 1000 BC. It was a staple food throughout the Andean region in the 1st millennium AD. ▷ 1.03, 1.28

POVERTY POINT CULTURE

Complex HUNTER-GATHERER culture of the lower Mississippi valley, North America, from about 1500 to 700 BC. It is named after the site of a ceremonial center with an impressive earthwork enclosure and platform mounds at Poverty Point, Louisiana, possibly influenced by Mesoamerican structures. Little is known about Poverty Point society or economy. ▷ 1.05

PRECERAMIC PERIOD

Period of ANDEAN CIVILIZATION, dating from about 3750 to 2000 BC. It is marked by the development of sedentary settlement and an increasing reliance on farming, the domestication of alpacas and LLAMAS, the continued exploitation of marine resources on the coast and gathered foods and hunting in highland areas, and the earliest construction of monumental architecture at ceremonial centers such as ASPERO. ▷ 1.28

PREDYNASTIC PERIOD

A period of 2,500 years of Egyptian history, between the beginning of farming in the Nile valley and the emergence of the first dynasties (c.2920 BC). Marked by increasingly sophisticated settlements, craftsmanship and religious beliefs, and by an increasingly hierarchical society, the Predynastic period saw the establishment of the main features of EGYPTIAN CIVILIZATION. ▷ 1.17

PTERIA

Site of a defeat of the Lydians by CYRUS the Great in 547 BC. It became a major settlement on the royal road from the ACHEMENID capital at SUSA to SARDIS, the capital of the satrapy of LYDIA, but its exact location is uncertain. Pteria may have been on the site of the former HITTITE capital, HATTUSAS. ▷ 1.15

PYLOS

MYCENAEAN palace site in MESSENIA (southwestern Peloponnese) and, according to Homeric legend, the stronghold of Nestor. Discovered LINEAR B tablets have provided important evidence of Mycenaean society and details of the last days of the palace before its destruction in about 1200 BC. ▷1.22

PYRAMID

A royal burial monument whose four triangular sides slope upwards to a sharp point. True pyramids developed from the earlier so-called STEP PYRAMIDS in OLD KINGDOM Egypt; by the 4th Dynasty, at Giza, they had reached a gargantuan size. Designed to house the bodies of the dead PHARAOHS, pyramids were always part of a much larger burial complex, including mortuary temples in which deceased rulers could be worshipped as gods. Pyramid building ceased at the end of the MIDDLE KINGDOM period. ▷ 1.17

QADESH

Battle between the PHARAOH RAMESSES II and the HITTITES (c.1285 BC), that took place at the town of Qadesh, central Syria, when the Hittites reacted to Ramesses' intrusion into Syria. The first documented battle in history, it was claimed as a victory by Ramesses, though Hittite sources suggest that it was a stalemate, or even defeat, from which Ramesses retreated. ▷ 1.12, 1.18

QAFZEH

MIDDLE to UPPER PALEOLITHIC cave site in ISRAEL with occupation layers containing MOUSTERIAN tools and animal bones. Most important are the skeletal remains of HOMO SAPIENS SAPIENS, dating from about 90,000 ya, suggesting the rapid spread of anatomically modern humans from Africa into Eurasia. ▷ 1.02

QI

A major feudal state of the ZHOU kingdom in northeast China from about 1100 to 250 BC, with a capital at Linzi. It grew in power during the SPRINGS AND AUTUMNS PERIOD and briefly became the leading state (hegemon) in the mid-7th century BC, under Duke Huan and his minister Guan Zhong. Its dominance waned due to internal strife and war with Song. ▷ 1.27

QIN

Feudal state in northwest China and the heartland of the ZHOU kingdom from about 1100 to 770 BC. Its capital was at HAO until barbarian attacks led to the transfer of the capital to LUOYANG. Its power waned during the SPRINGS AND AUTUMNS PERIOD and its revival as a leading power during the WARRING STATES PERIOD (c.480–202 BC) was largely due to the reforms of the 4th century prime minister, Shang Yang. These turned Qin into a centralized, militaristic state and ultimately led to Qin supremacy (from 250 BC) and the unification of China in 221 BC by its king, Zheng (Shi Huangdi). The Qin dynasty was soon overthrown by the Han, who took over the empire in 202 BC. ▷ 1.27

QUATERNARY PERIOD

Geological era following the Tertiary period, from about 1.6 million ya to the present day, that is represented by glacial and inter-glacial sediments and geomorphological features formed under PLEISTOCENE and Holocene environmental conditions. ▷ 1.01

RAMESSES II (THE GREAT)

Egyptian PHARAOH (r.c.1290–1224 BC). A man of immense ambition, he began his reign with a campaign into Syria that was checked by the HITTITES at QADESH. A subsequent peace treaty stabilized relations and allowed Ramesses to concentrate on a massive building program in Egypt, which included the temples at ABU SIMBEL in NUBIA. The last of the great pharaohs, his mummified remains have survived. ▷ 1.12, 1.18

REHOBOAM

King of ISRAEL (r.928–911 BC) and the son of SOLOMON. Rehoboam became increasingly unpopular and dealt harshly with dissent. Unable to suppress rebellion in the north, he was left in control of JUDAH and the capital, JERUSALEM. Jeroboam became king of Israel, inaugurating a period of dynastic instability. ▷ 1.14

RHODES

Island off the southwestern tip of Asia Minor. Its position made it a center for trade and the ambitions of its neighbors from Minoan times. Its greatest prosperity and proudest period of independence came in Hellenistic times, when it financed the Colossus of Rhodes, a vast statue astride its harbor entrance. Eventually outwitted by Roman diplomacy, the island was absorbed into the Roman empire in the 1st century BC. ▷ 1.22

RICE

Cereal plant (*Orzya sativa*) producing edible starchy grains, collected intensively by HUNTER-GATHERERS in China and southeast Asia. It was domesticated from about 7000 BC, with widespread wet-rice farming in the lower Yangtze region by about 5000 BC. Rice was the staple crop throughout east Asia by the 2nd millennium BC, and in eastern India by about 1000 BC. ▷ 1.03, 1.16, 1.26, 1.27

ROME (ANCIENT CITY)

From modest beginnings in the 10th century BC, Rome became the largest city of the ancient world and the center of the Roman empire. Tradition records a series of kings of

KINGS OF ROME	
Romulus (legendary)	
Numa Pompilius	c.715–673 BC
Tullus Hostilius	c.673–642
Ancus Martius	c.642–617
Tarquin I	c.616–579
Servius Tullius	c.578–535
Tarquin the Proud	c.535–509

Rome until 509 BC when the Roman republic was established.

Relatively little is known archeologically about the city in the regal and earlier republican periods; the extensive remains now visible mainly date to the later republic and empire. The city was embellished by the great patrician families and emperors, with major civic building projects such as forums, temples, theaters and circuses. As Rome's population grew, so did its infrastructure of roads, aqueducts and warehouses. Rome's political importance declined in the 3rd century AD as it was abandoned by the emperors for centers closer to the embattled frontiers. Following the fall of the western Roman empire in the 5th century, Rome's population declined dramatically, but the city retained importance as the leading Christian center in western Europe. ▷ 1.25

SABA

Ancient kingdom of southwest Arabia, known in biblical references as Sheba. Saba was founded by Semitic Sabaeans of the north from about 1200 BC. By the 7th to 5th centuries BC, it was a centralized state with IRRIGATION agriculture, monumental temples, and control over the Red Sea–Indian Ocean trade routes. ▷ 1.05, 1.06

SABEAN SCRIPT AND LANGUAGE

A writing system ultimately based on the proto-CANAANITE phonetic alphabet that was adapted by the Semitic-speaking Sabean people of southwest Arabia from about 1000 BC and used for record-keeping and monument inscriptions. ▷ 1.07

SABINES

A people of ancient Italy occupying the area northeast of ROME, along the west side of the Tiber valley. The Sabines figure largely in the legends of early Rome, though archeological data is scanty. Some recent excavations, however, reveal material culture similarities with LATIUM in the IRON AGE. The Sabines were finally defeated by Rome in 290 BC and were granted full citizenship in 268 BC. ▷ 1.25

SAKAS

INDO-IRANIAN pastoral nomad people of the central Asian steppes who raided the northeastern satrapies of the ACHEMENID EMPIRE in the late 6th and 5th centuries BC. CYRUS the Great built a chain of forts to defend the frontier against the Sakas and was killed fighting them in 530 BC. ▷ 1.06, 1.15

SAMARIA

A city in central Palestine that was founded by King Omri in about 880 BC as the new capital of ISRAEL. Some of Samaria's buildings of the 9th century BC have PHOENICIAN features. The city was destroyed by Shalmaneser V of ASSYRIA in 724 BC, after a three-year siege. ▷ 1.14

SAMARRAN CULTURE

Late NEOLITHIC culture of central MESOPOTAMIA, characterized by painted pottery styles with animal and human figures. Dating from about 6000 to 5500 BC, it follows the HASSUNA CULTURE and marks the extension of agricultural societies southwards. Samarran communities lived in large villages and developed large-scale IRRIGATION systems (at CHOGA MAMI), increasing crop yields and allowing for settlement of the Mesopotamian plains. ▷ 1.09

SAMNITES

A warlike OSCAN-speaking people of ancient Italy in the central-south Apennines, divided into a powerful confederation of the Caraceni, Caudini, Hirpini and Pentri tribes. Even after losing the Samnite wars, they supported Pyrrhus and Hannibal against ROME, fought in the Social War and against Sulla in the civil war. Latin colonies were established at Beneventum (268 BC) and Aesernia (263 BC), but Romanization was relatively slow. ▷ 1.25

SAN LORENZO

Earliest OLMEC ceremonial center, situated on a plateau beside the fertile Coatzacoalcos river plain. The main phase of building (c.1200–900 BC) involved construction work to raise the surface of the natural plateau, huge lateral ridges for access, mounds for timber houses (for an elite community of about 1,000 people), temple mounds, altars with stone carvings, and massive sculpted stone heads (portraits of Olmec kings or gods). It was destroyed in about 900 BC, when many sculptures were deliberately broken and buried. ▷ 1.28

SANXINGDUI

City occupied in the 2nd millennium BC, contemporary with the SHANG dynasty, that was recently discovered in central China. Found bronze objects indicate a high degree of technical sophistication and cultural complexity. The relationship between Sanxingdui and Shang China is uncertain. ▷ 1.27

SAQQARA

Important Egyptian site, close to MEMPHIS, and the burial place of many of Egypt's early kings, including NARMER. The most impressive monument is the STEP PYRAMID (c.2630 BC) built for the PHARAOH DJOSER. After THEBES became the focus for royal burials, Saqqara continued to be used for the burials of Memphis officials. ▷ 1.04, 1.17

SARDIS

Capital of the LYDIAN kingdom of western Anatolia from the 7th to 6th centuries BC, with a large citadel and the earliest known coin mint. It was captured, along with King CROESUS, by CYRUS the Great in 546 BC, and became the capital of a satrapy of the ACHEMENID EMPIRE. ▷ 1.15

SARGON OF AGADE (THE GREAT)

Akkadian king of KISH who founded the first imperial state (c.2334–2279 BC), ruling AKKAD and SUMERIA, north MESOPOTAMIA, the north LEVANT and ELAM. He controlled the maritime trade routes to the Persian Gulf, the Indus and the east Mediterranean, and the land routes to central Anatolia and Iran. He founded the city of Agade as a capital for his empire, but its location has not been discovered. His empire lasted for a century and reached its greatest extent under his grandson, NARAM-SIN, before it disintegrated in the early 22nd century BC. Sargon was a model for later Mesopotamian rulers and his life became the subject of many legends. ▷ 1.10, 1.11

SARGON II

King of ASSYRIA (r.721–705 BC), probably the son of TIGLATH-PILESER III, named after SARGON OF AGADE. Sargon II consolidated the conquests of his father, expanded Assyrian rule in URARTU (714 BC) and conquered south MESOPOTAMIA (710–07 BC). The Assyrian empire reached its greatest power and influence under his reign. He was probably killed in battle in Anatolia in 705 BC. ▷ 1.13

SARMATIANS

INDO-IRANIAN pastoral nomad people of the central Eurasian steppes who were closely related to the SCYTHIANS. The Sarmatians migrated into the Ural region in the 5th century BC, before conquering the Scythians and settling in the Ukraine and Balkans in the 4th–2nd centuries BC. ▷ 1.06

SAUL

First king of ISRAEL (r.c.1020–c.1006 BC), proclaimed ruler by the judge Samuel to unify the Israelites against the PHILISTINES and AMALEKITES. He was killed by the Philistines at the Battle of Gilboa. ▷ 1.14

SCYTHIANS

INDO-IRANIAN pastoral nomads of central Asia who migrated westwards and southwards in the 8th–7th centuries BC, displacing the CIMMERIANS and settling in the Ukraine (Royal Scythians) and the Caspian region (Pointed Hat Scythians). They are famous for their warlike character and rich tradition of metalworking, examples of which have been found in ROUND BARROW tombs. They were later absorbed by local populations or dispersed by further nomad invaders, such as the SARMATIANS, in the 4th–2nd centuries BC. ▷ 1.06, 1.15, 1.23

SEA PEOPLES

Groups of migrants of uncertain origin, who may have included elements from Libya, the northern Aegean, Asia Minor and even Sardinia. They raided widely around the eastern Mediterranean, as far south as Egypt, in about 1200 BC. Relatively little is known about them, though the HITTITE empire and the MYCENAEAN CIVILIZATION may have disintegrated as a result of their attacks. The Egyptians drove them off the Delta in 1180 BC, though one group, the Peleset (PHILISTINES) settled in Palestine, which is named after them. ▷ 1.12, 1.18, 1.22

SEMITES
Speakers of the Semitic languages, which originated in Arabia and western MESOPOTAMIA, and spread as the Semitic peoples migrated and conquered neighboring regions (3rd–1st millennia BC), either replacing existing populations or establishing ruling elites that imposed their own languages. These peoples include the Akkadians, AMORITES, CANAANITES, HEBREWS, ARAMAEANS, CHALDEANS, PHOENICIANS, Sabaeans and Arabs. ▷ 1.04, 1.05, 1.06, 1.07, 1.11, 1.12, 1.13, 1.14, 1.15

SENNACHERIB
King of ASSYRIA (r.704–681 BC) who maintained Assyrian dominance, though threatened by local or CHALDEAN and Elamite-inspired rebellions in BABYLONIA. He suppressed a revolt in Palestine (701 BC), and undertook six campaigns in Babylonia and ELAM, eventually destroying BABYLON in 689 BC. He moved the Assyrian capital to NINEVEH. ▷ 1.13, 1.14

SHALMANESER III
King of ASSYRIA (r.858–824 BC) who attempted, with varying success, to extend Assyrian dominion over the LEVANT and elsewhere. He was resisted at Qarqar in 854 BC by a coalition of Levantine states, including ISRAEL. The Assyrian empire entered a period of instability after his death. ▷ 1.13

SHAMSHI-ADAD
AMORITE king of SHUBAT-ENLIL (r.1813–1781 BC) who siezed control of ASHUR in about 1813 BC and established the first major territorial state in north MESOPOTAMIA. The kingdom declined thereafter and was under BABYLONIAN control by 1750 BC. ▷ 1.11

SHANG CIVILIZATION
The first state-organized urban culture of China, known from both historical and archeological sources, that was ruled by the Shang dynasty from their heartland in the Yellow river region. The semi-mythical founder of the dynasty, King Tang, is said to have deposed the last of the morally corrupt XIA kings in 1766 BC, though archeological evidence suggests a more gradual centralization from the 19th to 17th centuries BC.

A notable feature of Shang culture is their magnificent bronze work, using unique piece-mould casting processes to produce highly decorated ceremonial vessels and weaponry. A pictographic script, initally written on ORACLE BONES for divination purposes, was adapted for secular use, such

as inscriptions on bronze vessels. Shang cities such as ANYANG were built of rammed earth and timber, with massive ramparts, monumental buildings and large populations. Evidence from inscriptions, later histories and royal burials (accompanied by bronze and jade artifacts and human sacrifices) suggest that Shang society had a clan structure, with a strict social hierarchy and a warrior aristocracy engaged in constant warfare. Shang China became increasingly centralized, bureaucratic (with standard systems of measurement) and expansive. The last king of the Shang, DI-XIN, was overthrown by the ZHOU DYNASTY in 1122 BC. ▷ 1.05, 1.07, 1.27

SHANIDAR
MIDDLE and UPPER PALEOLITHIC cave site in the Zagros mountains, modern Iraq, with important MOUSTERIAN occupation levels. The site contains Neanderthal burials (including a disabled individual who must have been cared for by his companions). ▷ 1.01

SHEEP
Several species of sheep were domesticated in prehistory, the most important being *Ovis orientalis* in the Zagros mountains (by c.9000 BC) and *Ovis vignei* in central Asia (by c.4000 BC). It is possible that other species, such as the European *Ovis musimon*, were also domesticated. Sheep were important sources of meat in NEOLITHIC economies, and later became important for textile manufacture (WOOL). ▷ 1.03, 1.08, 1.09, 1.20, 1.21, 1.22

SHORTHUGAI
An INDUS CIVILIZATION settlement to the north of the Hindu Kush, near the Oxus (Amu Darya) river in north Afghanistan, 500 kilometers (310 miles) from the nearest Indus towns. It was probably a trading colony, founded by 2000 BC, for importing lapis lazuli and other raw materials. ▷ 1.26

SHOSHENQ I
Egyptian PHARAOH (r.945–924 BC) of Libyan extraction, who temporarily regained control of Palestine after a period of Egyptian weakness and withdrawal. ▷ 1.14, 1.18

SHUBAT-ENLIL
City in north MESOPOTAMIA that was founded as a new capital by King SHAMSHI-ADAD of ASSYRIA in about 1800 BC, on the site of an earlier city that had been abandoned in about 2200 BC. The city declined after his death and was destroyed by the Babylonians in about 1726 BC. ▷ 1.11

SICULI (SICELS)
The name given by the Greeks to the indigenous peoples of east Sicily in the later 8th century BC. It has not been possible to distinguish them archeologically from the other local groups, such as the Elymi. ▷ 1.25

SIDON
City on the Levantine coast that was founded in the 3rd millennium BC. Sidon was one of the most important PHOENICIAN city-states from about 1000 BC and became the most prosperous of the coastal cities after the annexation of the region by the Persian empire in about 530 BC. ▷ 1.14

SILBURY HILL
The largest prehistoric mound in Europe, situated in the AVEBURY late NEOLITHIC monument complex in the Kennet valley, England. It was built in three phases in the mid-3rd millennium BC for ceremonial purposes, and was sited so that only the top could be seen from contemporary monuments nearby, though its specific function is unknown. ▷ 1.20

SIWA
Remote oasis site in the desert west of Egypt, known for its oracle to Amun. An expedition under the Persian king CAMBYSES failed to reach it, but Alexander the Great succeeded in getting there, believing that the priests had saluted him as the son of Amun and thus the true PHARAOH. ▷ 1.15

SKARA BRAE
NEOLITHIC farming and fishing village on the coast of the largest of the ORKNEY Islands, northern Britain, inhabited in the 3rd millennium BC. The small nucleated group of stone-built houses linked by paved alleys, with central hearths and stone cupboards, were unusually well-preserved under wind-blown sand and occupation debris. ▷ 1.20

SKUDRA
Region of the southern Balkans (Thrace) on the north side of the Aegean, that was established as the only satrapy of the ACHEMENID EMPIRE on the mainland of Europe after the invasion by DARIUS I in 538 BC. It sent horses and weapons as tribute to the Persian emperor. ▷ 1.15

SLAVERY (ANCIENT WORLD)
Slavery, the ownership of one individual by another, was known throughout the ancient world, but Greece and ROME in particular depended heavily on slave labor. In Greece the subjection of the slave served to emphasize the freedom of the citizen. Slaves were used as domestic servants, on farms, in manufacturing and in mines, and their treatment ranged from the benign to the brutal. In Rome slaves were often seized as the fruits of victories, though a flourishing slave trade was also in existence. By contrast with Greece, in Rome slaves could be given their freedom, and many "freedmen" prospered as a result. Slavery was as prevalent in late antiquity as it had been in earlier times, and the coming of Christianity had no impact on the institution. ▷ 1.10, 1.22, 1.24

SMERDIS
Known as Bardiya in Persian sources and as Smerdis in Greek ones, he was the brother of CAMBYSES, king of Persia. Smerdis was involved in the mysterious events surrounding the death of CAMBYSES in 522 BC and the accession of DARIUS, perhaps as the murderer of Cambyses. Many scholars now believe that Darius murdered him in order to seize the throne himself. ▷ 1.15

SNOFRU
The first PHARAOH of the 4th Dynasty (r.2575–2551 BC) who played a crucial role in the development of the PYRAMID by filling in the space between the steps of a STEP PYRAMID, with the intention of creating the first true pyramid. In order to maintain stability, however, the angle of the sides of the pyramid had to be reduced when it was half built. The result was the unique "bent pyramid". Later pyramid builders were more successful. ▷ 1.17

SOGDIANA
Satrapy of the ACHEMENID EMPIRE in central Asia, to the east of the Aral Sea in modern Uzbekistan, conquered by CYRUS the Great in about 546–39 BC. The province sent horses, weapons and jewelry as tribute to the Persian emperor. ▷ 1.15

SOLOMON
King of ISRAEL (r.c.965–928 BC) and the son of DAVID. Solomon extended his empire through marriage alliances and military campaigns. His control of the trade routes between MESOPOTAMIA, the LEVANT, the Red Sea and Egypt allowed him to amass enormous wealth, which was spent on fortress building and public works such as the Great Temple at JERUSALEM. He reorganized the state administration, but his extravagance and exactions made him unpopular. ▷ 1.14

SOLON
Athenian politician who was awarded the task in 594–593 BC of asserting city authority over the powerful aristocratic families of ATTICA. His stated aim was to bring "good order". He curbed privilege based solely on birth and introduced a comprehensive code of law to which all citizens were equally subject. His reforms were threatened by the TYRANT PEISISTRATUS, but survived to be extended by KLEISTHENES. ▷ 1.24

SOLUTREAN CULTURE
European UPPER PALEOLITHIC tool industry dating from about 23,000–17,000 ya, following the GRAVETTIAN CULTURE. Solutrean toolmakers developed pressure-flaking techniques for the production of exceptionally fine bifacially-worked stone implements, notably leaf-shaped projectile points. They lived in a cold glacial phase, hunting large herd animals such as bison. ▷ 1.19

SORGHUM
Cereal plant with edible starchy seeds that was domesticated in southern Sudan by about 4000 BC. It was widely adopted throughout sub-Saharan Africa by about 1000 BC, as a reliable drought-resistant staple food crop, along with MILLET. ▷ 1.16

SPARTA
Important Greek city-state of the southern Peloponnese. Sparta's power rested on its highly trained HOPLITE forces and on the exploitation of the neighboring plain of MESSENIA. By the end of the 6th century BC, it was the dominant power in the Peloponnese and in 431 BC challenged Athens in the so-called Peloponnesian War. Gaining Persian support, Sparta won (404 BC), but its declining manpower and clumsy diplomacy meant the loss of its advantages. Defeated at Leuctra by Thebes in 371 BC, Sparta never recovered its power. Its rigid institutions and brutal training methods, including the state-supervised upbringing of all male children, were unique in the Greek world. ▷ 1.24

SPHINX, GREAT
Huge ancient Egyptian statue of a seated lion figure with a human head, carved from natural limestone, near the PYRAMID of KHEPHREN at Giza. The lion was traditionally seen as a guardian of the gates to the Underworld, which may explain its use here. The head is probably that of Khephren himself. ▷ 1.17

SPRINGS AND AUTUMNS PERIOD
Phase of the later (Eastern) ZHOU period in China from about 770 to 480 BC, named after the annals of the LU state. The decline of Zhou authority after the transfer of their capital to LUOYANG in 770 BC led to political fragmentation as rival states (dukedoms) within the kingdom struggled for power, some rapidly rising to hegemonic dominance but none sustaining that position (hence "Springs" and "Autumns"). The main hegemons were Zheng (late 8th century BC), QI (early 7th century BC), JIN (late 7th century BC and mid-6th century BC) and CHU (late 7th to early 6th centuries BC). The emergence of seven equally aggressive kingdoms from about 500 BC marked the beginning of the WARRING STATES period. ▷ 1.06, 1.27

SQUASH
Fruit of the gourd plant family, several species of which were domesticated in lowland areas of Central and South America by 3000 BC, becoming an important food crop in coastal Peru by 2500 BC (ASPERO TRADITION). ▷ 1.03, 1.28

STARCEVO
Early NEOLITHIC settlement beside the Danube in Serbia, occupied in about 6000–4000 BC. The site has given its name to the first Neolithic period in the central Balkans, characterized by TELL settlements, a distinctive pottery style and a mixed agricultural economy. ▷ 1.20

STATE
A form of political organization characterized by "legal-rational" institutions. It involved the codification of rights and obligations of all members of a community within a given territory according to defined social status, ideally implemented impartially according to established law (rather than personal or kin relations). State systems required bureaucracies and writing systems to preserve legal codes and to record precedents, and military institutions to guarantee rights and enforce obligations. Many early states were also theocratic, with elites drawing upon religious doctrines to justify their authority and political decisions. ▷ 1.04, 1.05, 1.06

STEP PYRAMID
A type of Egyptian PYRAMID constructed by raising a number of rectangular layers of stone of decreasing size, one above the other. The step pyramid was first seen at SAQQARA, where the architect Imhotep constructed one over the tomb of the PHARAOH DJOSER (c.2630). The inspiration behind it is believed to be the MASTABAS, an earlier type of Egyptian platform tomb. ▷ 1.17

STONE AGE
A subdivision of the THREE AGE SYSTEM. It was recognized in the 19th century that the idea of a discrete Stone Age is dubious as it subsumes several distinct stages of human biological and cultural evolution. The period was therefore subdivided into three separate periods: the PALEOLITHIC, MESOLITHIC and NEOLITHIC (Old, Middle and New Stone Ages). These terms are still widely used for general descriptive purposes.

STONE CIRCLE
Type of MEGALITHIC MONUMENT, consisting of stones arranged in a circle or ellipse, that is found in many parts of the world but is particularly associated with NEOLITHIC Europe. Stone circles vary greatly in scale, form, location and associations, but all were ceremonial in purpose, some taking account of astronomical alignments in the positioning and arrangement of stones. ▷ 1.20

STONEHENGE
Ceremonial enclosure and MEGALITHIC structure at the center of a concentration of NEOLITHIC and BRONZE AGE monuments on Salisbury Plain in WESSEX, Britain. The site has a long history of construction and use from about 3000 to 1000 BC, with three main building phases representing very different designs. Built in about 2400–2000 BC, the unique sarsen and blue-STONE CIRCLES, with carpentry-influenced design features, are oriented on summer solstice sunrise and winter solstice sunset. ▷ 1.04, 1.20

SUBARTU

Region to the northwest of ASSYRIA that is referred to in southern Mesopotamian texts of the 3rd and early 2nd millennia BC. SHAMSHI-ADAD of Assyria established his short-lived capital, SHUBAT-ENLIL, in Subartu in about 1800 BC, but the region was otherwise of little political or cultural significance in this period. ▷ 1.11, 1.12

SUMER, SUMERIA

The southernmost part of MESOPOTAMIA, and the region in which the first civilization developed in the 5th to 3rd millennia BC. Ubaidian settlers from central Mesopotamia established IRRIGATION systems for intensive farming from about 6000 BC, and introduced brick masonry, pottery and weaving. STATE formation and URBANIZATION in the 4th millennium BC led to the emergence of at least 12 city-states by about 2900 BC, with their own political and religious institutions and distinct cultural traditions. These states competed for regional dominance, the most powerful being KISH, LAGASH, URUK and UR.

Cultural developments in Sumeria during the URUK PERIOD (4300–3100 BC) and EARLY DYNASTIC (c.2900–2334 BC) include writing (Sumerian pictographs), urbanism, state institutions and sophisticated architecture and sculpture. Sumer was united with its northern neighbor, AKKAD, in the 24th century BC, first by LUGALZAGESI of Lagash and then by SARGON OF AGADE, before regaining political pre-eminence under the Third Dynasty of Ur (2112–2004 BC). Sumer merged with Akkad in the 2nd millennium BC (the whole region being known as BABYLONIA), and continued to influence later Middle Eastern civilizations until the Persian conquest in the 6th century BC. ▷ 1.04, 1.05, 1.07, 1.09, 1.10, 1.11

SUPPILULIUMAS

King of the HITTITES (r.1344–1322 BC). He established the Hittite empire as the leading state in the Middle East, conquering the western part of MITTANI and sacking the Mittanian capital, WASHUKANNI (c.1340 BC), fatally weakening the main rival to Hittite expansion. His conquests brought the Hittites into direct conflict with the Egyptians. ▷ 1.12

SUSA

City on the Karkeh river in southwest Iran, with origins in the 6th millennium BC. By 3000 BC it had grown into an urban center similar to those in SUMERIA. It was the capital of ELAM in the 3rd and 2nd millennia BC, with a citadel, palaces and temples, and from 522 BC it became the administrative capital of the ACHEMENID EMPIRE. ▷ 1.09, 1.10, 1.12, 1.13, 1.15

SWANSCOMBE

LOWER PALEOLITHIC site in southeast Britain, with stratified "Clactonian" chopper-tool and ACHEULIAN hand-ax industries, and the fossil remains (c.400,000 ya) of archaic HOMO

SAPIENS with cranial features intermediate between HOMO ERECTUS and HOMO SAPIENS NEANDERTHALENSIS. ▷ 1.01

SWARTKRANS

LOWER PALEOLITHIC cave site in South Africa with a sequence of deposits containing numerous fossil remains of AUSTRALOPITHECUS ROBUSTUS and a smaller number of HOMO HABILIS in higher levels, together with OLDOWAN-style tools. Later evidence of the use of FIRE, dating from about 1.6 million ya, may be related to activity by HOMO ERECTUS. ▷ 1.01

SYRACUSE

With its fine harbor and fertile territory in eastern Sicily, Syracuse was first colonized in 734 BC by the Corinthians and gradually became one of the most prosperous city-states in the ancient Mediterranean. Syracuse was able to hold its own militarily against the ETRUSCANS and – under Dionysius I – the Carthaginians (though with much greater difficulty). Despite immense prosperity in the 3rd century BC, Syracuse was conquered by ROME (212 BC) and became the capital of the Roman province of Sicily. ▷ 1.23, 1.25

TADMOR

City in Syria on a trade route across the Syrian desert from the Euphrates to the LEVANT that was probably a settlement from the 3rd millennium BC. Tadmor was ruled by ARAMAEAN kings from about 1200 BC, though it briefly came under Israelite control in the 10th century BC. It later became known as Palmyra. ▷ 1.11, 1.12, 1.13, 1.14

TARTARIA

NEOLITHIC settlement in Transylvania, Romania, where clay tablets dating to about 5000 BC have been found with incised signs, probably a system of notation. It did not develop into a writing system. ▷ 1.20

TARTESSOS

City on the Atlantic coast of Spain (probably modern Huelva), founded by native Tartessians by about 800 BC, and the capital of a powerful state by about 600 BC. It traded with the PHOENICIANS, who had a port nearby at GADES, exporting silver and other metals in return for pottery and luxury goods from the Mediterranean. The Tartessians were influenced by Phoenician styles of art and adapted their alphabetic script. Tartessos was conquered by the Carthaginians in the 4th century BC. ▷ 1.23, 1.25

TARXIEN

One of the late NEOLITHIC stone temple complexes on the Mediterranean island of Malta. It was built by an indigenous farming culture (c.3500–2400 BC), which originally came from Sicily (by 5000 BC), but developed a distinctive religious tradition. The Maltese

temples share symmetrical designs with lobed inner chambers, altars and monumental statuary. ▷ 1.20

TASSILI

A plateau region of the central Sahara (southern Algeria) where a rich tradition of ROCK ART (paintings and modified rock forms) flourished (c.6000–1000 BC). Representations of humans and animals indicate that the paintings were mainly the work of agriculturalists (primarily pastoralists), when the region was far less dessicated. There is archeological evidence of MILLET cultivation by 6000 BC and CATTLE-herding by 4000 BC. ▷ 1.16

TEHUACÁN

Desert valley of central Mexico, occupied from about 9000 BC, where especially dry conditions have preserved organic materials and artifacts, including evidence of very early agriculture (the cultivation of peppers and SQUASHES by c.6000 BC). The evidence from Tehuacán provides an exceptionally detailed picture of cultural change in the region. ▷ 1.28

TELL

Mound resulting from the long-term accumulation of debris from buildings and domestic refuse from a settlement. They are commonly found in areas where mud brick is used as the main building material, especially the Middle East and parts of southeast Europe. In the Middle East, where settlements have been occupied continuously for thousands of years, tells can be up to 30 meters (100 feet) high. The word comes from Arabic; alternative forms include *chatal* (Turkish) and *tepe* (Persian).

TELL AWAYLI

Settlement in southern SUMERIA that was founded in the early 6th millennium BC (UBAID PERIOD), with a large granary for the communal storage of agricultural produce. Centralized control of the collection, storage, and redistribution of key resources is a common feature of early complex societies and the development of social hierarchies and political institutions. ▷ 1.09

TELL MUREYBAT

NATUFIAN proto-farming settlement in the upper Euphrates valley in modern Syria, occupied from the 9th to the 7th millennia BC, with evidence of the cultivation of introduced wild cereal plants (einkorn WHEAT) in the 9th millennium BC, and the emergence of a fully agricultural pottery-using community by 6000 BC. ▷ 1.08

TEPE GAWRA

A settlement in central MESOPOTAMIA dating from the HALAFIAN period (c.5500 BC). The early temple, built in the UBAID PERIOD, contains the earliest examples of walls decorated with pilasters and recesses (c.5000

BC), a design feature of later Mesopotamian temples. ▷ 1.09

TEPE YAHYA
Settlement in southern Iran occupied from the 5th millennium BC, with evidence of the earliest bronze metallurgy to use arsenic to improve the casting properties of smelted ores (c.3800 BC). In the 3rd millennium BC it was a major center for the manufacture of soapstone vessels and seals. ▷ 1.10

TERRA AMATA
LOWER PALEOLITHIC occupation site found in fossil beach deposits in southern France, dating from about 230,000 ya. Evidence of oval brushwood shelters (potentially the earliest known human structures) is disputed by most archeologists. ▷ 1.01

THEBES (EGYPT)
The Greek name for the southern Egyptian town of Waset. Thebes rose to prominence after its ruling family initiated the MIDDLE KINGDOM and its local god, Amun, became the dominant Egyptian deity. During the NEW KINGDOM period Thebes, the religious capital of Egypt, reached the height of prosperity, with enormous temples to Amun and other gods erected at LUXOR and KARNAK. ▷ 1.18

THERA
Island in the southern Aegean that was the scene of an immense volcanic eruption in about 1626 BC, which some historians believe may have given rise to the Atlantis legend. Its most flourishing town, Akrotiri, has been rediscovered beneath the lava, providing magnificent examples of MINOAN-style frescoes. ▷ 1.22, 1.24

THESSALY
Large region of northeastern Greece, made up of two plains enclosed by mountains, with little access to the sea. For much of its history Thessaly was a federation of states with only the occasional ruler (e.g. Jason, the TYRANT of the 4th century BC) exercising strong central control. The plains were easily subdued by Philip II of Macedon in the 4th century BC. ▷ 1.24, 1.25

THOLOS
A circular building. The term often refers to the vaulted "beehive" tombs of the Mycenaeans that originated in MESSENIA and reached their most sophisticated form at MYCENAE in the 14th century BC (as in the "Treasury of Atreus"). ▷ 1.22

THRACIANS
People of uncertain origin who occupied the southern Balkans between the Aegean and the Danube (Thrace) from the 7th century BC, known from early historical texts (Herodotus) and archeological sources. They were ethnically heterogenous, with a horse-riding elite, possibly drawn from warrior

pastoralists, who migrated into eastern Europe in the early 1st millennium BC. The Thracians developed close trading and cultural links with the Greeks, and had established a STATE system by the 5th century BC. ▷ 1.05, 1.06, 1.12, 1.15, 1.23, 1.24, 1.25

THREE AGE SYSTEM
An evolutionary classification of human culture, based on tool technologies and materials (STONE AGE, BRONZE AGE and IRON AGE), first proposed by the Danish archeologist Christian Thomsen in 1816–19. It is now accepted that the scheme has no analytical value, being applicable in strict terms only to Eurasia and north Africa (with different temporal parameters in different regions). It is considered too crude a means of characterizing the complexity and variety of ancient cultures, and too simplistic as a way of representing cultural change. The terms Bronze Age and Iron Age are sometimes still used for broad descriptive purposes.

TIBETO-BURMESE
HUNTER-GATHERER peoples with closely-related languages who lived in the Himalayan region and who adopted transhumant PASTORALISM from about 1500 BC. They were influenced by contacts with herding communities in India and by the steppe pastoralists of central Asia. ▷ 1.04

TIGLATH-PILESER I
King of ASSYRIA (r.1115–1076 BC). He resisted invasions by HURRIANS and KASKAS of Anatolia, but failed in his attempt to revive Assyrian dominance by controlling ARAMAEAN settlers. The empire declined after his death, and was reduced to control of the region around ASHUR. ▷ 1.12

TIGLATH-PILESER III
King of ASSYRIA (r.744–727 BC) who re-established Assyrian dominance in the Middle East. Once governor of Calah, he deposed Ashur-nirari V and reorganized the empire as a centralized state with a professional army and a provincial administration under direct royal control. He curbed the power of URARTU and imposed Assyrian rule on BABYLONIA and the LEVANT, resettling conquered populations in border areas. ▷ 1.13, 1.14

TIN
Metal used in COPPER-alloy metallurgy, forming about 10 percent of bronze, added to strengthen and harden cast objects. Tin ore sources were of considerable significance in the ancient Old World, and major deposits were exploited in Europe and Asia from the 3rd millennium BC, with large-scale regional trading networks dating from about 2000 BC. ▷ 1.10, 1.21, 1.23, 1.25, 1.26, 1.27

TINGIS
PHOENICIAN trading colony (modern Tangiers) on the Atlantic coast of Africa, to the west of

the Straits of Gibraltar. It was founded in the 7th century BC as a port for west African trade. By about 500 BC, Tingis was the capital of a province of the Carthaginian empire. ▷ 1.23, 1.25

TORRALBA-AMBRONA
Group of LOWER PALEOLITHIC sites in central Spain where ACHEULIAN hand-ax industries dating from about 600,000–200,000 ya have been discovered, along with evidence of elephant butchery, wooden spears and the use of FIRE. ▷ 1.01

TRES ZAPOTES
An important early OLMEC ceremonial center (c.1200 BC) to the west of the Tuxtla mountains (where basalt for monument construction was obtained), near the Gulf coast in central Mexico. It was the last major Olmec center to be occupied after the destruction of LA VENTA in about 400 BC. ▷ 1.28

TRIPOLYE-CUCUTENI CULTURE
Late NEOLITHIC and early Copper Age culture of the west Ukrainian steppes and Carpathian mountains, dating from about 4200–3800 BC. It is characterized by large fortified villages, painted pottery, and COPPER and gold artifacts such as those deposited in the VARNA cemetery. Tripolye-Cucuteni communities were among the first to domesticate HORSES. ▷ 1.20

TROJAN WAR
Legendary war in which a massed force of Greeks attacked TROY after the abduction of Helen of SPARTA by Paris of Troy. The Greeks eventually sacked the city after a ten-year siege. The war was a major theme in epic poetry and forms the background to HOMER'S ILIAD. The legend may rest on actual events of the MYCENAEAN period. ▷ 1.22

TROY
Ancient city on the eastern side of the entrance to the Dardenelles. Its prosperity resulted from the control of sea routes to the Black Sea and east–west land routes. The complex site was occupied, with short interruptions, from 3000 BC until the 9th century AD, and its detailed history has proved difficult to interpret. No clear evidence of a Greek or MYCENAEAN siege has yet been discovered, though the site was destroyed by fire twice in the 13th century, and again in about 1100 BC. ▷ 1.22

TRUNDHOLM
Ancient bog in Zealand, Denmark, where an outstanding example of middle BRONZE AGE metal craftmanship, the "Chariot of the Sun", was deposited in the mid-2nd millennium BC. The composite cast-bronze model, which consists of a horse pulling a vertical disk (gold-plated on one side), mounted on a wheeled carriage, probably had religious significance. ▷ 1.21

TURDETANIANS
People of southern Spain, related to the
Tartessians, who traded with PHOENICIAN and
Greek colonies, and later with Carthaginian
cities on the Mediterranean coast, in about
900–200 BC. They developed an indigenous
sculptural tradition influenced by Greek and
Phoenician art, and by about 500 BC had
established several kingdoms with urban
centers, such as Porcuna. ▷ 1.25

TUTANKHAMUN
Egyptian boy-PHARAOH (r.1333–1323 BC).
Tutankhamun was of little importance historically, but achieved worldwide prominence
when his unplundered tomb was discovered
in the VALLEY OF THE KINGS in 1922. ▷ 1.18

TUTHMOSIS I
Probably the greatest PHARAOH of NEW
KINGDOM Egypt, Tuthmosis I (r.1504–1492
BC) founded the Egyptian empire in the
LEVANT, as well as extending Egyptian
power into NUBIA. He was the first pharaoh
to be buried in the VALLEY OF THE KINGS.
▷ 1.12. 1.18

TUTHMOSIS III
Egyptian PHARAOH (r.1479–1425 BC) of the
NEW KINGDOM period who became sole ruler
in 1458 BC after the death of his domineering
stepmother, HATSHEPSUT. A fine military com-
mander, Tuthmosis III systematically reduced
the cities and kingdoms of Syria and
Palestine, thus consolidating the Egyptian
empire in the Near East. ▷ 1.18

TUTHMOSIS IV
Egyptian PHARAOH (r.1401–1391 BC) of the
NEW KINGDOM period. By marrying his son
to the daughter of the king of the rival Near
Eastern state of MITTANI, Tuthmosis IV gained
a 50-year period of stability for Egypt and an
ally against the growing power of the HITTITE
empire of Anatolia. ▷ 1.12

TYRANT
In the turbulent period (650–500 BC) when
the Greek city-states were evolving their
political systems, it was common for single
rulers to seize power – often with popular
support – from the aristocratic elite. The
term tyrant, possibly PHOENICIAN in origin,
was used to describe a ruler who had gained
power by his own efforts rather than by
inheritance. Tyrants were not initially associated with oppressive government. Many,
such as PEISISTRATOS of Athens, were able
rulers who enjoyed widespread popular
support because they challenged aristocratic
privileges. As citizen bodies became more
confident, however, one-man rule became
an anathema, and most tyrants were overthrown or expelled from their cities. ▷ 1.24

TYRE
A port on the Levantine coast that had
become the leading PHOENICIAN city by the
10th century BC, establishing trading colonies
throughout the Mediterranean, including
Carthage. It was sacked by the Babylonian
king, NEBUCHADNEZZAR, in 574 BC but
remained an important port into Roman
times. ▷ 1.13, 1.14, 1.15, 1.23, 1.25

UBAID PERIOD
Late NEOLITHIC period in which farming
communities similar to those of the SAMARRAN
and HALAFIAN cultures settled in south
MESOPOTAMIA in about 5900–4300 BC. They
built large-scale IRRIGATION systems and their
distinctive CERAMICS are found throughout
Mesopotamia from about 5200 BC. Farming
villages in this period grew into small towns,
such as ERIDU (by c.5000 BC), some with
temple buildings, establishing a pattern of
urban development and religious architecture
that was central to Mesopotamian civilization.
▷ 1.09

UGARIT
Levantine port that became a major state in
the 2nd millennium BC, when it handled
Cypriot, MYCENAEAN, HITTITE and Egyptian
trade. The cosmopolitan character of Ugaritic
culture is evident from trade goods, artifacts
and records written in four languages and
seven scripts. The city was destroyed,
probably by SEA PEOPLES, in about 1200 BC.
▷ 1.08, 1.09, 1.10, 1.11, 1.12, 1.13, 1.14

UJJAIN
One of seven sacred Hindu cities, located
in the upland area of central India, founded
in the 6th century BC as the capital of the
powerful Avanti kingdom. Ujjain was defended by massive earth ramparts enclosing
an area about 1.5 kilometers (0.9 miles)
in diameter. ▷ 1.26

ULU BURUN SHIPWRECK
Shipwreck on the south Anatolian coast
dating from the 14th century BC. Its varied
cargo, which included COPPER ingots; bronze
weapons; pottery from Greece, Canaan and
Cyprus; Anatolian TIN; gold jewelry; Egyptian
scarabs, and a range of faience, ivory and
glass objects, provides a unique insight into
the late BRONZE AGE Aegean system of trade.
▷ 1.22

UMBRIANS
Term applied to various geographical,
linguistic and cultural entities. Umbria
formed part of the 6th region of Italy under
Augustus. Umbrian was an INDO-EUROPEAN
Italic dialect of central Italy, attested in a
number of inscriptions, notably the Iguvine
bronze tables. ▷ 1.25

UMMA
Sumerian city that competed with LAGASH,
URUK, UR and AKKAD in the 3rd millennium
BC. It briefly achieved regional hegemony
under King LUGALZAGESI (c.2350 BC), who
defeated Lagash and united SUMER and Akkad
under one ruler for the first time. Conquered
by SARGON OF AGADE in about 2330 BC, it
never regained its former power. ▷ 1.10

UNETICE CULTURE
Culture of north-central Europe dating from
about 2500 to 1500 BC, whose features widely typify the Early BRONZE AGE cultures of
temperate Europe, including rich single
burials under ROUND BARROWS, the widespread use of bronze (from c.2000 BC), the
development of CHIEFDOMS, and long-distance
trade in bronze, amber, faience and gold
prestige goods. ▷ 1.04, 1.21

UR
City in SUMERIA that became a major city-state
in the EARLY DYNASTIC period (c.2900–2334
BC), and at times the most powerful city in
MESOPOTAMIA. The famous "Royal Cemetery"
of the 26th century BC, with spectacular grave
goods and human sacrifices (slaves, attend-
ants and guards), suggests a powerful and
brutal ruling elite. It competed with rival
cities such as KISH, LAGASH and UMMA, and
was briefly pre-eminent in the 25th century
BC under the First Dynasty of Ur (the first
dynasty known from written records).
After a period of domination by Akkadian
and Gutian rulers in the 24th–22nd centuries
BC, the city revived under the Third Dynasty
of Ur (2112–2004 BC), which established an
extensive empire in southern Mesopotamia.
The great ZIGGURAT built by UR-NAMMU was
one of the most impressive structures in
ancient Mesopotamia. After the sack of Ur by
the Elamites in 2004 BC, the city gradually
declined in religious and commercial importance until the massive rebuilding works of
the Neo-Babylonian kings, NEBUCHADNEZZAR
and NABONIDUS, in the 6th century BC. It was
abandoned in the 3rd century BC, when the
local IRRIGATION system failed. ▷ 1.09, 1.10,
1.11, 1.12, 1.13

UR-NAMMU
First king of the Third Dynasty of UR
(r.2112–2095 BC), who established a new
imperial state in MESOPOTAMIA, 80 years after
the collapse of the Akkadian empire. His
success stemmed largely from control of the
trade routes into the Persian Gulf. ▷ 1.11

URARTU
Mountain region between Anatolia and the
Caspian Sea, inhabited in the 2nd and 1st
millennia BC by Hurrian-speaking peoples.
By 850 BC Urartu had become a major state,
conquering and developing neighboring
areas as far as the Caucasus and upper
Euphrates. Its power waned in the 8th
century BC, as the Neo-Assyrian empire
expanded, culminating in 714 BC in SARGON
II's defeat of Rusas (the last Urartian king
with imperial aspirations) at Lake Urmia.
Urartu was conquered by Armenian
invaders in the 7th century BC. ▷ 1.05,
1.07, 1.12, 1.13

URBANIZATION
Process leading to the formation of urban settlements, in which most inhabitants are engaged in non-agricultural activities, living in dense agglomerations of houses, elite residences, public buildings and commercial quarters. Urban life is distinctive in terms of its social complexity, structured by multiple corporate, political and legal institutions (also associated with STATE systems), social stratification, economic specialization and cultural heterogeneity. The earliest cities developed in MESOPOTAMIA from the 5th to 3rd millennia BC, and in the Indus valley and China from the 3rd to 2nd millennia BC. ▷ 1.03, 1.04, 1.09, 1.10, 1.26, 1.27

URNFIELD CULTURES
Although culturally diverse, late BRONZE AGE societies in Europe widely adopted a shared funerary tradition of individual cremation burial in funerary urns that were placed in large cemeteries, sometimes numbering thousands of graves (e.g. Leubingen). This tradition originated in eastern Europe in the mid-2nd millennium BC, spreading to the Rhine and Italy by about 1200 BC and the Atlantic coast by about 1000 BC. ▷ 1.05, 1.06, 1.21, 1.25

URUK
City in SUMERIA that developed from an UBAID farming village, becoming an urban center in the 4th millennium BC (its name is given to the URUK PERIOD of Mesopotamian history). It was a major city-state in the EARLY DYNASTIC period (c.2900–2334 BC), and remained an important religious and commercial center until the 1st millennium BC. ▷ 1.09, 1.10, 1.11, 1.12

URUK PERIOD
Period of Mesopotamian culture following the UBAID PERIOD. During the Uruk period the first civilization in the world developed in SUMERIA (c.4300–3100 BC), marked by processes of STATE formation and URBANIZATION that included the invention of the earliest script for record-keeping, increasingly intensive IRRIGATION agriculture, and the widespread adoption of new technologies (COPPER metallurgy, the potter's wheel, the PLOW and wheeled transport). ▷ 1.09, 1.10, 1.11, 1.12

URUKAGINA
The last king of the 1st dynasty of the city of LAGASH in southern SUMERIA (c.2350 BC). His law code is the earliest surviving record of state legislation and governmental powers, particularly in relation to temple authorities. ▷ 1.10

VALDIVIA TRADITION
Long-lived culture (c.3800–1700 BC) of the PRECERAMIC PERIOD, around the Gulf of Guayaquil, Ecuador. Valdivia communities were sedentary, largely dependent on fishing, shellfish collecting and MAIZE cultivation.

Their CERAMICS were the earliest in South America (from c.3000 BC). ▷ 1.04, 1.28

VALLEY OF THE KINGS
Valley to the west of the Nile at THEBES, used as a burial place by the PHARAOHS of the NEW KINGDOM. Sixty-two tombs were constructed, but most were later discovered and robbed of their rich contents. The exception was the tomb of TUTANKHAMUN, whose opulence revealed the magnificence of what has been lost. ▷ 1.18

VAN LANG
Earliest complex CHIEFDOM society in southeast Asia, based on intensive RICE farming, which emerged in the Red River (Song koi) delta, in the region of modern Hanoi in Vietnam, by about 500 BC. The early history of the area in Vietnamese legends refers to the kingdom of Van Lang (Land of the Tatooed Men), ruled by the legendary Hung dynasty. ▷ 1.06

VARNA
Early Copper Age cemetery (c.4600–4100 BC) in the Danube basin, close to the Black Sea coast. More than 280 burials of men, women and children have been found, with an extraordinary range of artifacts including pottery, gold jewelry and decorative fittings, COPPER tools and weapons, and shell beads. The range and richness of the grave goods may indicate the early development of a complex social hierarchy. ▷ 1.20

VINCA
Large, late NEOLITHIC TELL site in modern Serbia that gave its name to the Vinca culture of the central Balkans (c.5500–4500 BC). It is characterized by large, long-lived agricultural villages and distinctive painted pottery, including figurines and models. ▷ 1.20

VIX
Early IRON AGE (HALLSTATT D) female burial in a timber mortuary house beneath a ROUND BARROW in central France, dating from about 520 BC. It contained a four-wheeled cart, fine metal objects, including a gold diadem, and a huge bronze *krater* (wine mixing vessel) and painted pottery cup from Greece, indicating long-distance trade with the Mediterranean. ▷ 1.23

WARRING STATES PERIOD
Last phase of the later (Eastern) ZHOU period in China (c.480–220 BC), when widespread rejection of Zhou overlordship led to the emergence of seven powerful and aggressive kingdoms competing for dominance, the strongest being QI, CHU and QIN. By about 250 BC, Qin had gained supremacy and finally unified China in about 220 BC. ▷ 1.27

WASHUKANNI
Capital of the HURRIAN kingdom of MITTANI, possibly at the unexcavated site of Tell al-

Fakhariyeh to the east of the Euphrates in northern Syria. It was sacked by the HITTITES in 1340 BC and by the Assyrians in about 1300 BC. Nothing is known of its history, layout or buildings. ▷ 1.12

WATER BUFFALO
See CATTLE

WAVY LINE CERAMICS
One of the earliest CERAMIC traditions in the world, made by HUNTER-GATHERERS in sub-Saharan Africa from the Hoggar massif (Algeria) to the Upper Nile (Sudan), before the adoption of agricultural practices, in about 8000 to 6000 BC. Its name derives from the distinctive incised decoration made by combing catfish spines across the vessel surfaces. ▷ 1.16

WAYWAKA
Burial site in the southern Peruvian Andes where thin sheets of gold foil and a metal-working tool-kit were found with a male inhumation of about 1440 BC. This forms the earliest evidence of metallurgy in the Americas. ▷ 1.28

WEI
Feudal state of the ZHOU kingdom (c.1100–250 BC), with a capital city at Chaoge. It played a minor role in the SPRINGS AND AUTUMNS PERIOD but became a leading state in the WARRING STATES PERIOD, particularly during the reign of Duke Wen (c.424–387 BC). ▷ 1.27

WESSEX CULTURE
Early BRONZE AGE culture of southern Britain (c.2000–1500 BC), characterized by groups of large ROUND BARROWS and a rich burial tradition, with grave goods such as bronze daggers, gold work, amber, jet and faience jewelry. These objects demonstrate links with Brittany and central Europe, and the widespead use of bronze. ▷ 1.05, 1.21

WHEAT
Cereal plant species, including emmer, einkorn and spelt wheat, that was domesticated in the FERTILE CRESCENT and Anatolia from about 9000 BC, becoming staple food crops throughout the Middle East, Europe and north Africa by 5000 BC. They were especially important for milling flours suitable for making breads and biscuits. ▷ 1.03, 1.08, 1.09, 1.16, 1.20, 1.22

WHEEL
Circular frame or disk mounted on a central pivot for mechanical purposes, especially for wheeled transport and pottery manufacture. The earliest evidence of the existence of the wheel is wheel-thrown pottery from MESOPOTAMIA, dating from about 4500 BC. Wheeled vehicles were probably first used in the 4th millennium BC, invented either in Mesopotamia or on the west Eurasian steppes

(carts and wagons), and had spread to Europe and India by about 3000 BC. The potter's wheel was also invented independently in China (before 3000 BC). ▷ 1.03, 1.10, 1.20, 1.21, 1.27

WINDMILL HILL
The largest early NEOLITHIC enclosure in northwest Europe, near AVEBURY in southern Britain, built in about 3600 BC. It consists of three concentric circuits of causewayed ditches with internal banks, about 350 meters (1,150 feet) in diameter. It probably had a ceremonial purpose. ▷ 1.20

WOOL
Animal fiber obtained from live animals (mainly SHEEP, GOATS and camelids) that was used to make strong, relatively coarse textiles, including clothes, blankets and carpets. Woollen fabrics were made from about 4000 BC (in MESOPOTAMIA), though the earliest surviving examples date to the 2nd millennium BC (from Egypt, Denmark and China). ▷ 1.03, 1.09, 1.22

WU
Large feudal state of the ZHOU kingdom, with a non-Chinese population, named after its capital city. It gradually grew in power during the SPRINGS AND AUTUMNS PERIOD to become the dominant state in southern China by the late 6th century BC (replacing CHU). It was conquered by the neighboring kingdom of Yue in 473 BC. ▷ 1.27

XIA DYNASTY
Legendary 1st dynasty of China (c.2205–1766 BC), founded by YU THE GREAT. There is no archeological or contemporary literary evidence of the Xia dynasty or states in this period, though later literary references may have been based on earlier texts written on materials that have not survived. ▷ 1.27

XIANYUN
Tribal people of northern China who lived beyond the northwest frontier of the ZHOU kingdom in the early 1st millennium BC. Their attacks on the Zhou heartland from the late 9th to early 8th centuries BC led to the abandonment of the ancient capital at Han. ▷ 1.27

YAM
Plant species of the genus *Dioscorea*, with edible tubers, that is found in tropical and subtropical regions and is widely cultivated as a staple food source. The domestication of yams may have occurred as early as about 5000 BC in New Guinea (sweet potatoes) and about 3000 BC in west Africa. ▷ 1.03, 1.16

YAN
Northern feudal state of the ZHOU kingdom (c.1100–250 BC), with a capital city at Ji. It played only a minor role in the power struggles of the SPRINGS AND AUTUMNS

PERIOD, as the authority of the Zhou dynasty declined (from c.770 BC). ▷ 1.27

YANGSHAO CULTURE
The earliest farming culture in China with a full agricultural economy (MILLET, PIGS, GOATS and SHEEP), dating from about 5000 to 3200 BC. It developed from indigenous proto-farming societies on the light fertile loess plains of the Yellow river and its tributaries. Yangshao communities lived in large settlements of substantial timber houses and had a rich material culture, with painted pottery, textiles and jade carvings. ▷ 1.27

YAYA-MAMA RELIGIOUS TRADITIONS
Tradition of religious architecture and iconography of the Lake Titcaca region in the high Andes from about 600 to 400 BC, in the area later ruled by the Tiahuanaco state (established by c.AD 500). ▷ 1.06, 1.28

YONG
People who lived to the southeast of SHANG territory, mentioned in late Shang records (from c.1150 BC) when military campaigns conducted by King DI-XIN were directed at hostile barbarians in eastern China. ▷ 1.27

YU THE GREAT
Legendary king and founder of the first ruling dynasty of China, the XIA. In later literary sources he was said to be the chief minister and then successor of the emperors Yao and Shun, and to have ruled China from about 2205 BC. ▷ 1.27

YUE QI
Steppe nomad people of the Altai-Gobi region, also known as the Kushans, who raided the northern states of ZHOU China in the 8th to 2nd centuries BC, until they were forced to move westwards by the expansion of the fierce Xiongnu nomads of Mongolia. ▷ 1.06

ZAPOTECS
People of the OAXACA VALLEY region of south-central Mexico, who developed state societies in the 1st millennium BC, with several ceremonial centers (notably Monté Albán) and the first writing script in the Americas (Zapotec hieroglyphic, used for royal names and calendrical records), from about 800 BC. The cultural and political relationships between Zapotec, OLMEC and Maya states in the 1st millennium BC remain uncertain, though extensive trade networks existed for the exchange of OBSIDIAN, jade and other important materials. The height of Zapotec power and architectural achievement was reached during the 1st to 7th centuries AD. ▷ 1.06, 1.07, 1.28

ZAWI CHEMI SHANIDAR
Proto-farming settlement located in the Zagros mountains, in modern Iraq. It was occupied between the late 10th and early

9th millennia BC, with a subsistence economy based on the intensive management of wild SHEEP herds and wild cereal cultivation. The site provides some of the earliest evidence of animal and plant domestication. ▷ 1.08

ZEBU
See CATTLE

ZEDEKIAH
Last king of JUDAH (r.c.597–586 BC). His attempt to rebel against Babylonian rule in 587 BC led to the destruction of JERUSALEM by NEBUCHADNEZZAR, Zedekiah's imprisonment, and the deportation of his subjects. ▷ 1.14

ZHOU DYNASTY
Ruling dynasty of China (1122–256 BC) that was established by King Wu, who overthrew the last of the SHANG kings, DI-XIN. Wu justified his usurpation by claiming the "Mandate of Heaven", which served as a model for all later imperial ideologies in China, and a feudal system of rule that relied on the obedience of vassal dukedoms.

The Zhou period is divided into two phases, the Western Zhou (1122–770 BC), when the capital was located in their heartland at HAO, and the Eastern Zhou (770–256 BC), initiated when barbarian attacks forced the removal of the capital to the less vulnerable city of LUOYANG. Detached from their heartland, the authority of the Zhou dynasty declined. In the early Eastern Zhou period, also known as the SPRINGS AND AUTUMNS PERIOD (770–480 BC), rival dukedoms vied for dominance, some achieving temporary hegemony, while paying nominal allegience to the Zhou king. The fragmentation of the Zhou state in the late Eastern Zhou period (largely coterminous with the WARRING STATES PERIOD, 480–221 BC) finally ended when the last Zhou king was deposed by the triumphant QIN dynasty in 256 BC.

The Zhou period is notable for the spread of urbanism throughout China, its rich artistic tradition, and for the establishment of a fully literate culture and the political and philosophical traditions that pervade much of later Chinese history (especially Confucianism). ▷ 1.05, 1.06, 1.27

ZHOUKOUDIEN
LOWER PALEOLITHIC cave site in northern China, with occupation levels dating from about 500,000 ya. The site contains chopper- and flake-tool industries associated with important fossil remains of HOMO ERECTUS. ▷ 1.01

ZIGGURAT
Rectangular stepped mound on which Mesopotamian temples were built in the 3rd to 1st millennia BC (possibly symbolizing sacred mountains). Most ziggurats were built of mud brick, with an exterior fired-brick casing, ornamental facades, and stairways and ramps for access to the shrines. ▷ 1.09, 1.11

Text, timelines and maps

The authors and publishers readily acknowledge the work of a large number of scholars and published works, on which they have drawn in the preparation of this atlas. Many of these works remain in print, and can be used as reliable secondary reading on the many topics covered in this atlas. Among them are the following:

al Faruqi, Ismail Ragi (ed) *Historical Atlas of the Religions of the World* (New York and London 1974)

Allchin, B and R *The Birth of Indian Civilization: India and Pakistan before 500 BC* (London, 2nd ed 1994)

Bahn, Paul G (ed) *Cambridge Illustrated History of Archaeology* (Cambridge and New York 1996)

Baines, John and Malek, Jaromir *Atlas of Ancient Egypt* (Oxford and New York, 1980)

Barraclough, G (ed) *The Times Atlas of World History* (4th ed , London 1993 and New York 1994)

Beek, MA *Atlas of Mesopotamia* (London 1962)

Blunden, Caroline and Elvin, Mark *Cultural Atlas of China* (London and New York, 1986)

Boardman, J *The Greeks Overseas* (London 1964)

Bolton, Geoffrey (ed) *The Oxford History of Australia* (Oxford and Melbourne 1994)

Bonsall, C *The Mesolithic in Europe* (Edinburgh 1989)

Chadwick, Henry and Evans, Gillian R (eds) *Atlas of the Christian Church* (London and New York, 1987)

Champion, T, Gamble, C, Shennan, S and Whittle, A *Prehistoric Europe* (London 1984)

Chang, KC *The Archaeology of Ancient China* (Yale 1977)

Chard, CS *Northeast Asia in Prehistory* (Madison, USA 1974)

Coe, Michael, Snow, Dean and Benson, Elizabeth *Atlas of Ancient America* (London and New York, 1986)

Coe, Michael *Mexico: from the Olmecs to the Aztecs* (London and New York 4th ed 1994)

Cohn-Sherbok, D *Atlas of Jewish History* (London and New York 1994)

Coles, JM and Harding, AF *The Bronze Age in Europe* (London 1979)

Connah, G *African Civilizations: Precolonial cities and states in tropical Africa* (Cambridge and New York 1987)

Cook, JM *The Persian Empire* (London 1983)

Cornell, Tim and Matthews, John *Atlas of the Roman World* (London and New York, 1982)

Cotterell, A *East Asia* (London 1993, New York 1995)

Crawford, M *The Roman Republic* (London 1978, Cambridge, Mass 1993)

Cunliffe, Barry (ed) *The Oxford Illustrated Prehistory of Europe* (Oxford and New York 1994)

Davies, JK *Democracy and Classical Greece* (London 2nd ed 1993)

Davis, Norman *Europe: a History* (Oxford and New York 1996)

de Lange, Nicholas *Atlas of the Jewish World* (London and New York, 1984)

Elliott, JH (ed) *The Hispanic World* (London and New York 1991)

Fagan, Brian M *The Journey from Eden: the Peopling of our World* (London and New York 1990)

Fagan, Brian M *Ancient North America* (London and New York 1995)

Fagan, Brian M *People of the Earth* (New York and London, 7th ed 1992)

Fage, JD and Oliver, R (eds) *The Cambridge History of Africa* (Cambridge and New York 1975–)

Fage, JD *An Atlas of African History* (London 1978)

Falkus, M and Gillingham J *Historical Atlas of Britain* (London and New York revised ed 1987)

Fiedel, SJ *Prehistory of the Americas* (Cambridge and New York, 2nd ed 1992)

Freeman-Grenville, GSP *Historical Atlas of the Middle East* (New York 1993)

Frye, RN *The Heritage of Persia* (London 2nd ed 1976)

Gamble, C *The Palaeolithic Settlement of Europe* (Cambridge 1986)

Gamble, C *Timewalkers: the Prehistory of Global Colonization* (Stroud 1993, Cambridge, Mass. 1994)

Gaur, A *A History of Writing* (London 1984, New York 1994)

Gilbert, Martin *The Atlas of Jewish History* (London and New York 5th ed 1996)

Green, MJ *The Celtic World* (London and New York 1995)

Grosser Historischer Weltatlas (3 vols (Munich 1981)

Hall, DGE *A History of South-east Asia* (London 4th ed 1981)

Hood, S *The Minoans* (London and New York 1973)

Johnson, Gordon, Bayly, C and Richards JF *The New Cambridge History of India* (Cambridge 1987–)

Johnson, Gordon *Cultural Atlas of India* (London 1995, New York, 1996)

Kemp, BJ *Ancient Egypt* (London 1989, New York 1992)

Kinder, H and Hilgemann, W *Atlas of World History* (2 vols, Munich, London and New York 1974)

Kuhrt, A *The Ancient Near East* (2 vols, London and New York 1995)

Kulke, H and Rothermund, D *A History of India* (London 1990)

Langer, William L *An Encyclopedia of World History* (5th ed, London and New York 1973)

Levi, Peter *Cultural Atlas of the Greek World* (London and New York, 1984)

Ling, T *A History of Religion East and West* (London 1968)

Mallory, JP *In Search of the Indo-Europeans* (London 1989, New York 1991)

Moore, RI (ed) *The Hamlyn Historical Atlas* (London 1981)

Moseley, ME *The Incas and their Ancestors* (London and New York 1993)

Murray, Oswyn *Early Greece* (London 2nd ed 1993)

Phillipson, DW *African Archaeology* (Cambridge, 2nd ed 1993)

Roaf, Michael and Postgate, Nicholas *Cultural Atlas of Mesopotamia and the Ancient Near East* (London and New York, 1990)

Roberts, JM *The Hutchinson History of the World* (London 1976)

Rogerson, John *Atlas of the Bible* (London and New York 1985)

Scarre, Dr Chris *Past Worlds: The Times Atlas of Archaeology* (London and New York, 1988)

Schmidt, KJ *An Atlas and Survey of South Asian History* (New York and London 1995)

Schwartzberg, Joseph E (ed) *A Historical Atlas of South Asia* (Chicago and London, 2nd ed 1992)

Sharer, RJ *The Ancient Maya* (Stanford Ca 5th ed 1994)

Shepherd, William R. *Shepherd's Historical Atlas* (New York and London, 9th ed 1974)

Sinor, D (ed) *The Cambridge History of Early Inner Asia* (Cambridge 1990)

Smith, BD *The Emergence of Agriculture* (New York 1995)

Taylour, W *The Mycenaeans* (London and New York 2nd ed 1990)

The Times Atlas of the World (London and New York, 8th ed 1990)

Todd, M *The Early Germans* (Oxford and Cambridge, Mass. 1992)

Twitchett, D and Fairbank, J (eds) *The Cambridge History of China* (15 vols, Cambridge and New York 1978–91)

Vincent, Mary and Stradling, RA *Cultural Atlas of Spain and Portugal* (London 1994, New York 1995)

Walbank, FW *The Hellenistic World* (London 3rd ed 1992, Cambridge, Mass. 1993)

Watson, F *India, a Concise History* (London and New York 1993)

Whittle, A *Neolithic Europe: a Survey* (Cambridge and New York 1985)

Artwork

Artwork references have been assembled from a wide variety of sources. Any individual or institution who can demonstrate that copyright may have been infringed is invited to contact Andromeda Oxford Ltd.

Photographs

Introduction Telendos: Images Colour Library.